ASPECTS OF GRIEF

Bereavement in Adult Life

Jane Littlewood

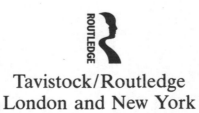

Tavistock/Routledge
London and New York

First published 1992
by Routledge
11 New Fetter Lane, London EC4P 4EE

Simultaneously published in the USA and Canada
by Routledge
a division of Routledge, Chapman and Hall, Inc.
29 West 35th Street, New York, NY 10001

© 1992 Jane Littlewood

Typeset in Times by
Falcon Typographic Art Ltd, Edinburgh & London
Printed in Great Britain
Mackays of Chatham PLC, Chatham, Kent

British Library Cataloguing in Publication Data

Littlewood, Jane Lesley, 1955–
Aspects of grief: bereavement in adult life.
I. Title
306.88

Library of Congress Cataloging in Publication Data

Littlewood, Jane, 1955–
Aspects of grief: bereavement in adult life/Jane Littlewood.
p. cm.
Includes bibliographical references and index.
1. Grief. 2. Bereavement – Psychological aspects. 3. Death –
Psychological aspects. I. Title.
BF575.G7L57 1992
155.9'37—dc20   91–21388 CIP

ISBN 0–415–02816–7
ISBN 0–415–07176–3 (pbk)

For Malc and Reggie

CONTENTS

List of tables   viii
Acknowledgements   ix
Introduction   xi

1 THE WAY WE DIE   1

2 RITUALS AND MOURNING CUSTOMS   20

3 EXPERIENCES OF GRIEF   40

4 MODELS OF BEREAVEMENT:
   SEARCHING FOR MEANING   60

5 MODELS OF SOCIAL SUPPORT AND
   PROFESSIONAL SUPPORT NETWORKS   78

6 INFORMAL SUPPORT NETWORKS   97

7 THE DEATHS OF CHILDREN IN
   CHILDHOOD, ADOLESCENCE AND ADULTHOOD   122

8 THE DEATHS OF PARTNERS AND PARENTS   148

   Bibliography   175
   Name index   186
   Subject index   189

TABLES

1   Control of the dying process   2
2   Dying trajectories   5
3   Awareness contexts   9
4   The structure of funeral rites   24
5   Relationships between different aspects of funeral rites   28
6   A comparison of theories relating to stages of grief   53
7   Percentages (and numbers) of parents agreeing and refusing to discuss their bereavement according to age and sex of child   136

ACKNOWLEDGEMENTS

This book grew out of research concerned with the ways in which people who have been bereaved come to terms with their loss, and the ways in which they are helped or hindered by their culture in their attempts to do so. Many people who had lost relatives and friends were kind enough to agree to contribute. I would like to thank them all for their time, and to acknowledge the courage it takes to speak openly about painful experiences. I hope that they will feel fairly represented by what is written here.

The work has also benefited greatly from the many other researchers who have written about this area in an attempt to promote a more open discussion of the processes of dying and bereavement.

I would like to thank individually David Stonestreet of Routledge for his patience, Malcolm Nicholas for his support, and Cathie Ward, Gwen Moon, Anne Smith, Vivian Dhaliwal and Myra Hunt for their help in translating the manuscript into typescript.

INTRODUCTION

This book is concerned with the issue of bereavement in adult life. It is about the ways in which people experience grief, and the ways in which bereaved people are experienced by others. At any given moment in time, approximately one in four members of the adult population will have experienced the death of someone close to them within the previous five years. For some people, this will be one of many experiences of bereavement, and for others it will be their first encounter with death. Whilst the impact of the loss of a loved person can vary from the bearably painful to the emotionally catastrophic, very few people will manage to avoid this type of loss although, perhaps, most of us would wish to.

Many of the examples of experiences which follow the death of a loved person used throughout this book are taken from my own research. They are concerned with bereavement in modern Western societies and specifically relate to the experiences of those living in England and the Netherlands. It is within this cultural context that they should be considered.

Death raises profound social and cultural issues and some of these issues are discussed in Chapter 1. Attitudes towards death and dying in Western societies have been characterised by denial and avoidance by many researchers in the area. Consequently, the chapter commences with a brief history of attitudes towards death, and considers the implications of the social settings in which deaths typically occur in contemporary Western societies. The importance of having a period of time in which to prepare oneself for the possibility of a death occurring is discussed in this chapter, as is the development of the hospice philosophy, which encapsulates attitudes towards dying as a process and death as an event alternative to those found in the general community. The final part of Chapter 1 briefly considers contemporary attitudes towards what might be considered a 'good' death and looks at the paradoxical relationship between people's beliefs about the death they would wish to die and what is known about deaths which are difficult for people to come to terms with.

Under ordinary circumstances most societies dispose of corpses with rituals, and the second chapter of the book is concerned with the ritual processes and systems of belief which are associated with death. Relationships between the dead and the living are not simply extinguished at the point of physical death, however that might be defined. In most societies those who had a close relationship with a person who has died see themselves, and are seen by others, for a greater or lesser period of time, depending upon the society, to have been 'touched' in some way by death. Therefore, people who have been bereaved are associated, in their own and other people's minds, with the dead as well as the living. Up to a point, the way a society approaches death characterises the way in which it treats people who have been bereaved, and the avoidance of such people, together with a disinclination to talk openly about death, are recurring themes of this book. The social and psychological implications of the corpse, for the living, are also addressed in this chapter, and it is suggested that the presence or absence of the corpse, together with societies' beliefs about the relationship between body and soul can affect not only funeral rituals, but the process of grieving itself. The specific example of the decline of mourning customs and the scale of funeral rites in England is also discussed.

Whilst appropriate rituals might be helpful to adults who have been bereaved, it is suggested that the more recent forms of ritual associated with death reflect rather more support for the society in general than for people who are grieving over a particular death. Perhaps in complex multi-racial societies the only rituals which might support a person who has been bereaved are those spontaneously generated or adopted by the people themselves. Consequently, the final part of the chapter looks at the smaller scale rituals of everyday life and at their relationship with the giving and receiving of supportive exchanges.

Chapter 3 is concerned with the wide range of subjective experiences, somatic, psychological and emotional, which are associated with contemporary experiences of grief in adulthood. Bereavement is known to result in an increased risk of morbidity, both psychological and physical, and mortality. Although the metaphor of dying from a broken heart is an old one, it is also a powerful one which has at least some basis in reality.

The experiences associated with the grieving process vary over time, and the ways in which experiences are often organised are addressed in this chapter. There would appear to be no time limit to grief, and changes associated with the loss of a loved person probably continue indefinitely. Since the person who has been bereaved is involved in other social relationships which also undergo change, the consequences of a death can be far-reaching indeed. Depending upon relationship and circumstance, we are all affected by the deaths of others whether we choose to acknowledge this or not.

The grieving process does not always proceed along a relatively uncomplicated course, and factors associated with complications to the normal processes and experiences associated with grief are discussed in Chapter 3. It is suggested that the processes associated with both complicated and uncomplicated grief involve a series of contradictions. These contradictions must be resolved if the person who has been bereaved is to regain any level of ordinary psychological functioning or general sense of well-being.

Chapter 4 documents some of the many theories which have been forwarded to explain aspects of the grieving process. These theories are particularly wide-ranging, since relatively few of them have been generated specifically to explain the processes and experiences associated with grief. Theories which focus on our common biological and evolutionary characteristics account for grief in terms of the activation of two biological response mechanisms, which compel the person who has been bereaved towards anxiety and/or depression. Alternatively, other theorists have looked at the species-specific survival value of fear of separation from the group in general, and from people who are significant to us in particular.

The psychodynamic explanations of grief largely originated from studies of depression, which is itself one of the many experiences which commonly follow the loss of a loved person. Psychodynamic explanations of human behaviour tend to focus their attention upon an individual's childhood experiences, and the ways in which such experiences are adapted to and interpreted over time. This particular range of theoretical orientations has been vitally important in terms of promoting an understanding of the consequences of bereavements occurring during childhood.

Outside theories which focus upon a person's internal biological and psychological preoccupations, there are other perspectives which consider the social and subjective meaning of bereavement. Attachment theory is one of the main theories to offer an explanation of the development, maintenance and loss of relationships in both childhood and adult life. This theory has been complemented by several others which seek to place attachments in their social context by looking at the meaning certain relationships have in particular societies and at particular times.

One key aspect of the bereavement process which is known to affect the outcome of grieving is the presence and quality of social support offered to people, both before and after the occurrence of a death. Chapter 5 looks at some of the general models of social support which might be relevant to bereavement, and at some specific studies which have addressed the issue of the extent to which professionals and lay volunteers can play a role in the support of people who have been bereaved. It is suggested here that support programmes provided by professionals, volunteers and charitable organisations play an extremely important part both in the prevention and the amelioration of complications arising during the grieving process. However, it is also suggested that, at the present time, only a minority of people who have been bereaved have, or seek access to, these valuable sources of support following a death.

Chapter 6 is concerned with the range of informal support available to people who have been bereaved. In very general terms informal sources of support following a death, due to the intensely personal meaning of close relationships, tend to be the ones which most people who have been bereaved would prefer to use. However, the usual pattern of informal supportive exchanges following a death effectively results in bereaved people supporting other bereaved people and in some instances the stresses associated with this pattern of support are too great for everyone involved. Furthermore, some people who have been bereaved simply do not have access to appropriate sources of informal support, and it is suggested that this aspect of the situation is, in some cases, enough in itself to complicate the processes associated with bereavement.

Another aspect of the process of grieving which is known to be of importance, in terms of outcome, is the circumstances which surround a particular death. Chapter 7 is concerned with these circumstances, and focuses upon the impact which the deaths of children, in childhood, adolescence and adulthood have upon the child's parents.

Whilst deaths occurring in the younger age ranges are rare in contemporary Western societies, they are also likely to be perceived as untimely and, therefore, generally difficult to come to terms with. It is also the case that the causes of deaths in childhood are many and varied, and the cause of death is important inasmuch as different patterns of access to support, different periods of time in which to anticipate the death and the developmental age of the child at death can all affect the process of parental grieving.

The eighth and final chapter of the book is concerned with two other bereavements associated with losses commonly occurring during adult life: the deaths of parents and the deaths of partners. Chapter 8 looks at the impact of these losses in themselves and at the importance of particular types of relationships in terms of their effects upon the process of grieving.

The range of issues known to affect the process of grieving tend to be inter-related and part of a complex web of personal interpretations, actual experiences and circumstances surrounding the death. Consequently, in the final chapters of the book, reasonably detailed examples of people's recollections of their experiences have been included.

For the most part, these recollections are not commented upon in any great detail in the text because they are aspects of grief and, as such, are open to a multitude of different interpretations.

1

THE WAY WE DIE

'The tame death is the oldest death there is.'
Ariès (1983)
The Hour of our Death

INTRODUCTION

It is difficult to consider reactions to bereavement without looking at
social and cultural attitudes towards death and dying. An increase in
average life expectancy and changes in patterns of mortality have made
deaths outside the older age ranges relatively rare occurrences. Many
people now reach middle age without having any direct experience of
bereavement. However, research in the area would indicate that coping with death and dying remains profoundly problematic for people
in Western societies. Furthermore, it has been suggested that the difficulties associated with these areas have accumulated rather than diminished.

Consequently the first part of this chapter looks at some of the evidence which suggests that death and dying are surrounded by a series
of cultural contradictions and distortions. The second part is concerned
with the social context in which death occurs and some ways of dying
which have been associated with difficulties for the survivors. The third
part of the chapter focuses upon the attempts of health professionals
to provide improved services for people who are dying, and the final
part identifies some of the problems involved in the provision of services in an environment which may be hostile to their aims and objec-
tives.

ATTITUDES TOWARDS DEATH

Ariès (1974, 1983) has looked in detail at changing attitudes towards
death in Western societies from the Middle Ages to the present day. The
contemporary situation would appear to be bleak. According to Ariès, the

1

history of dying is one in which both control of the dying process and the place of death have changed. At the risk of oversimplifying his scholarly work the main variations may be represented as shown in Table 1.

Table 1 Control of the dying process

| | | Death | |
Time	Control	Place	Support at the time of death
Middle Ages	Held by the dying person	In the community	Communal
	Held by the dying person's family	In the home	Family
Present Day	Held by the medical profession	In the hospital	None*

* i.e. outside a small group of health professionals who have sought to change practice in the area.

Ariès characterises the contemporary situation as one in which death has been rendered invisible – simply 'conjured away'. The majority of deaths now occur in institutions with the dying person isolated from the everyday activities of the society and, perhaps more importantly, from other people. This way of dying contrasts unfavourably with his portrayal of deaths in earlier times where dying people remained in full control of their deaths, dying in the heart of their particular community. Up until the point of death itself dying people had a key role to play in what were undoubtedly social proceedings – that of preparing themselves and others for their death, a 'tame' death.

At the present time Ariès believes us to be both ashamed and afraid of death. The dying provoke unease, embarrassment and disquiet. It is seen to be appropriate that they are quietly removed from the community, to die in isolation. This isolation also seems to affect the bereaved. As living reminders of the unspeakable truth of death they may be avoided rather than supported, effectively quarantined – as Gorer (1965) puts it, 'mourning in reverse'.

Ariès (1983) identifies four models of dying in the present day which correspond to the social and historical changes he identifies. These models have profoundly different implications for people who are dying and people who have been bereaved. Again, at the risk of oversimplifying a complex analysis, the models would appear to have the following components:

MODEL 1 The tame death in which death is a sad, inevitable but natural end to life.

MODEL 2 The romantic death in which death is a great event. An event which confirms and deepens the meaning of an individual's life.

MODEL 3 The modern death which involves the isolation of the dying and their carers. Death is a meaningless event which could happen to anybody at any time. It is dying which is feared.

MODEL 4 The modern death which involves the total isolation of the dying person. Death is simply ignored, subsumed in everyday reality, an event which must be managed as quickly and as cleanly as possible.

Ariès believes that it is models three and four which capture the way of death in contemporary Western societies (particularly for young adults). Whilst there must be as many ways of dying as there are of living, the awful isolation associated with model 4 has a nightmarish quality about it; there is nothing tame about this way of dying.

Illich (1977) is another critic of the contemporary way of dying. He contrasts a past acceptance of mortality with the contemporary denial of it. He calls contemporary attitudes towards death 'primitive'. Rather than seeing death as a natural, inevitable end to life we seek to attach blame to someone or something because we hold the irrational belief that death, particularly premature death, should ultimately be avoidable:

> the witch hunt that was traditional at the death of a tribal chief is being modernised. For every premature or clinically unnecessary death, somebody or something can be found who irresponsibly delayed or prevented a medical intervention.
>
> Illich (1977)

Illich argues that this situation has arisen out of a misguided notion of progress and a belief that advances in medical science and technology would ultimately be able to conquer death itself. Gorer (1965) identified a similar tendency and was bemused by an apparent underlying belief that death was potentially avoidable if one met certain behavioural standards and requirements.

In an early essay on the subject Gorer (1955) argued that death had replaced sex as contemporary society's major taboo topic. He was concerned with what he called the 'pornography' of death and the presentation of dying in an unrealistic framework. People can see the mechanics of death portrayed by the media without experiencing the reality of grief. People die and those who cared about them seek revenge rather than comfort, live to fight another day and feel better by the following morning. Gorer believed that, as the actual experience of deaths in the community became rarer and fewer, and fewer people either saw

3

corpses or experienced bereavement, a relatively realistic view of death had been replaced by a voyeuristic, adolescent preoccupation with it. At the time he was writing he believed that the 'horror comic' and the 'horror movie' epitomised such tendencies. If one wished to extend his ideas to the present day then some aspects of the media presentation of various issues might provide examples. Peter Tatchell makes the following comments about the presentation of news connected with the virus believed to cause AIDS.

> To Fleet Street AIDS was a new cocktail which embodied all the ingredients on which sensationalist journalism thrives, homosexuality, venereal disease, disfigurement, disability and death.
>
> Tatchell (1986)

Whilst there are many other authors who discuss the denial of death and its inadequate, unrealistic portrayal in popular culture, these authors have not been without their critics. For example, Kaufmann (1976) questions a whole range of authors from Feifel (1959) onwards over the denial of death. He points out that art and literature have always addressed these issues in depth and continue to do so. Furthermore, there have been many books written by bereaved people about bereavement, for example, Lewis (1961) and more recently Heike (1985). However, Smith (1982) suggests that, whilst the literature relevant to professionals who work in the area grows daily, the general public seems unaware of this growing body of literature. Kalish (1985) is of the view that despite courses in death education becoming widely available, particularly in the United States, their actual impact may only be marginal. In short, it does not simply seem to be a question of the presence of portrayals of death and dying but rather one of the predisposition to acknowledge what is, and always has been, there.

Overall the evidence would seem to suggest that death and dying have, at least in broad cultural terms, been 'conjured away' as Ariès suggests. Despite criticisms of the implicit romanticism of this analysis (Elias 1985) the process of dying in contemporary Western societies must in existential terms be an extremely lonely one. Many people would appear to die in an isolation almost too terrible to contemplate.

DYING IN HOSPITAL: DEATH AS A SOCIAL EVENT

According to Turner (1987), approximately 80 per cent of people who die in the United States do so in hospital. In the United Kingdom Cartwright *et al.* (1973) put the figure at approximately 57 per cent (hospital or similar institution).

A number of studies have focused upon death and dying in hospital. Some concentrate upon the social processes surrounding death (Glaser and Strauss 1965, 1968; Sudnow 1967) whilst others look in more detail at the psychological consequences of these social processes (Hinton 1967; Kübler-Ross 1969).

Sudnow emphasises the ways in which dying is routinised and thereby moulded to fit the day to day functioning of the hospital as an organisation. His work suggests that, even at the point of death itself, considerations of social worth and status are paramount. For example, he noted that differing amounts of effort were made to revive people who were suspected of being 'dead on arrival' at a hospital. He associated the degree of effort with perceptions of the social worth of the person involved – the greater the social worth, the more strenuous the resuscitation attempts. In extreme cases such considerations would appear to be acted out upon corpses. He interpreted his observations of the apparent disrespect shown to the corpses of suicide victims in terms of the social unacceptability of the act of suicide. Presumably, if people did not value their own lives then the social constraints which prevented others from desecrating their corpses were taken to be inapplicable.

Although Sudnow's work may be criticised on the grounds that few alternative explanations of his observations were considered, perhaps the observations themselves should not be too surprising. If Ariès (1983) is to be taken seriously, then Sudnow's work could be interpreted as a study of some of the ways in which the occurrence of an event which should not occur is dealt with, i.e. by aggressively invoking and adhering to the very norms and mores of everyday reality which are under threat. However, this is not necessarily the only or the best way that exposure to death and dying may be dealt with.

Glaser and Strauss (1965) also conceptualise dying as a form of 'status passage'. This passage is guided by beliefs concerning appropriate and inappropriate behaviour. These beliefs are ordered into a series of expectations about dying ('dying trajectories') which are believed to define various forms of 'normal' and 'abnormal' ways of dying. One function of casting ahead a dying trajectory is to limit, perhaps unrealistically, the uncertainty that those attending people who are dying may feel about the event of death. A summary of their findings is given in Table 2.

Table 2 Dying trajectories

Time of death	Occurrence of death within foreseeable future	
	Certain	Uncertain
Known	Some accidents	Radical surgery
Unknown	Terminal illness	Chronic illness

In the case of some accidents (e.g. road traffic accidents) the time of death may be known or its occurrence in the near future predicted with some degree of certainty. For example, a person may be found to be dead on arrival at a hospital or so badly injured that no effective treatment is available. Alternatively, if radical surgery is required then death may become a probability or a risk rather than a virtually certain outcome.

In the case of terminal illness the situation is one in which death is reasonably certain to occur in the foreseeable future but the precise timing, i.e. in days, weeks or months, remains uncertain. The case of chronic illness is associated with an even higher degree of uncertainty over both whether or when death may occur as a result of the condition.

Glaser and Strauss were mainly concerned with deaths occurring in hospital. Obviously, not all deaths do occur in hospital although most are associated with a hospital setting at one time or another. For example, most accident victims would presumably have little contact with a hospital prior to their death. Whilst degree of contact with a hospital is one variable associated with different dying trajectories, the potential for an individual's actual awareness of impending death is another.

Kalish (1985) has suggested that if people are given a choice they would choose to die in old age of a cause which is associated with no period of hospitalisation or prior warning. A sudden death. Paradoxically the death most people say they would like to die may be one of the most traumatic for the people who cared about them to come to terms with. Both age at death and perceptions of the suddenness of a death are important, if somewhat contradictory, factors which may affect reactions to bereavement. Parkes (1972) has indicated that unanticipated deaths may be associated with complications arising during the bereavement process. Kaufmann (1976) suggests that there is an association between death and old age which may make deaths in the older age ranges less difficult to come to terms with than the deaths of younger people. Also, Illich (1977) has indicated that premature deaths are those most likely to be associated with a tendency to seek revenge or allocate blame for the death. Furthermore, both Gorer (1965) and Parkes (1972) forward a 'timeliness' hypothesis which implies that deaths believed to be timely, i.e. generally those occurring in the older age ranges, seem to be less distressing for people who have been bereaved than 'untimely' deaths, i.e. those occurring in the younger age ranges. Nevertheless, it must be said that 'timeliness' may equally well be a function of the state of a relationship and the perceptions of the two people involved. Age may not necessarily be an important factor. For example:

A man in his seventies expressed anguish over the death of his wife, also in her seventies. They had married in their fifties and he felt that she had been badly abused by her first husband. He wanted to have the time to 'make all that up to her' – he felt that he hadn't had long enough.

A woman in her forties still grieved deeply for her mother seven years after the death. The women felt her mother had survived a hard, unhappy life in poverty with very little material comfort or emotional support. She had hoped to be able to share some of her own happiness. Her mother died long before she felt she had shared enough.

However, actual evidence from studies which have looked at reactions following the death of an elderly person are inconclusive. Parkes summarises the situation as follows:

> while age may be a factor in determining the intensity of grief, pathological reactions are not confined to the young.
>
> (1972: 155)

Furthermore, the position is complicated by the fact that advancing age itself may lead people to consider the issue of mortality in more depth. In a culture which, to say the least, does little to facilitate any real understanding of death and dying in the general population, advancing age increases the likelihood of a direct confrontation with these issues. It is possible that anticipation of death and the development of a belief system to account for it may be more common amongst older people. Perhaps it is the absence of these considerations which makes death and bereavement extremely difficult to cope with for younger people, rather than the presence of them making death and bereavement appreciably easier for those who are older.

In my own study (Littlewood 1983) relatively few people under 45 years of age had considered death or dying until their bereavement. Alternatively, relatively few people over 65 had not considered some of the issues involved. However, although many older people had thought about death, their thoughts were largely confined to deaths occurring amongst the elderly. In general, the development of a system of beliefs about dying did little to assuage the grief elderly people felt in connection with the deaths of younger people. Despite some people holding vivid memories of deaths which had occurred in their youth, they also held a belief in progress together with the idea, perhaps best expressed by a grandmother whose grandson had died of leukaemia, that:

> these sorts of things shouldn't be happening in this day and age. In my time they were common enough, I lost two [children] myself – but these days. . . .

7

She went on to blame the 'negligence' of the medical profession for having failed to diagnose the problem earlier.

Alternatively it would seem that some elderly people who had died managed to help the people who cared for them both before and after their deaths. Through acceptance, planning, discussion and reminiscence some elderly individuals would seem to have had the courage and ability to 'tame' their own deaths in a way which was beneficial to their survivors. Unfortunately these people were in the minority.

Except for the victims of sudden accidents or fatal heart attacks it would seem that very few people can escape at least some knowledge of their impending deaths. The issues surrounding the awareness of one's death occurring in the foreseeable future are extremely complex. This complexity is compounded if people are seen as part of a social network rather than as isolated individuals. Glaser and Strauss (1968), in looking at the awareness of impending death a terminally ill person may have or be given, identify three types of awareness contexts, i.e. 'open', 'mixed' and 'closed'.

An open awareness context is one in which the terminally ill person is aware of his or her prognosis and is able to discuss the implications openly with medical personnel, family and friends. Everyone knows and acknowledges that the person is dying and all are willing to communicate openly about the subject.

Mixed awareness contexts are those in which some members of the dying person's social network know of the prognosis but others (often including the dying person themselves) do not. Mixed awareness contexts, particularly those which involve the dying person being kept in ignorance of the terminal nature of his or her disease may be particularly difficult to maintain over time. For instance, as the terminal illness progresses, the dying person may come to suspect that their condition is considerably worse than they had been led to believe. A person in such a position may attempt to gain information in various, usually indirect, ways. It may be very difficult for a person who is dependent upon medical personnel and/or families for support to ask the direct question – a question which would invariably challenge the validity of previous communication.

Another variation of a mixed awareness context arises when everyone knows of the fact that a given person is terminally ill but everyone chooses to pretend otherwise. The major difficulty here is that everyone is simply assuming what other people may know and communication patterns may be dictated by false assumptions. Such mutual pretence may lead to a dying person unnecessarily isolating himself or herself in order to protect other people, and friends and relatives wondering, after the death has occurred, who 'knew' what.

A closed awareness context is one in which an attempt is made, usually by the medical personnel and the terminally ill person's family, to keep the prognosis from the person. Again, this can prove to be an arduous task if the pretence has to be maintained over any length of time. Furthermore, it may serve to alienate the dying person from their friends and relatives. A range of awareness contexts is given in Table 3 which hopefully gives an indication of the complexity associated with communicating with people who are terminally ill.

Table 3 Awareness contexts

Terminally ill person's awareness	Patterns of social organisation and communication in society, community, family, hospital or home		
	Open	*Mixed*	*Closed*
Open	A	B	C
Mixed	D	E	F
Closed	G	H	I

In terms of the dying trajectories identified by Glaser and Strauss, it is only in the case of terminal illness that death in the foreseeable future must be faced by someone. However, the designation of a terminal illness is itself a social event, usually a clinically conferred status, which may bear little relation to the dying person's perception of their condition. It is by no means inevitable that all of those involved will either know, or be prepared to admit, that a given illness has reached its terminal phase.

Indeed, the clarity of the category itself is open to question. From a philosophical perspective it may be argued that death is the only certainty in life and, therefore, may give life meaning. However, as Sartre (1958) has pointed out, the uncertainty of death's timing makes it unlikely that it will or even can give meaning to the processes of life. At one level we all face certain death at an uncertain time but death within the foreseeable future is not something that many people, other than those who know they are terminally ill, routinely confront. Nevertheless, the issue of timing remains of paramount importance. Unfortunately, prognoses are frequently imprecise and uncertainty concerning the timing of death is something we all share, to a greater or lesser extent.

In considering the impact a terminal prognosis may have it is not surprising that considerable debate has surrounded whether or not a person should be told. These debates tend to revolve around the concepts of helplessness and control. Those who believe that it may be better for some people not to know of their terminal prognosis believe that telling a person that they are dying may rob them of all hope for the future, destroying the quality of their remaining life and possibly hastening their death. Seligman (1975) identified a condition which he called learned helplessness. In such a condition people come to believe that there is nothing they can do to influence the outcome of events. Seligman associates this condition with depression and, in certain cases, with death. Many people who prefer those who are dying to remain unaware of the fact believe that the delivery of a terminal prognosis may precipitate a form of helplessness, leaving the person demoralised, depressed and without hope for the future.

Those who believe it better to tell a person who is dying the truth about their condition feel that the person is robbed of the control of their remaining life if they are kept in ignorance of their impending death. To a certain extent the withholding of such information excludes the dying person from the taken-for-granted reality of others and may unnecessarily isolate them. Also, the person may eventually become an object of pity in the eyes of their carers, further corroding the dying person's support network at a time when they are probably in desperate need of supportive relationships. Furthermore, evidence suggests that, even if people are not expressly told of their condition, they know of it nevertheless (Kübler-Ross 1969). In these instances the dying person may be attempting to protect those around them by feigning ignorance to their carers. The situation is one in which no-one can be sure of who is protecting whom from what. People who are dying may wish to be able to use their time more profitably. For example:

A 70-year-old woman who was dying of a breast cancer which had metastasised to her lung talked about her condition at some length. She felt that, overall, she had enjoyed a good life and achieved many worthwhile things. She hoped to live long enough to see her grand-daughter's wedding and to be well enough to go to the reception. Her husband was a great support to her although as far as she was concerned he did not suspect what she knew, i.e. that she was dying. She could not bear to tell him because it would take away his hope of her recovery. Upon the return of her husband she left to talk briefly with a neighbour. Her husband was distraught, he knew his wife was dying but could not bring himself to speak of it because it would take away her hope of recovery. They talked often of the past but lived 'from day to day' in the present. He desperately wanted to care for her at home but felt he lacked the material resources to do so. He could not try to obtain them because that would mean 'telling the truth'. Both were doing what they thought to be in the best interests of the other. Both were isolated and both were desperate.

Debates surrounding awareness contexts will no doubt continue, but at the level of the institution it would seem likely that a particular awareness context will be dominant and that individuals will be expected to accept this. Acknowledgement of the need for more flexible approaches to the issue of the awareness of dying may well be under-stated because of this factor. Sudnow's work (1967) would suggest that the dominant awareness context in the institutions he investigated was a closed one, arguably mirroring socio-cultural attitudes towards death. Glaser and Strauss's

(1965, 1968) work may be taken as illustrative of the many contradictions and confusions which arise out of attempts to deal with an event which in cultural and institutional terms may be an example of what Douglas (1987) has called 'an unspeakable truth'. Whilst some people who are terminally ill may neither have nor necessarily want any knowledge of their impending death, sooner or later their carers will almost certainly be told of the prognosis. Some research has suggested that forewarning of a death may help those who have been bereaved to adjust to their loss.

ANTICIPATING GRIEF

The term 'anticipatory grief' was first used by Lindemann (1944) in connection with people who showed no overt manifestations of grief at the time of a death, but who had already apparently experienced normal grief prior to the death occurring. However, there is some controversy over whether or not a period of anticipatory grief is helpful to people in the later stages of their bereavement. Parkes and Weiss (1983) suggest that sudden deaths are likely to lead to difficulties and Glick, Weiss and Parkes (1974) concluded that the opportunity for anticipatory grieving decreased the likelihood of psychological difficulties thirteen months after the death. Kalish (1985) summarises the findings in this area and concludes that anticipatory grief does occur in some cases, is associated with greater calm at the time of death, and that some bereaved people gain the capacity for effective functioning more rapidly if they have time to anticipate the death.

The helpfulness or otherwise of a period of anticipation prior to a death would appear to be dependent upon a number of factors. One important area of debate is about the way people respond to the threat of the death of a loved person. Research findings on this point are contradictory. Some evidence indicates that some people respond by 'letting go' of the relationship (Bugen 1977), whilst other evidence indicates that some people intensify their commitment to the dying person (Vachon et al. 1980). Unfortunately both courses of action may be problematic.

The first body of evidence may be taken to suggest that anticipatory grief may help the survivors at the expense of the dying person. Fulton and Fulton (1971) suggest that mourning may finish before the death has occurred leaving the dying person alone and abandoned. Volkan (1975) has also commented upon what he calls the 'waiting vulture' syndrome – a situation in which the relatives gather around the dying person, heads down, shoulders hunched, silently waiting in the belief that 'nothing can be done'.

In my own study (Littlewood 1983) some people reported that they had grieved the loss of the relationship long before the death itself had occurred.

11

Whilst the impact of their reactions upon the dying person may only be inferred, examples of such experiences may be of interest.

A woman in her seventies who had nursed her husband for many years felt that she had 'lost all her love for him' long before he died. Following the amputation of a leg fifteen months before his death her husband became increasingly withdrawn and resentful. The woman felt that he had been completely changed by his period of hospitalisation and was no longer the person she knew. She felt that his actual death had little impact on her as she'd come to feel that she was caring for a stranger – she had effectively lost her husband at the time of his operation.

Another woman in her fifties started to grieve for her father at the time he was admitted to residential care. He was suffering from senile dementia and she 'knew he was as good as dead when he had to go away'. She said she felt little reaction to the news of his actual death.

It seems possible that long periods of time during which the dying person is mentally 'absent', together with the belief that the situation is likely to be permanent, may precipitate reactions similar to those which usually occur after a physical death. Furthermore, it seems reasonable to suggest that people who experience such reactions may regain the capacity for effective functioning more rapidly than those who do not. However, it must be said that the impact such a reaction may have on the dying person could be devastating.

Paradoxically, whilst letting go of a relationship may be helpful to a person about to be bereaved (possibly at the expense of the person who is dying), intensifying a relationship may be helpful to the dying person – possibly at the expense of the person who is about to be bereaved. Sanders (1983) and Vachon *et al.* (1982) have suggested that a period during which a death may be anticipated might be conducive to the social support of the person about to be bereaved. Presumably, people who might wish to care for the person who is about to be bereaved, if they have some prior warning of the death, are better prepared. However, in some cases where the person who is to be bereaved intensifies the relationship with the person who is dying, social isolation may result as the person who is about to be bereaved focuses all of their time and attention upon the person who is dying. For example:

A woman in her forties whose teenage daughter had died of bone cancer was 'very close' to her daughter during her terminal illness. She felt that no-one could care for her daughter as effectively as she herself could and believed that the act of momentarily leaving her daughter's bedside had precipitated her death. In caring for her daughter who was an only child this woman eventually lost most, if not all, of her social contacts including her husband. On the day of her daughter's funeral she was about to accept the advice of friends who suggested that she should ignore her daughter's wishes and take flowers to the crematorium when she heard her daughter say 'Don't let them influence you mother'. After that they seldom did; literally years after her daughter's death this woman relied primarily on her daughter for social approval and social support.

The situation may be further complicated by the issue of awareness contexts. Anticipatory grief in the best of circumstances may be difficult to cope with due to attempts by those who are about to be bereaved to protect the dying person from further pain. However, if the dying person is unaware at whatever level of their condition then a prolonged period of pretence could actually worsen the strain for survivors. Clearly anticipatory grief is a complex phenomenon. Nevertheless, if most people now die of chronic illnesses then most survivors could be given at least some time in which to anticipate the death. Therefore, further research into the area of the impact of anticipatory grief might go some way to identifying under what circumstances a period of anticipation may be helpful to those about to be bereaved. So far the impact of anticipatory grief upon survivors has been considered, but what of the position of the dying themselves? The seminal work of Kübler-Ross (1969) addressed their position and, in her major theoretical contribution to the area, she identified five stages of the dying process associated with deaths occurring in hospital. The five stages are as follows:

1. Denial and isolation

According to Kübler-Ross almost all people make use of denial when they first have the knowledge that they are dying. Denial can be a healthy strategy which enables people to control shock and to pace their inter-pretation of information when they first realise that they are terminally ill. Later on isolation may be used. Isolation involves maintaining a cognitive understanding of an event without acknowledging its emotional impact. Again this can be a positive response which protects the person from despair and maintains their enjoyment of day to day activities.

2. Anger

Following a period of denial and isolation the dying person becomes angry and resentful. Anger may be directed at anyone; for example, society, self, carers, God or the world in general may all be the subject of a dying person's intense rage. Such anger may be extremely difficult to cope with and may lead to the dying person being avoided and further isolated by their carers. Alternatively, anger may be responded to in punitive ways. Neither response would seem to be particularly helpful to the dying person since avoidance and/or disapproval may only isolate them further.

3. Bargaining

The third stage Kübler-Ross identifies is that of bargaining. Bargains are usually made in secret and involve attempts to negotiate more time or greater relief from pain.

4. Depression

When death is finally acknowledged to be inevitable feelings of loss overwhelm the person and they become depressed. Sadness, guilt and a sense of worthlessness often accompany this depression and many people who are dying believe they must have done something to deserve their fate.

5. Acceptance

The final stage Kübler-Ross describes is that of acceptance. This is not necessarily a happy state. The dying person may lose all interest in their surroundings and their carers. Less and less energy is available for life and the person seems to need to 'get on with dying'. Perhaps if it were not for its negative connotations, withdrawal might be a more accurate description of this stage.

Several questions have been raised concerning Kübler-Ross's work, and whilst these questions are important they in no way detract from the work's considerable impact in terms of bringing the isolation and fears of the dying into the public arena. Whilst most workers in the area agree that the responses to dying described by Kübler-Ross are familiar, there is considerable doubt over whether or not they are recognisable, non-overlapping occurrences.

Fitchett (1980) found that only a quarter of health care professionals and students could agree in the identification of a given case as being that of someone in a stage of acceptance. Almost as many thought the case was that of someone in the stage of denial. Furthermore, when experience was controlled for, it would appear that it was the more experienced workers who tended to talk in terms of denial whilst the least experienced workers and students presumed acceptance.

Shneidman (1973) has also noted that the stages described by Kübler-Ross do not appear to be uni-directional. In particular, alternation between acceptance and denial was frequently noted, which may go some way to explaining the grounds for the confusion found by Fitchett.

However, such results are not necessarily surprising when contemporary attitudes towards death are taken into account. Interpretation will always present difficulties. For example, Ariès (1983), in identifying what he believes to be the predominant ways of dying in modern society, describes them in terms of a surface acceptance of death together with a more or less successful denial of the emotional impact of the event. Acceptance or denial will probably always be dependent upon the perspectives of the people involved, particularly since both may be present in the same person at the same time. Furthermore, work in connection with awareness contexts might lead one to suggest that denial may function as an inter- as well as intra-personal defence mechanism, thereby increasing the difficulties associated with any interpretations made in this area.

In all probability the stages of dying identified by Kübler-Ross apply to dying in a specific social context (i.e. hospitals in Western societies). There may be many other reactions to impending death. Dying in hospital and the receipt and interpretation of knowledge regarding death-related issues raises a series of complex cultural contradictions. The difficulties experienced at the level of individual people and their carers should not be underestimated. The isolation, identified by numerous researchers, of people who are dying would seem to be potentially overwhelming. The tangled web of individual and group protection, deception and defence is difficult to appreciate and may be impossible to interpret with any real degree of confidence.

THE HOSPICE ALTERNATIVE: A DIFFERENT WAY OF DYING

Increasing knowledge and understanding of the problems faced by dying people and their carers undoubtedly stimulated the growth of the modern hospice movement. Young (1981) characterised the hospice movement as having to face the taboo nature of death in order to overcome the fear of dying. He suggests that the hospice movement goes some way to restoring death to its natural and dignified state rather than allowing it to remain associated with a daunting, dehumanising and frightening process. Whilst the origin of the modern movement is frequently taken to be the launch by Cicely Saunders of St Christopher's hospice in England, Hillier (1983) points out that the movement has a much longer history. In the Middle Ages the term hospice was associated with a waiting place for travellers, including those who were ill or dying. However, the origins of the contemporary movement may be traced to the foundation, by the Irish Sisters of Charity, of a hospice in Dublin. The hospice was founded at a time of great need. The potato famine in Ireland left many people sick and dying, and in England where pain and sickness were believed by equally

15

many to be a punishment for sin, people who were terminally ill were not on the whole treated well in the Poor Law establishments. In 1900 the Irish Sisters of Charity opened St Joseph's convent in London, and in 1902 they opened St Joseph's hospice for poor people who were dying.

Hillier suggests that the opening of St Christopher's hospice may be interpreted as a move towards a more ecumenical, medical model for the provision of care. Davidson (1979) has pointed out that at least four distinct models of modern hospice care may be identified, and more recently Gilmore and Gilmore (1988) have suggested that the movement is towards a more secular model of care. Nevertheless, despite these changes, St Christopher's still provides the basic model of modern hospice care which is as much a philosophy as it is a pattern of service delivery.

In terms of philosophy, hospice is a concept of care which involves recognising the uniqueness and importance of the dying person and their carers. There is a commitment to respecting this uniqueness and to meeting needs on an individual basis. Whilst hospital care tends to focus upon disease, hospice care may be said to focus upon the person. Perhaps most importantly, hospice involves a change in perspective from 'nothing more can be done' to 'we must provide the best kind of human care possible for this person'.

In terms of service delivery the modern hospice combines both institutional care and home care for people who are terminally ill. Because of successful home care programmes, hospices can treat many people during the course of a year. Modern hospices usually provide a combination of the following:

1. in-patient services: including specialist knowledge of pain relief;
2. out-patient services to the home via professional and/or volunteer networks which enable many dying people to be cared for in the community;
3. support for bereaved people.

Hospice care attempts to see the individual as part of a broader social network and consequently attempts to meet the needs of those caring for dying people as well as those of the dying person themselves. The hospice movement has also made a great contribution to the area of pain control. By promoting an understanding of the multi-faceted aspects of pain and by treating pain before it begins, the role of pain in terminal illness, and the associated fear of it, has been greatly diminished.

Most studies which compare hospice care to the care of dying people in other settings show a broad range of advantages. Hinton (1979) found that people dying in hospices were less anxious and less depressed than a comparable group of people dying in another institution. Parkes (1978) also compared people dying in a hospice to people dying elsewhere and found that those dying in the hospice were more mobile and experienced less pain. In addition, their carers reported less anxiety, fewer somatic symptoms, visited more often and were more involved with the day to day care of the dying person.

However, hospice care may not be available for everyone and may be inappropriate for some people. For example, it may be unsuited to a person's needs or the person may suffer from a condition which requires equipment which is not readily available in a hospice setting. Furthermore, hospices have been criticised on the grounds that they segregate dying people from the rest of the community. However, as hospices develop more community links and expand their contribution to the education of health professionals, it is hoped that any barriers which may exist will be broken down. Perhaps the hospice movement, with its focus upon the individual and the insistence that people can and should die their own way, has gone some way towards making a 'tame' death a distinct possibility – always assuming that this is what the dying person wants.

A GOOD DEATH: SAFE OR SANITARY?

Whilst major improvements in the care of people who are dying have undoubtedly been made, the impact of these improvements upon cultural attitudes towards death may be marginal. Despite the growth, particularly in North America, of death education courses, the actual impact of these courses has been questioned by Kalish (1985). He believes that the enthusiasm which characterised the early work in the area of death awareness may have been overwhelmed by what he calls 'bureaucratisation'. Instead of challenging the prevailing norms and values of society the movement was apparently challenged by them, and death and dying became sanitised in the process. Kalish fears that the contemporary situation may be one in which people do 'd and b' (death and bereavement) after their coffee breaks, a situation where much may be known at the cognitive level but little understood at the emotional level.

Perhaps misinterpretations of Kübler-Ross's work provide another example of this tendency. Kastenbaum (1975) has suggested that anxiety and a lack of structure amongst health professionals working with dying people led them to apply Kübler-Ross's findings in a particularly rigid manner, thereby giving themselves a falsely secure knowledge base. The stages, taken by some people to be immutable, were seen as the norm, leaving any deviation from them in danger of being labelled pathological. It is possible that the tendency towards adopting a fixed view of Kübler-Ross's work was more difficult to avoid than had been anticipated. In addition, in a later work Kastenbaum (1988) suggests that those involved in the broader social context in which hospices operate may have very different views of their contribution when compared to those within the hospice movement. Specifically he argues that hospices may be seen as having the potential

17

to deliver a 'safe' death: a death which is dignified and private, a death which takes place outside the general social context – a death which Ariès might be more familiar with than Saunders. Kastenbaum points out that not all causes of death can easily be made 'safe' in this way. For example, for various reasons, people dying from the AIDS syndrome may not be in a socio-cultural position to die 'safely'. It would seem possible that some deaths may be more difficult to re-tame than others.

Whilst these views may be seen to be extremely pessimistic, it would appear reasonable to suggest that, if powerful cultural forces are acting upon an area, then attempts to change any understanding of it will be met with considerable resistance. Marris (1986) has postulated that a 'conservative impulse' and a resistance to change are inevitable parts of life which operate at all levels in society. He used research concerning bereavement as the cornerstone of an argument which strongly suggests that change, if it can be achieved at all, can be achieved only relatively slowly and at considerable psychological cost to all those involved.

Parkes (1975), in a consideration of the ways in which individuals deal with what he calls 'redundant world models', indicates that there may be several different ways of coping with information which threatens previously held expectations and 'realities'. It might be suggested that Kalish and Kastenbaum are focusing upon strategies which involve incorporating ideas about dying and bereavement into the dominant cultural pattern. However, this way of interpreting information about people who are dying or who have been bereaved may be only one of many potential responses to change in this area, even if it is the dominant response. Obviously, the processes and struggles associated with achieving major changes in cultural mores and values are beyond the scope of this chapter. Nevertheless, there is little doubt that they have a profound impact upon the ways in which dying as a process and death as an event are experienced. Despite a high level of improvement in knowledge and standards of care, the evidence would seem to indicate that the potential problems associated with cultural representations of and expectations about death and dying remain considerable.

It would still seem to be the case that dying people risk facing isolation, misunderstanding, denial and fear. Perhaps the contemporary idea that a good death is one in which a person avoids, because of the suddenness of the event, exposure to such risks should cause little surprise. However, most people will not experience a 'good' death and perhaps the hospice movement has gone some way to re-taming the more likely ending to life.

It would seem too, that people who have been recently bereaved, because of their close association with the process of dying, are also at risk of isolation, misunderstanding, denial and fear. Nevertheless, it cannot be said that the bleak scenario painted by Ariès is inevitable:

18

We ignore the existence of a scandal that we have been unable to prevent; we act as if it did not exist, and thus mercilessly force the bereaved to say nothing. A heavy silence has fallen over the subject of death. When this silence is broken, as it sometimes is in America today, it is to reduce death to the insignificance of an ordinary event that is mentioned with feigned indifference. Either way, the result is the same: Neither the individual nor the community is strong enough to recognise the existence of death.

(1983: 613–4)

2

RITUALS AND
MOURNING CUSTOMS

'We are unable to maintain our former attitude towards death and
have not yet found a new one.'

Freud (1915)
Thoughts for the Times on War and Death

INTRODUCTION

Whilst death may mean different things to different cultures, it would
seem that all human groups, under ordinary circumstances, dispose of
corpses with ritual (Habenstein and Lamers 1963). The rituals associated with the disposal of the dead vary widely. However, there is a
widespread belief that funeral rites are a source of valuable social support to the society in general and to those who have been bereaved,
in particular. Indeed, the decline of mourning customs, particularly in
England, has been related to a decline in valuable communal support
for people who have been bereaved. Consequently, the first part of
this chapter looks at some of the anthropological evidence which has
been taken to suggest that death-related rituals are helpful to those
who are bereaved. An attempt has been made to identify the potential
relevance of these observations to the contemporary situation and to
evaluate the extent to which death-related rituals may be helpful to
bereaved people.

The second topic this chapter is concerned with is some of the major
interpretations of the role actual mourning customs in England, from the
Victorian era to the present day, may have played in terms of facilitating
the bereavement process. The third part of the chapter is concerned with
the relevance of the smaller scale rituals which Goffman (1972) argues we
all use to organise our everyday lives, expectations and interactions and the
final part is concerned with the actual experiences of bereaved people who
have undergone funeral rites.

RITUALS

According to Taylor (1980), rituals represent 'the symbolic affirmation of values by means of culturally standardised utterances and actions'. A distinction is usually made between calendrical rites and rites of passage. Calendrical rites are those which occur annually or seasonally and rites of passage are those which occur when individuals or groups move from one social status to another. Funerals are obviously examples of the latter group of rites, i.e. rites of passage. However, the status changes involved in funeral rituals are relatively complex.

Clearly, the status of the corpse is involved but the status of all those who were related to the corpse also undergoes social changes. The position of the dead person is relatively unproblematic. Specifically, a funeral ritual changes the dead person's social status from being alive and a member of society to being acknowledged as officially (in social terms) dead, and therefore no longer a member of the social group. The position of people who have been bereaved is rather more complicated. Most societies presume, for various lengths of time, that those who were socially related to the person who has died remain socially close to the world of the dead. Only after time has elapsed are people who have been bereaved allowed to be fully active members of the society again. Taylor (1980) has further identified the following functions of rituals, all of which would presumably apply to funerals.

1. Validation and reinforcement of values in the face of psychological disturbances:
    Obviously, any death in any society causes, to a greater or lesser extent, psychological disturbances. Funerals, from this perspective, would be expected to represent the core values of the society which have been threatened by the occurrence of a death.

2. Reinforcement of group ties:
    In the case of funerals the relationship between the dead person and other members of the society would be affirmed. This affirmation of the social worth of the dead person would also, presumably, have the effect of reinforcing the group ties of the survivors of the death.

3. Aiding status change by acquainting people with their new role:
    Funerals also act to socially confirm the status changes which must be undertaken by the survivors of a death. For example the social status of being a husband or wife would change to that of being a widower or widow.

Given the apparent benefits of rituals it might be supposed that rituals are invariably helpful to those undergoing them. However, there has been considerable debate in the literature concerning both the relevance and the helpfulness of rituals in contemporary society.

21

If it is believed that ritual behaviour restores social equilibrium when changes in social interaction have occurred, then a very positive view of rituals and ritualisation emerges. However, as Leming and Dickinson (1985) have pointed out, rituals can also have extremely negative functions inasmuch as they may cause, or more probably channel, tensions inherent in a society or groups of individuals without necessarily offering a resolution of the conflicts and tensions involved. Obviously, some social conflicts cannot easily be resolved and in such instances rituals may cause those involved in them to focus sharply on the conflict rather than on the issue of its resolution. The marked tendency of 'political' funerals to result in, not to mention from, violence in divided communities would be an obvious example of the problems they describe. In this example, the group ties of one group are affirmed in terms of their opposition to another group – thereby increasing the overall degree of social tension rather than decreasing it.

Vizedom (1976) has argued that contemporary opinions concerning the efficacy of rituals in terms of their ability to facilitate harmonious change are unrealistic. In an extensive review of the literature she has suggested that contemporary societies, particularly in times of change, have persistently overestimated the power of ritual transformations.

She notes that concern over adolescence as a developmental stage resulted in a review of less complex societies together with a belief that the rituals associated with such societies, i.e. those that changed children into adults, could simply be taken out of the social context in which they arose and used in a very different kind of society. Vizedom is of the belief that rituals can assist passages from one status to another only in societies which are relatively homogeneous and static. Thus, she contends that changes in the nature of contemporary societies severely limit the extent to which rituals can facilitate changes in a given individual's status. She concludes that, though it may be widely believed, it has yet to be demonstrated that, in any contemporary cultural context, rituals facilitate transitions.

Martinson, Deck and Adams (1986) make a similar point in their identification of a series of myths about bereavement. One of the myths they identify is the myth that cultural rituals are always effective in preventing negative sequelae after a death has occurred. However, the belief that funeral rituals must be of help to people who have been bereaved would appear to be a particularly strong one. For example, Gorer (1965), Marris (1986) and Parkes (1972) all comment upon the lack of ritualisation surrounding deaths in contemporary society and assume that this must somehow be detrimental to people who have been bereaved.

VAN GENNEP AND RITES OF PASSAGE

Van Gennep's seminal work on rites of passage was written at the turn of the century and translated into English in 1960. The work is often cited in connection with the helpfulness of funeral rites. Van Gennep was concerned with a wide range of rites of passage of which funerals were an important sub-set. His thesis was that all rituals involving passage from one state to another, be it single–married, child–adult or alive–dead, shared a single tripartite structure of rites. The first series of rites involve separation. These rites of separation serve to separate the individual or group from their previously held social status or position. The second series of rites involve transition. During the rites of transition the individual or group is between social states and is often physically or symbolically excluded from the society. The third and final series of rites are those of incorporation. These are the rites by which the individual or group is incorporated into the new social state or position. Van Gennep believed that this general structure was adhered to in most societies and was related to the social necessity of recruiting people who develop, grow old and die into fixed and relatively unchanging cultural systems. In short, rites of passage are necessary because societies outlive their individual members.

As Huntington and Metcalf point out:

> There is a deceptive simplicity to Van Gennep's notion, which at first sight seems to amount to little more than an assertion that rituals have beginnings, middles, and ends. However, Van Gennep was the first to notice just how similar are the beginnings, middles and ends of an extraordinarily wide range of rituals. Van Gennep emphasized that these similarities are not random analogies but part of a single general phenomenon.
>
> (1979:8)

Van Gennep's consideration of funerals is of particular interest. He initially anticipated that rites of separation, i.e. of the dead from the living, would be extremely prominent with rites of transition and incorporation only slightly elaborated. However, he found that rites of separation were few in number whilst the transition rites 'have a duration and complexity sometimes so great that they must be granted a sort of autonomy' (1960: 146).

Following his survey of death rituals throughout the world, he came to the conclusion that the theme of transition rather than separation dominated funeral symbolism. Furthermore, the deceased's next-of-kin (however that might be culturally defined) were subject to these rites along with the dead person. Van Gennep's conceptualisation of the passage of the dead person and their relatives is given in Table 4.

Van Gennep's work has been widely quoted in the literature concerned with dying and bereavement (e.g. Abse 1985). However, it must be said that Van Gennep himself did not claim that rites of passage in general or funeral rites in particular actually eased the transitions for passengers. However, the structure of the rites themselves facilitates an understanding of the ambiguity which often surrounds people who have recently been bereaved.

23

As Kübler-Ross (1983) has pointed out, funeral rites of separation are relatively straightforward and simply involve the public acknowledgement that a person significant in our lives has died.

However, rites of transition involving the social and the personal acceptance of the meaning of death are far more complicated and subject to a great deal of social negotiation in terms of the acceptance or otherwise that the death of someone significant to us has occurred. Perhaps, with the benefit of hindsight, it should not be surprising to find that it is these rites which dominate funeral symbolism. Further difficulties arise when rites of re-incorporation are considered. For many people in contemporary Western societies there would appear to be little if anything in the way of a formal acknowledgement that a person who has been bereaved can and/or should be permitted or required to re-engage in the normal day to day activities of the particular society. If Van Gennep's analysis is accepted then perhaps it might be anticipated that the major problems facing people who have been bereaved are likely to occur after, rather than be resolved by, the funeral ritual.

Table 4 The structure of funeral rites

Rites	The dead person	Those who are bereaved
Separation	From the living members of society	From the living members of society
Transition	From the world of the living towards the world of the dead	From the world of the dead towards the world of the living
Incorporation	Into the world of the dead	Into the world of the living

Rites of passage and re-incorporation

For many people in Western societies re-incorporation into the mainstream of social life may become problematic. Without the support of any social or ritual sanctions it becomes difficult to determine when a period of grief has socially, if not personally, ended. Under these circumstances it is often difficult to estimate any degree of adjustment to the loss. Interestingly enough, in an early study Glick, Weiss and Parkes (1974) used remarriage as an indication of adjustment to the loss of a spouse. Obviously, marriage is a rite of passage in itself and it might be suggested that, for some people, undergoing another rite of passage may be attempted in order to achieve normality following a bereavement.

In my own study (Littlewood 1983) remarriage was one of the commonest reasons given for refusing to be interviewed in depth about the loss of the first spouse. The following comments, made by a remarried 47-year-old man, whose first wife had died two years' previously, may serve as an example: 'I feel that that part of my life is over now, I'm back to normal and it wouldn't be a good idea to talk about it.'

Paradoxically, it would appear that being on the brink of birth, marriage or remarriage was a common reason for volunteering to be interviewed about bereavement. For example, a father whose daughter had died of leukaemia over a year before he was interviewed felt that, although he didn't want to talk about this experience of bereavement in depth, he did want to let the hospital know that he was better. It was particularly important to him because he'd felt he'd completely broken down after his child died but he was back to normal now and looking forward to the birth of twins in a few months' time. Despite anthropological theory indicating otherwise, some people in contemporary Western societies hold the belief that undergoing another rite of passage following a death may serve as the final funeral rite, i.e. that of re-incorporation. The importance of this 'rite' in everyday language is the role it plays in getting the person 'back to normal'. Whilst it must be hoped that the belief will work the magic people hope for, obviously this is an outcome which cannot be assured.

> A woman, in her twenties, whose father had died, was very clear that her reason for marrying so soon after her father's death was 'to get back to normal'. However, the transformation she'd hoped for had not occurred. Nevertheless, she was expecting her first baby in a few months' time and that, she thought, 'would do it'.

For many women the desire to have a child following a bereavement can be particularly strong. Whilst, on one level, having a baby may be viewed as a rite of passage, other motives may be involved. For example, one woman described wanting a child to 'look after and cuddle' as being a recurring reaction following the deaths of people close to her and many widows reported finding it helpful to have contact with other people's young children following the deaths of their husbands (Littlewood 1983).

In the case of parents who have lost children, Videka-Sherman (1982) has suggested that having another baby is one of the signs of positively adjusting to the loss. Her work in general would suggest that a shift away from preoccupation with the dead child and the past towards activities in the present is necessary if parents are to cope adequately with the death of their child. However, it must be said that there may be many reasons other than positive ones which may motivate people in this respect. For example, if there is a belief amongst members of the general population that undergoing another rite of passage will somehow serve to re-incorporate them back into normal life, it might be the case that some people undertake such rites to avoid the bereavement process rather than to signify symbolically that, for them, that process is at an end. Furthermore, Cain and Cain (1964) identified a group of children who had apparently been deliberately conceived literally to 'replace' a child who had died. Whilst this sample was taken from a child guidance clinic and the authors were clearly focusing on a sample of children with problems, the children's parents appeared to be locked into a chronic pattern of mourning. Apparently the birth of these 'replacement' children served to further chronically complicate the bereavement process for the parents, which in turn caused relatively severe problems for the children.

Rites of passage and the period of transition

The theme of transition which Van Gennep identified as being particularly lengthy and important in funeral rites has been investigated independently by Turner (1969). According to Turner, a long transitional period in rites of passage in general may be extremely beneficial to the passengers of these rites. Turner argued that the transitional period is one in which people are 'betwixt and between' social states and therefore people meet as true equals and social considerations of status, power and worth do not apply. Consequently, long periods of transition may be times of respite and communality. Obviously, Turner's analysis is rather more relevant to rites of passage which involve large numbers of people undergoing the same rite at the same time. However, his observations may be extremely relevant in the case of people who have been bereaved by the occurrence of a disaster which affects a whole community.

Miller (1974) poignantly describes the aftermath of Aberfan, a disaster in which many children from a mining village in Wales lost their lives. According to Miller, the situation was one in which communal grieving and healing were handled relatively well by the community itself, with a minimum of external intervention. People were described, in keeping with Turner's hypothesis, in terms of their coming together as equals with a common purpose. For a long period of time social barriers were lifted and the solidarity of the community facilitated the expression of grief.

Alternatively, Erikson (1979) documented the aftermath of a similar disaster in Buffalo Creek, USA. In this case an intervention programme in which people were randomly placed in caravan parks was undertaken. However, the relocation of people from the disaster-struck community had extremely adverse effects:

two years after the flood, Buffalo Creek was almost as desolate as it had been the day following, the grief as intense, the fear as strong . . . they rarely smiled and rarely played . . . they were unsettled and deeply hurt.

(Erikson 1979: 137)

Given the relatively long period of time experiences of grief are known to continue, Turner's observations would suggest that support groups for survivors and relatives of the dead following disasters which take place outside established communities may serve as a particularly useful focus of support in both the short and the long term.

Systems of rituals and beliefs

In an influential essay translated into English in 1960 Hertz was concerned with funeral rites in societies where the dead person was considered to be in limbo, i.e. between the world of the living and the world of the dead, for some period of time after physical death had occurred. These types of rituals have been cited as being particularly helpful to those who have been bereaved (e.g. Smith 1976) since they involve the social acknowledgement of a continuing relationship with a dead person whose social identity is slowly extinguished over an extended period of time. However, Hertz's analysis is also of interest because he looks at funeral rituals in terms of their representing complete systems of rites and beliefs. At a general level of analysis Hertz suggests that funeral rituals involve three main elements, i.e. the corpse, the soul and the mourners. It is the relationship between these elements of funeral rituals which explains aspects of funeral rites in societies. Consequently, this analysis has the potential to explain change as well as continuity in the mourning customs of any given society. A summary of the analysis is presented in Table 5.

The focus on rituals and beliefs as part of a coherent structure is a useful one since it reminds us that rituals occur in specific social contexts and aspects of them cannot simply be transferred from one context to another and be expected to maintain the same meaning.

For example, Turner (1987) has identified the increasing secularisation of Western societies as being an important factor which contributes towards the difficulties associated with coping with dying and bereavement. Hertz's analysis would suggest that changes in cultural beliefs, inasmuch as they affect the relationships between the soul, the corpse and the mourners, might result in changes in aspects of funeral rituals. From this perspective funeral rituals reflect the broader system of social and cultural beliefs and change in accordance with them.

Many observations concerning changes in funeral rituals may be usefully explained by reference to Hertz's thesis.

27

The relationship between the soul and the dead and the corpse and the burial

According to Hertz the nature of the relationship between the soul and the dead and the corpse and the burial affects the form of funeral rites which in turn expresses a given culture's beliefs associated with the metaphorical relationship between the body and the soul. Jung (1933) postulated that the major dilemma for modern 'man' was that he had lost, and consequently needed to search for his 'soul'. Jung's analysis would suggest that Western societies over-emphasise the rational and consequently under-emphasise other aspects of human potential. In his consideration of death Jung was of the opinion that a strong desire to do something for the dead had virtually been rationalised out of existence. There would appear to be no rational justification for taking such actions, so they simply could no longer be taken – at least not in public.

Table 5 Relationships between different aspects of funeral rites

Cultural beliefs	Relationship	Aspects of funeral rites
1. The soul and the dead	1 + 2	*The form of rites* which expresses the metaphorical relationship between body and soul.
2. The corpse and the burial	2 + 3	*The scale of rites* which express the social order.
3. The living and the mourners	1 + 3	*Duration of rites* which expresses the involvement of the living and the dead during the gradual extinction of the deceased's social identity.

In this context, it is interesting to note that the early supporters of an essentially new form of funeral rite in England, i.e. that of cremation, explicitly equated cremation with rationality and progress. Cremation was discussed in terms of its expression of a modern, enlightened view of the relationship between body and soul which in cultural terms had become disconnected. Furthermore, cremation was believed to have several advantages over burial: in general, it was seen as a more scientific way to dispose of a body and, in particular, it involved the use of technology rather than manual labour to achieve its aim.

In Gorer's study cremation was more popular than burial; out of sixty-seven cases forty were cremations and the remainder burials. Gorer was of the opinion that 'In many cases, it would appear, cremation is chosen because it is felt to get rid of the dead more completely and finally than does burial' (1965: 35–6). However, as Ariès indicates, it might be a mistake to

> interpret the disappearance of the body in cremation as a mark of indifference or neglect. The relative of the cremated person rejects the physical reality of the site, its association with the body, which inspires distaste, and the public character of the cemetery. But he accepts the absolutely personal and private nature of regret. For the cult of the tomb he has substituted the cult of memory in the home.
>
> (1983: 577)

The relationship between the corpse and the burial and the living and the mourners

According to Hertz, an analysis of the relationship between the corpse and the burial and the living and the mourners might provide evidence concerning the scale of funeral rites which express a given society's social order. In this context it is interesting to note that social historians have recently begun to uncover a darker side to the Victorian 'celebration' of death. If the scale of funeral rites can be seen as an expression of the social worth of the dead person and their relatives then treatment of those deemed less worthy in social terms is of particular interest. Richardson (1988a) has traced the origins of a fear of 'death on the parish' which she found amongst elderly poor and working-class Londoners back to the early nineteenth century and the Poor Law (Amendment) Act. This act was designed to deter all but the most desperate from seeking public assistance and its principles were ruthlessly upheld. Those who failed to provide for themselves in death were taken naked, wrapped only in paper or a strip of calico stretched over the corpse. Relatives were denied the customary farewell and were allowed no say in where the burial might take place. Given the scale of death rites prevalent at the time, a more brutally calculated statement of the social worth of the poor is difficult to imagine.

Richardson (1988b) illustrates another expression of the social worth of the poor in her examination of the Anatomy Act. The Anatomy Act permitted the use of the bodies of certain people who died in the workhouse for the purpose of dissection, in practice frequently irrespective of the dead person's wishes or previously held religious beliefs regarding the relationship between body and soul.

It might be suggested that the mourners of a dead person would feel inclined under such circumstances to protect the memory of that person by going to great lengths to secure appropriate funeral rituals. Cannandine (1981) points out that the cost of these rituals was considerable and frequently came at a time when families could least afford it. Taylor (1983), in her consideration of the social history of mourning dress, makes a similar point. By the middle of the nineteenth century people who had been bereaved were concerned over the potential for being publicly shamed by their failure to carry out the Victorian etiquette of death correctly. Those on low incomes experienced particular difficulty and burials were often delayed while people struggled to raise enough money for a respectable funeral.

The relationship between the soul and the dead and the living and the mourners

One of the most important aspects of the duration of funeral rites is believed to be that of time limitation (Gorer 1965; Parkes 1972; Marris 1986). It is argued that, if the length of time the mourners are to spend in mourning is ritually stipulated, then this acts as an important aid to the bereaved person's re-entry into social life. However, if, as Hertz suggests, the duration of rites results from the relationship the soul and the dead are believed to have with the living and the mourners, then it could be argued that modern funeral rites are, in social terms, appropriately time-limited, i.e. they extend only for the time it takes to dispose of the body.

Both Van Gennep and Hertz indicate the close association between the person who has died and those who have been bereaved by the death. It would seem reasonable to suggest that, if contemporary Western societies effectively deny death in public, then they will also limit the scope for public expressions of bereavement. Mourners are in a particularly difficult position inasmuch as they may be expected to ignore, in terms of social interactions outside the group of mourners, the often devastating impact of their bereavement. Furthermore, the contemporary situation is one in which those who have been bereaved are expected to re-engage in social activities fairly soon after a death has occurred. For example, it is relatively rare for bereavement leave to be given by employers and, when it is, it seldom extends for much more than a week. The next part of this chapter considers a brief history of the development of mourning customs in England and raises the issue of the relationship between the prevalence of death and bereavement in the community, mourning rituals and social support.

MOURNING CUSTOMS IN ENGLAND

The Victorian celebration of death

The Victorian celebration of death has, almost universally, been cited as a helpful rite of passage for mourners. Most references to Victorian funeral rituals owe much to Gorer's (1965) study of contemporary England. This interpretation of the lack of ritual in contemporary society was based upon what has become an extremely powerful historical perspective which basically assumed that the Victorian era was a 'golden age' for grief. The belief that Victorian rituals of mourning provided support and guidance for those who were bereaved is an exceptionally strong one. Gorer was of the belief that the wearing of clothes which symbolised mourning was also helpful inasmuch as the clothes facilitated the identification of recently bereaved people and thereby elicited appropriately supportive behaviour from the wider community.

There would appear to be a general consensus amongst researchers in the area that death-related rituals must somehow be of help to the mourners. However, it remains undemonstrated exactly how such rituals, in themselves, could help to assuage the grief of the survivors. Nevertheless, Marris continues this tradition in the following way.

> Traditionally, full mourning in England would begin with the shutter-ing of the house, and the hanging of black crèpe while the dead person was laid out in his or her old home. The funeral procession itself was decked with as much pomp as the family could afford or its sense of good taste suggested. Thereafter the nearest relatives wore black for several months and then half-mourning for a while, gradually adding quiet colours to their dress . . . and when the period of mourning is over it [the family] can take up the thread of life without guilt because the customs of society make this its duty.
>
> (1986: 29–30)

However, the work of researchers other than Gorer does not necessarily lead to such optimistic conclusions. Recently, social historians have begun to cast doubt on Gorer's analysis. As previously mentioned, both Richardson (1988a,b) and Cannandine (1981) indicate that the Victorian celebration of death was unavailable for certain groups in the society and associated with considerable, and presumably stressful, financial hardship for others. Furthermore, Cannandine points to the fact that there appears to be little direct evidence concerning whether or not individuals did, in fact, find it helpful to be partly excluded from society for a year or more following the death of a family member. Also, Taylor (1983) makes the point that, in reality, it was women rather than men who were compelled to wear clothing which symbolised mourning. It must also be mentioned that Queen Victoria, who presumably would have had the utmost benefit of all available ritual support following the death of Prince Albert, remains to this day one of the most often cited examples of someone who experienced a chronically complicated bereavement reaction.

One of the factors which complicates any appreciation of the supportive role of rituals in connection with bereavement is that of the general mortality rate in the community. In terms of patterns of mortality, death would have been no stranger to the average Victorian adult. Cholera epidemics, the infectious diseases of childhood, accidents in the workplace, high maternal mortality rates and high infant mortality rates virtually ensured that most adult Victorians would have had at least one personal experience of bereavement. It was commonplace for parents to grieve the loss of at least one of their children and for young children themselves to possess a vivid sense of death at an early age. The range of available support and experience of bereavement in such a community with or without the ritual acknowledgements must have been considerable. Furthermore, the sheer arbitrariness of death must have facilitated a general sense of fatalism associated with the acceptance of death as being an inevitable and highly visible fact of life. The relationship between rituals and social support is a complex one and unfortunately, at least in the case of mourning customs in England, ceremony and ubiquitousness seem to be strongly related, thereby making it difficult to draw any firm conclusions. However, social change proceeded at an extremely rapid pace and by Edwardian times experiences of mass bereavement were becoming increasingly rare. As public health dramatically improved and life expectancy rose, expectations changed rapidly. It was about this period in English history that Illich (1977) suggested that optimism concerning the further potential for the rapid progress of society in general and medical science in particular led to a belief that death itself could eventually be totally, as in a certain sense it had been partially, conquered.

It is also at this point in time that Cannadine's (1981) analysis takes serious issue with Gorer's. Gorer associated the decline of Victorian mourning customs with the onset of World War I. Gorer's position would suggest that the sheer ubiquitousness of bereavement brought about a decline in mourning customs. However, Cannadine's position would suggest essentially the opposite, i.e. the decline in mourning customs simply mirrored the decline in mortality rates which started in the late Victorian, early Edwardian period. Cannadine further suggests that death, once so commonplace and arbitrary, was seen in a rather different light in this period. Once conquered, death became glorious and was firmly placed in the realms of the exotic and the exciting:

if the celebration of death was on the wane from the 1880s onwards, the glorification of death – of death on active service, in battle, in the front line, for one's country – was markedly on the increase. The growing international tensions of these years combined with the ever-widening appeal of ideas of social Darwinism, and the stridently athletic ethos of the late-Victorian and Edwardian public school, produced an atmosphere in which soldiering and games were equated, in which death was seen as unlikely, but where, if it happened it could not fail to be glorious.

(1981: 195)

Many of those so recently spared the possibility of an early death from infectious diseases went on to lose their lives in young adulthood – on the battlefields of World War I.

World War I

During World War I bereavement once again became a virtually universal experience. Almost every family experienced the loss of at least one adult male member. Approximately 30 per cent of all young men lost their lives. However, the communal reaction to this loss did not lead to a revival of Victorian mourning rituals but rather to the creation of a new form of ritual.

Again, it would seem to be the case that the ritualisation of mourning is associated with large numbers of dead. However, the deaths associated with World War I were different from those associated with the earlier period. Specifically, the war radically changed the relationship between the corpse and the burial and the living and the mourners.

The young men who lost their lives in World War I died away from home and most of those who mourned them had no opportunity to see the corpse or attend its burial. For many people there was the added uncertainty implied by the receipt of a telegram which informed them that their relative was 'missing' and only 'presumed dead'. As Cannadine notes:

In April 1917, for instance Bonar Law learned that his second son, Charlie, was missing after the Battle of Gaza. For many weeks, on the strength of a German newspaper report, it was thought that he might be a German prisoner of war, and this frail hope seemed to have been triumphantly substantiated in June when a message was received from the Vatican saying that he was a prisoner in Turkish hands. But jubilation and relief turned to dust when it later transpired that the crucial word 'not' had been omitted from the Vatican telegram.

(1981: 214)

Perhaps, under such circumstances, the dramatic increase in public interest in spiritualism which followed World War I should not surprise us unduly.

33

Given the absence of a corpse and the presence of very real uncertainty concerning the reality of the death, many bereaved people, in the inter-war years, turned, for comfort to spiritualism. For example:

> We say your departed certainly return, they often stand at your side as in former days, though not being clairvoyant you fail to see them. They speak to you, but not being clairvoyant you do not hear them. They try to impress you with an awareness of their presence, though you deem that sudden thought of them just a fancy of your own and nothing more.

> (Thomas 1928: 194–5)

Presumably, the attraction of spiritualism lay in its potential to both fulfil wishes and legitimise experiences. As Chapter 3 will indicate, what is common to experiences of bereavement is not the fact that the dead are neither seen nor heard following the death but its opposite, i.e. hearing and experiencing the presence of the dead person, which is a relatively common experience amongst bereaved people. An interpretation of such experiences which involved the belief that the dead lived on obviously proved difficult for many people to resist. However, at the public level the significance of World War I lay in the evolution of a new ritual and a permanent reminder of the war, i.e. Armistice Day and the Cenotaph. In the week following the erection of the Cenotaph over a million people visited it and more than 100,000 wreaths were laid. Furthermore, war memorials were erected all over the country as people sought to ensure that the dead were not publicly, as they would not be privately, forgotten. Obviously, Armistice Day is a calendrical rite rather than a rite of passage as such. Equally obviously, funeral rites were difficult if not impossible to secure for those who died in war-time conditions. Consequently, one of the considerations involved in naming the Tomb of the Unknown Soldier was that any mother, in the absence of a body, a named grave or the resources to visit a grave, might mourn her son there. Clearly, millions of bereaved people wanted some sort of public recognition of their loss. Equally clearly, the Victorian celebration of death would not do.

World War II

In terms of rituals, those developed in the context of World War I were simply extended to World War II, presumably because the circumstances were not sufficiently different to warrant change. In terms of casualties, the country fared far better than it did in World I War, but, in terms of a global understanding of death rather than a personal understanding of bereavement, the situation changed dramatically. The mass murder of people in concentration camps and the horrors of Hiroshima and Nagasaki left a legacy of the possibility of either intentional or accidental global destruction.

1950s denial and pornography

During the 1950s the early contemporary research concerning the avoidance, perhaps an understandable one, of death began to be published. It is in this context that Gorer's (1955) influential essay, referred to in Chapter 1, must be placed. Once again, death was no longer an everyday event and bereavement, particularly outside the older age ranges, became a relatively uncommon experience. However, Gorer's analysis indicated an increase, rather than a decrease, in public interest in these issues. In this respect Gorer's (1955) analysis of attitudes towards death in the 1950s shares some similarities with Cannandine's (1981) analysis of attitudes towards death in the Edwardian era. Specifically, in both cases a decrease in public prevalence led to an increase in public interest. However, it is here that the similarity ends. Two world wars separated these analyses. In Cannadine's work the public face of death was frankly exotic and vaguely romantic. Gorer, however, portrayed a rather different picture – the new public face of death was one of dirt, shame and pornography. Death, and by association bereavement, was now the province of the voyeur rather than the hero.

The death awareness movement

The death awareness movement flourished in the USA from the early 1960s to the mid-1970s. The movement was widespread and some of its many purposes were as follows:

1. to challenge the denial of death;
2. to facilitate humane programmes of care for dying people and appropriate programmes of support for people who have been bereaved;
3. to offer realistic courses in death education for professionals who work with people who are dying or bereaved;
4. to offer realistic courses in death education for the community in general.

The late 1960s and early 1970s saw many critical analyses of the ways in which death and dying were dealt with by contemporary Western societies together with the development of an alternative approach, i.e. the hospice movement. However, Kalish (1985), an early advocate of death awareness, is of the opinion that the movement has lost some of its momentum. Specifically:

> bureaucratization seems to have taken place. What had been exciting new ideas and programs have become routine. Hospices are spending immense time and effort on third-party payments, cost-effectiveness, reducing health costs and institutional linkages: all necessary to be

sure, but with little focus on the individual needs of the individual dying person or that person's family members.

(Kalish 1985: 14)

Perhaps the best that can be hoped for is that people who have been bereaved may begin to consider new ritual expressions of grief appropriate to themselves and their mourning group in greater numbers – perhaps we have a long way to go.

Social support and the rituals of everyday life

Whilst most anthropological research has focused upon relatively large-scale social rituals, the value of rituals in terms of generating social support has been a major theme developed by most researchers in the area. However, researchers concerned with the structure of rituals and systems of rituals and beliefs are often vague concerning the specific ways in which support is mobilised. One possible exception is the work of Durkheim (1915). Whilst Durkheim emphasised that the renewal of common social values and the strengthening of social bonds were the basic functions of rituals, he was concerned to identify the mechanisms by which these functions might be achieved. Funeral rites formed a very important part of his analysis which emphasised the need for detailed knowledge of peoples and cultures in order to understand the extremely subtle dynamics of social interaction.

For example:

Durkheim's description continues in this vivid fashion to portray the mourning obligations of various categories of kin. The reports from several areas of the continent are the same people (according to rather precise formulae) gouge their faces, slash their thighs, burn their breasts and attack their friends. Much of this activity is so ferocious that it is not uncommon for mourning to add to the death toll.

(Huntington and Metcalf 1979: 30)

However, the analytical emphasis in the anthropology of religion had shifted away from 'rather precise formulae' and few studies were concerned with the intimate knowledge of social interaction which would be required to pursue this mode of analysis. It was not until 1972 that Goffman investigated the sociological implications of this approach in his consideration of the rituals of everyday life. Goffman pointed out that only in secular societies can the ubiquitousness, strategy and location of the small-scale rituals of everyday life be ignored. Ritual is defined here as a perfunctory conventionalised act through which an individual portrays his/her respect and regard to some object or person. According to Goffman these small-scale rituals have a vital role to play in social organisation and social support. Furthermore, a characteristic of them is that their successful performance depends upon a complex and detailed analysis of social position, social status and social role.

Following Durkheim's analysis of religious rituals, Goffman suggests that rituals may be divided into two classes, i.e. the positive and the negative. The negative types of ritual obligations involve the donors avoiding the recipients of the rites and essentially staying away from them. For the recipients this would signify that they have a right to be left alone. Positive ritual consists of the various ways in which homage can be paid to the recipients and involves the donors moving closer to recipients in order to affirm and support the relationship. For the recipients this would signify their right to receive support. However, the relationship between rituals used in this context and the complex nature of social networks, social status and social support will be the subject of Chapter 6. The final section of this chapter looks at the experiences of individuals who have undergone funeral rituals in the 1980s.

Perceptions of funeral rites in the 1980s

The overall pattern of changes associated with funeral rituals would seem to indicate that participating in these rituals in the contemporary context would not necessarily be helpful for people who have been bereaved. This decline in the helpfulness of mourning customs, be it related to a lack of ritualisation or a lack of relevant experiences in the community, may be compounded by another difficulty identified by Turner (1987). Turner is of the opinion that the increasing secularisation of Western societies has made dying and bereavement particularly difficult transitions to cope with. Furthermore, since most funeral rituals have their bases in religious belief systems it might be suggested that changes in those belief systems, particularly those with regard to the possibility of an afterlife, may be associated with changes in the funeral rituals themselves.

However, at the individual rather than the social level, evidence concerning the role religious beliefs may play in offering support to people who are dying and those who are bereaved is, itself, by no means clear. Leming and Dickinson (1985) suggest that high levels of religious commitment are essentially similar to low levels of religious commitment in terms of the anxieties associated with death and bereavement. Alternatively, moderate levels of religious commitment would seem to be associated with particularly high levels of death-related anxiety. Whilst it might be argued that it is the uncertainty associated with moderate levels of religious commitment which provokes high levels of anxiety, it might equally well be argued that the condition of uncertainty is increasingly the position of the majority of the population.

In my own study (Littlewood 1983) the majority of the participants reported relatively low levels of religious commitment. Whilst the vast majority of people had attended the funeral associated with their bereavement, the lack of agreement regarding the helpfulness or otherwise of funeral rituals was striking. Almost as many people reported their experiences in terms of the ritual being an ordeal which had to be undergone, as those who found the ritual helpful to them. Many of the people interviewed were of the belief that the funeral would provide a meaningful framework within which they might begin to interpret their experiences of bereavement, and were disappointed when, as far as they were concerned, it did not.

However, it was surprising to note that relatively few people tried adopting another system of religious beliefs in order to interpret their experiences. Of those who did make such an attempt, 3 per cent were approached in their homes by Jehovah's Witnesses or Latter Day Saints and none of these people found their encounters to be particularly satisfactory. No-one changed their beliefs because of these visits and, in all cases, the contact was of extremely short-term duration. A further 9 per cent sought out spiritualists but, again, for most people the contact was as unsatisfactory as it was short term. Only one person maintained contact with a spiritualist medium for more than one month, and the other participants were either dissuaded by relatives from further attendance and/or found the information they received too vague and, therefore, unsuited to their felt needs.

In terms of wearing clothing which was believed to symbolise bereavement the vast majority of people who attended the funeral service did so, but only on the day of the service itself. Less than 20 per cent of those interviewed wore clothing symbolising mourning following the funeral service and of those who did so the vast majority were elderly (i.e. over 65 years of age) and continued the practice for less than one month following the death. Less than 5 per cent of those who were interviewed wore mourning for any length of time greater than one month.

The most popular gesture made in connection with a bereavement was sending a floral tribute to the funeral service. Over 85 per cent of people participating in the study did so. The second most popular gesture, made by 49 per cent of participants, was making a donation to charity.

Interestingly enough, both avoidance and voyeurism were identified by some people as being particularly distressing experiences following the death of a loved person. To a certain extent rituals enact the needs of the society and in the contemporary context mourners may be in a particularly difficult position insomuch that it might be argued that they are effectively expected to ignore, in terms of social interactions outside the group of mourners, the often devastating impact of their bereavement. Should this prove difficult or impossible, then bereaved people may face the prospect of others, particularly those on the periphery of the mourning group, avoiding them. The tendency for people, apparently for no reason, to avoid those who have recently been bereaved is frequently cited by bereaved people as being a particularly upsetting experience for them (Littlewood 1983; Littlewood, Hoekstra-Weebers and Humphrey 1990). Avoidance may well express the ambivalence that people who are acquaintances of a bereaved person feel about what they should or should not say. For many people, colleagues and workmates who say little or nothing about the death also cause distress. One woman postal worker felt that the lack of acknowledgement of her husband's death afforded to her at her workplace contributed to her mental breakdown. It was, as she put it, 'As if he'd never existed in the first place'.

Voyeurism is also an experience with which many people who have been bereaved are familiar and it is one that most find extremely upsetting. In the contemporary situation it usually takes the form of people wanting to see a dying person or a dead body simply to satisfy an impersonal curiosity or asking a person who has been bereaved for overly detailed information.

It is within such a cultural context that the more personal experiences of grief must be interpreted. The range of personal experiences associated with grief is the subject of Chapter 3.

3

EXPERIENCES OF GRIEF

'Suffering is a form of change which people experience. It is a mode of becoming – it is meaningless or meaningful.'

Soelle (1976)
Suffering

INTRODUCTION

Research regarding the nature of bereavement has progressed from many different theoretical perspectives. However, the descriptive literature regarding the experiences associated with grief is remarkably uniform. This apparent uniformity persists despite, as Bowlby (1980) notes, information about grief being gathered for different purposes, using different methods, by different people. The term grief is taken here to refer to the experiences which arise following the death of a loved person. Although bereavement is, by definition, a state involving loss it does not necessarily follow that unhappiness will be associated with the loss. Grief, on the other hand, is inevitably associated with unhappiness and suffering. It may be possible to be bereaved without feeling grief but it is difficult to grieve without being bereaved, although bereavement need not involve the loss of a person. Grieving is a process which is universally associated with pain, confusion and distress. However, it would seem to be a necessary process, if the person involved is to regain or develop a sense of understanding and well-being.

The first part of this chapter looks at the range of experiences which have been described in connection with the process of grief. The second part is concerned with how such experiences tend to be organised over time and identifies the range of experiences associated with uncomplicated grief. The final part focuses upon the range of factors which are believed to be associated with complicating the grieving process.

EXPERIENCES ASSOCIATED WITH GRIEF

It is difficult to disentangle the complex range of experiences associated with grief. However, major researchers in the area (Lindemann 1944; Parkes 1972; Worden 1982; Kalish 1985) have identified a wide range of experiences which may be divided into the categories of physical sensations and health concerns, thoughts and feelings, and behaviour.

In an early piece of work Engel (1961) likened grief to a disease and, whilst this view has been questioned by researchers, many people consult a doctor following the death of a loved person. The physical sensations associated with grief are often experienced as frightening. Many bereaved people refer to being wounded, torn, ripped, hollow or broken – the metaphor is clearly one of physical injury.

Following Worden (1982), the physical sensations commonly reported by bereaved people are as follows:

1. Experiences of hollowness or tightness. Hollowness tends to be associated with the stomach or abdomen and tightness with the chest, shoulders and throat.
2. Oversensitivity to noise.
3. A sense of depersonalisation in which nothing, including the self, feels real.
4. Breathlessness which is often accompanied by deep sighing respirations.
5. Muscular weakness.
6. Lack of energy and fatigue.
7. Dry mouth.

Although the physical sensations associated with grief may be frightening, they are not, in themselves, cause for concern. However, many studies have indicated that significant increases in mortality and morbidity follow the death of a loved person. Young, Benjamin and Wallis (1963) found a major increase in the death rate of widowers, aged 54 and over, during the first six months following their bereavement, whilst Maddison and Viola (1968) have found increased morbidity in widows. Kalish (1985) has suggested that increases in mortality and morbidity are not confined to widows and widowers, and may be common to the loss of any loved person. Rowland (1977) is of the opinion that the greatest risk of illness or death is during the first six months of bereavement.

Numerous thoughts and feelings have been reported by people who have been bereaved. Most studies concentrate upon the following, relatively common, range of experiences.

Shock

Shock is usually associated with sudden deaths, but even in situations where the death of a person has long been expected, shock following the news of the actual death may still be experienced.

Numbness

Numbness is usually experienced relatively soon after a death has occurred. The person appears to be void of any feeling and their responses are typically slow, automatic and cold. One man retrospectively described the experience as 'going onto automatic pilot'.

Disbelief

Disbelief that the death has actually occurred is a common and usually transient reaction to bereavement. It may be more likely amongst people who were not present at the death and did not, for whatever reason, see the body.

Anxiety

Anxiety following the death of a loved person can take many forms. Some people suffer from a persistent sense of being unsafe in the world, whilst others may experience panic attacks. Worden (1976, 1982) suggests that anxiety may stem from two sources. The bereaved person may fear that they will not be able to survive without the dead person and/or may be afraid of being overwhelmed by feelings of grief. Many people appear to become extraordinarily helpless following news of a death, and, particularly if the dead person was someone the bereaved individual normally relied upon for emotional support, the bereaved person may come to doubt their capacity to cope with their loss.

Another source of anxiety is associated with an increased awareness of death in general and of one's own mortality in particular. In my own study (Littlewood 1983) many people who had lost parents in adulthood felt a strong sense of anxiety concerning the prospect of their own deaths. A middle-aged woman described her reaction to the death of her father in the following way: 'I just feel that I'm next, there's nobody between me and death now.' People may also be anxious about their own deaths because they feel that they may leave others unprotected.

A 28-year-old woman whose husband was killed in a road traffic accident expressed her strong anxiety over her own death in the following way.

I keep thinking something's going to happen to me, that I have cancer, or I'll be killed or something. The kids would be on their own then.

42

I'm terrified of dying before they grow up. I have nightmares about it.
I keep thinking that I might not live to see Amy's next birthday. . . .
I know I shouldn't dwell on it but I can't help it.

Additionally, many people are anxious about their sanity and are afraid
that their grief will literally send them mad. Lewis (1961), writing about
his reaction to the death of his wife, has observed that grief can feel very
much like fear.

Sadness

Sadness is a common feature of grief and requires little explanation. The
sadness associated with grief may be overwhelming at times and is often,
although not invariably, associated with episodes of crying.

Relief

Relief following a death is not an unusual reaction to bereavement. Relief
may be felt for many reasons. The dying person may have suffered and their
carers may feel relieved that this has ended. Relief may also follow long
periods of uncertainty regarding the probability of a death. Pincus (1976)
has suggested that some young adults who have lost parents feel a sense
of freedom and emancipation following the death. However, such feelings
probably coexist uneasily with feelings of guilt. Relatively less common
are feelings of euphoria following a death. Bowlby (1980) discusses such
reactions and is of the opinion that, if they occur over long periods of time,
they bode ill for future adjustment to the death. Eason (1985) reports a
relatively unusual example of euphoria in the parents of a child killed in an
accident. Having been deeply shocked by the death, the young girl's father
wrote about a visit to the funeral director in the following way.

On the Tuesday afternoon he rang to say that she was ready to view
at the Chapel of Rest. We therefore decided to go the following
morning. Together with Kay's mother we were shown into a small
viewing room and the job he had done had to be seen to be believed.
Amy looked absolutely beautiful and he had used some photographs
to get her hair just as Kay used to do it. I cried a little, but Kay was
so aghast at the sight she could not cry. She had taken a pair of socks
to ask Michael to put them on. He, in turn, suggested that she do it
herself. Her mind had caused her to think that Amy would be cold
without her socks. . . . I don't know if what happened in the florist's
can be explained or not, but it was very unusual. We walked in feeling
on air as the way Amy looked had had some effect on us. For a couple
who had lost a young child, we were laughing and joking, showing off
the photographs Michael had returned to us and generally gave the

impression we were ordering flowers for a party rather than a funeral. From the florist we took the long way home driving to a small market town near to where we lived. We walked round the town, holding hands and laughing like a couple of young love birds. The feeling was very, very strange. However, we arrived home at about 1.00 pm and, as soon as I opened the front door, we changed back to as we had been before we left.

In my own study (Littlewood 1983) a 19-year-old woman observed a similar reaction in her mother:

They brought my sister's body to the house and put it in the front room. My mother wouldn't move out of the room and sat holding her hand. She seemed to be deliriously happy and we thought she'd gone mad. We all sat in the kitchen and didn't know what to do. When they came to take us to the chapel my mother wouldn't let her go and went hysterical. She screamed and sobbed. I was frightened and my Dad went upstairs. The undertaker said it was all right and he went and talked to her. She calmed down after that.

It might be the case that viewing the body may, for some people, lead them to feel that the dead person has been 'recovered' in some way and a temporary sense of euphoric relief may be one of many responses to the situation.

A slightly more unusual variant of euphoria may occur in instances where a terminal illness has been diagnosed. One woman in my own study (Littlewood 1983) was shocked to realise that her mother, upon learning her husband's terminal prognosis, bought herself several new outfits and expressed great concern over her appearance. Jones (1988) in writing of her own experiences during her husband's terminal illness makes the following observations:

I was more surprised to find how sexual is death. I now understand how a person whose partner is dying might, in some circumstances, go out and couple violently and casually. It would neither shock nor startle me, yet I might have lived all my life without this knowledge.

Almost immediately Stanley went into hospital, I went out and bought new clothes; a pretty blouse, some knickers. . . . For a few days I went with the same high excitement I had felt when Stanley and I first met. . . .

Somehow I knew I had felt all these things before, recognised them, but I never identified them until I was telling a young married woman of our acquaintance. She looked at me, tears in her eyes, and said, 'Don't you know? You were courting!' And that was it.

In many ways grief is like falling in love – backwards. Perhaps it should not surprise us too much to find that some people, for short periods of time, might experience euphoria in an attempt to reverse this painful process.

Meaninglessness and despair

A sense of meaninglessness commonly follows a major bereavement. The bereaved person may feel that the external world makes little sense to them since their internal world is so badly damaged. The past may frequently be seen to be as meaningless as the present and the future. Since there may appear to be little point in continuing to participate in a meaningless environment thoughts of suicide are not uncommon. Although relatively few people actually commit suicide following the loss of a loved person many people think about it. Parodoxically, thoughts of suicide may be helpful inasmuch as the person is continuing to identify one way out of what appears to be an intolerable situation.

Loneliness

As Weiss (1974) has indicated, there are different types of loneliness. One sort of loneliness which is commonly associated with grief is the loneliness arising from the loss of a 'special' person to interact with. Loneliness may also be caused by lack of company in general. Unfortunately, lack of company, particularly in the time which follows the funeral, may also be associated with grief.

Confusion and difficulty in concentrating

Grief is often associated with confusion. People who have been bereaved may find it difficult to concentrate, prioritise or otherwise order their thoughts. Tasks which were relatively simple to perform prior to the death may become major obstacles or be perceived as being too difficult to cope with.

Anger

Anger is one of the commonest, and perhaps one of the most disturbing reactions, associated with grief. Anger may be directed towards the person who has died, others believed to have caused the death (or failed to prevent it), the self or society in general. Many people know that their anger is irrational and this knowledge adds to their general feelings of confusion and disorientation. Worden (1982) suggests that anger should be targeted towards the deceased since other strategies can cause major problems for people who have been bereaved. Anger directed towards other people may alienate them and, in severe cases, anger directed towards the self may result in suicidal behaviour.

Guilt

Guilt, over acts or omissions, is another experience which often follows the death of a loved person. Guilt in connection with not being kind enough to the dying person or not being present at the death are particularly common.

Worden (1982) has suggested that irrational guilt following a bereavement is amenable to reality testing. However, for some people irrational guilt may be a chronic complication of their bereavement process. For example, 'I just know it's my fault that's all. He was my son and now he's dead, so I couldn't have done right by him and that's the end of it.' Alternatively, guilt which has some basis in reality is almost always associated with complications arising during the bereavement process.

Preoccupation with thoughts of the deceased and events leading up to the death

Most people who have lost a loved person are preoccupied by their image. Thoughts of the dead person take up much of the bereaved person's time and energy. Such thoughts coexist uneasily with the pain they frequently provoke. Events leading up to the death may be obsessively reviewed in an increasingly desperate attempt to understand what has happened. Many people feel that the death could have been prevented or that the review might reveal more details about the cause of it. A woman whose 17-year-old sister had been killed in a road traffic accident in which no other vehicle had been involved described her family's review of the death in the following way:

> It went on for months, it went over and over and over. We just couldn't understand it, she wouldn't have swerved for no reason. We thought it might have been an animal or something – she liked animals – and that might have caused it.

Unfortunately, some people find it impossible to come to an explanation of the death which is acceptable to them.

Yearning

Yearning or pining for the dead person frequently occurs. However, as Volkan (1985) has suggested, a strong desire to recover the dead person is often matched by an equally strong fear of doing so. A person who is grieving seems to wish for a return to a past situation, in which the dead person is present and is constantly frustrated by the knowledge that this cannot be achieved. However, the deceased is still desired even though it may be known that this desire cannot be fulfilled.

Sense of presence

As Parkes (1970) has noted, a strong desire to recover the dead person is, in some instances, associated with the belief that the person is still in the immediate environment. Some people who are grieving sense the presence of the dead person. Whilst this usually occurs in places familiar to and associated with the dead person and is often a short-lived experience, this is not always the case.

A woman whose father had died of stomach cancer took a trip to the coast six months after the death. She suddenly felt that her father was present in the crowd and believed that he 'accompanied' her for the rest of the day. She had not experienced any similar feelings prior to her visit.

Visual and auditory hallucinations

Many people believe that they 'see' and/or 'hear' the dead person. These experiences may be interpreted in different ways, some people find them frightening whilst others take comfort from them. Visual and auditory hallucinations are usually found, if they occur at all, in the first year following the death. However, elderly people seem particularly likely to report auditory hallucinations which affect them for a number of years. In my own study (Littlewood 1983) 20 per cent of elderly people living alone in the community reported auditory hallucinations lasting for over one year. Much of this communication seemed to concern the sexual division of labour within the home. For example one man frequently 'heard' his wife giving him advice about cooking and one woman 'heard' her husband advising her about the maintenance of the house. None of the elderly people involved seemed to be particularly disturbed by their experiences and, in general, it was the younger age ranges who were afraid when they 'saw' or 'heard' their dead relative.

The range of behaviour disturbances following the loss of a loved person is probably best characterised as a series of contradictions. The major behavioural characteristics of those who are grieving appear to be as follows.

Sleep disturbances

Difficulties in being able to get to sleep and early morning waking are common amongst people who have been bereaved. A feeling of dread and despair upon waking is equally common. A middle-aged widow described the situation in the following way:

> I'd finally get to sleep about two in the morning and wake up at dawn. For a split second I'd wake and feel all right, then I'd remember, it'd all come flooding back and I'd wish I'd never woken up in the first place.

Appetite disturbances

Loss of appetite frequently follows bereavement and substantial weight loss may occur. Worden (1982) points out that, whilst undereating is a far more common response than overeating, overeating may occur in some cases.

Forgetfulness

Since grief is often characterised by a preoccupation with the image of the dead person, forgetfulness over everyday matters and activities may occur. Such forgetfulness may add to the bereaved person's anxiety considerably.

Dreams

Disturbing dreams, particularly those about the deceased, are not uncommon. Parkes (1972) has observed that even in dreams where the dead person is apparently alive there is often some indication that all is not well. As with the case of auditory and visual hallucinations, dreams are interpreted in different ways by different people. Also, many dreams seem to reflect the ambivalence described by Volkan (1985), i.e. desire to regain the dead person together with a dread of achieving that desire. Perhaps two examples may serve to illustrate the ambivalent reaction to dreams about the dead person. The first example is from a 24-year-old woman whose father had died six weeks prior to her dream and the second example is from an 18-year-old woman whose sister had died three months prior to the relevant dream.

> It was a confusing dream, it started in the churchyard by his grave, I heard someone say 'Yes, but he lived for another three years after that you know'. Then I was back at the house and he was in the bed he died in, but looking much better, then in the kitchen talking about how his treatment had given him a good few years. When I woke up I was frightened and confused. I couldn't work out whether he was alive or dead. When I realised that he'd died, I felt a flood of relief go through me – it was over for both of us and he wouldn't have to suffer any more.

I dreamt my sister came into the bedroom looking for me. She asked me to go with her. I was excited, in the dream, I knew she'd find me again. As I tried to get out of bed I looked at her – she was standing in the shadows and I could only see one side of her face. I just knew that the other side would be something terrible and woke up screaming.

Alternatively, not dreaming of the dead person may cause anxiety. One woman in her forties felt that she had failed to mourn her husband properly because 'I never saw him again – not even in dreams'. Furthermore, a man in his fifties felt concern over his wife because, following the death of his mother, he had a dream in which she told him that she was 'all right' – he felt that until his wife communicated with him in this way that she would not be able to rest in peace.

Reminders of the dead person

Objects, people or places associated with the dead person may be actively sought or actively avoided. Furthermore, people who have been recently bereaved may be given advice to do either. For example, a woman in her thirties burned all of her husband's possessions, including the bed he died in on the night of his death. She did so on the advice of her sister and the GP in attendance at the death. Retrospectively, she felt that she had acted prematurely and kept his wedding ring in a box which was virtually a shrine. Lewis (1961) in recording his reactions to the death of his wife pointed out the difficulties associated with avoiding reminders of the deceased. His wife's memory permeated his past and he felt her presence in places where they had never been together. Many people keep or wear articles of clothing or jewellery belonging to the deceased, and possession of such articles may be seen to be of vital importance. For some people, the disposal of items which once belonged to the deceased is seen as a positive step towards an improvement in their situation. For example, a widow in her mid-forties who had kept her husband's work clothes felt that a significant step was made when she felt strong enough to dispose of them. Perhaps Marris (1986) captures the situation when he describes the pull of the past and the lure of the future as being characteristic of attempts to escape the pain of the present. Unfortunately, not all of those who grieve manage to recover from their loss. For example, a woman in her forties whose 3-year-old son, a Down's Syndrome child, had died unexpectedly kept photographs of the child hidden under the floorboards. Her family refused to talk about him and when alone she retrieved her photographs of him as reminders because she said 'they'll never take my lad from me again'. The child had been fostered soon after his birth and had died at his foster parents' home. The woman had desperately hoped for his eventual return and five years after the death felt:

> I can't resign myself to it – at one level I know but daren't let it sink
> in. If I ever let go and accepted it [her grief] I'd explode – it's too
> deep and it's been there for a long time.

Whilst some people find reminders of the dead person comforting others
may find them painful. A woman in her fifties, who was involved in
removing her mother's possessions from the hospital made the following
comments:

> I felt that was all that was left of her, a few things in a bin-liner. When
> we eventually cleared the house it was the same sinking feeling – her
> life packed in boxes and cases, all that she was reduced to those few
> things, there was no meaning, no life.

Another woman in her fifties kept her mother's belongings in a locked
trunk and refused to open it because she felt that to accept the loss of
her mother would mean accepting the loss of her past and her identity:
'If I look upon her things I will become nothing – to know that they are
here and she is not is enough'. Worden (1982) suggests that such marked
withdrawal from reminders of the deceased may not be a particularly
helpful coping strategy. However, it would appear that avoidance of the
reality of the death may take the form of keeping, as well as avoiding,
reminders of the dead person. Perhaps it is coping styles which avoid the
reality of the loss whatever form they take which, when maintained over a
long period of time, are not particularly helpful to those who have been
bereaved.

Searching/calling for the deceased

Both Bowlby (1980) and Parkes (1970) have noted the importance of the
desire to search for the dead person. For many people searching for
the dead person is an activity which involves actually calling out for
the deceased and/or looking for the person in familiar or unfamiliar
places.

> A man in his eighties experienced great difficulty in accepting the
> death of his wife. His children often found him in the cemetery where
> his wife was buried. He was invariably in an agitated state and fre-
> quently called his wife's name. He had great difficulty understanding
> why he could not find her – his family had told him that this was where
> she had gone.

> A woman in her thirties whose son had died in hospital found herself
> searching for him at a local annual fair. Her son had attended the fair
> the previous year and she was temporarily of the belief that she might
> find him there.

50

For other people the actual searching behaviour is inhibited by the knowledge that a search will be fruitless. However, the desire may still be present.

Searching for a dead person has also been observed to take more indirect forms. For example, Bowlby (1980) has suggested that many people search for the dead person through creative work or other forms of activities. As Parkes (1970) has indicated, searching is frequently associated with finding, and the dead person is often 'found' in various places – in oneself, in an object, in another person, in a piece of work or in the generation of an acceptable explanation of the death. Whilst it may be necessary, for some people, to 'find' the dead person again before they can adjust to the death finding may in itself be a source of anxiety. Furthermore, 'finding' the dead person may delay or perhaps prevent adjustment to the loss. The following example may serve to illustrate the point.

> A woman in her sixties felt little grief over the death of her aunt. She believed her aunt's spirit had resided in their mutual pet – a black labrador dog. She was at a loss to explain why, when several years later her dog died, she was overcome by grief and despair. The few friends she had were apparently unsupportive inasmuch as they could not understand the intensity of her feelings.

Restlessness

Grief is often characterised by restlessness. People who have been bereaved often feel agitated, as if they should be engaged in some activity, but, at the same time, feel incapable of action. Pacing the floor, driving or walking the block may all be undertaken, without apparent success. It is possible that restlessness may be associated with the inhibition of calling or searching for the deceased since the only activity which can be perceived as worthwhile (i.e. finding the dead person or preventing the death) is acknowledged to be impossible. Nevertheless, the desire to take this course of action persists. The following example may illustrate the paradoxical nature of the restlessness which so often afflicts people who have been bereaved.

> A man in his forties whose wife died unexpectedly from a heart attack described a situation in which he constantly searched for something to do but found himself incapable of initiating any action. Small tasks, for example the payment of household bills, proved too much for him and boredom permeated his day to day activities. He described his dilemma in the following way: 'I was hopeless, couldn't do a thing pacing up and down, planning to go out, do the ironing – anything – but when it came to it, I could do nothing. I was bored but I couldn't do anything even though I wanted to. It was so frustrating – I wanted to scream all the time.'

Apathy

Despite, or perhaps because of, intense preoccupation with the dead person and events surrounding the death, people who have been bereaved are very often apathetic. The world seems to be meaningless and there may be little motivation to participate in day to day activities. A coldness towards others and a lack of understanding of others' needs may often be present, together with an inability to comprehend why any activity could be perceived as worthwhile. Such apathy may be interspersed with periods of crying, anger, restlessness or guilt.

Crying

Grief is often, although not always, accompanied by crying. Many people are afraid of the intensity of their emotions and their apparent inability to control them. Crying is often perceived by people who have been bereaved as a sign of self-indulgence or weakness and, as such, may often be controlled or avoided. Some people find themselves unable to cry.

A woman in her twenties did not cry over the death of her father. Following the death she described a situation in which something 'froze and became hard' inside her. The chance discovery of a tape of her father's voice, several months after the death, precipitated uncontrollable sobbing.

Crying is an activity which is bounded by cultural constraints, and many people attempt to control this expression of sadness, often because they are afraid of upsetting others or of making other people 'lose control'.

A man in his fifties felt he could not cry over the death of his daughter because his wife, who was distraught by the loss, may 'go mad if she let it all out'. He also described a desire to protect their other children and felt that a display of tears from him would precipitate even greater sorrow in them. Two months after the death he 'broke down completely' at his sister's house, and expressed relief over the fact that he never cried at home.

The presence or absence of crying in itself may tell little of the nature of grief.

Social withdrawal

For many people who have lost a close relationship there appears to be little point in communicating with other people. The preoccupation with the dead person may be so intense that all other social relationships fade into insignificance. Often all but close relatives or helpers are avoided and social contacts may be permanently lost to the bereaved person.

Substance abuse

The consumption of alcohol and tobacco in people who have been bereaved is known to increase in those who used them prior to the death. Although no relationship between alcoholism and bereavement has been directly proven, it seems reasonable to suggest that bereavement may precipitate dependence upon alcohol. It also seems reasonable to suggest that an increase in the consumption of tobacco and alcohol may account for some of the increased incidence of morbidity in the recently bereaved. The use of tranquillisers in connection with bereavement has been the subject of considerable debate. Overall they would appear to be contraindicated in terms of their effect on bereavement outcome. However, as Stedeford (1984) has indicated, in certain cases they may provide temporary relief or respite depending upon the person's circumstances.

THE ORGANISATION OF GRIEF OVER TIME

Experiences of grief are multiple and varied. It is difficult to organise them in terms of a logical sequence of events and, indeed, contradictory impulses may present themselves in any one person at the same time. However, major researchers in the area (Averill 1968; Parkes 1972) have suggested that grief may be conceived of in terms of a series of stages or phases. Also, Kübler-Ross's (1969) five stages of dying have been applied to the grief process by Kalish (1985). A comparison of these theories may be found in Table 6.

Table 6 A comparison of theories relating to stages of grief

Researcher:	*Averill (1968)*	*Kübler-Ross (1969)*	*Parkes (1972)*
Stages of grief:	Shock Despair Recovery	Denial Anger Bargaining Depression Acceptance	Numbness Pining Depression Recovery

It can be seen that the theories are remarkably similar if it can be accepted that Averill's stage of despair encompasses Parkes's stages of pining and depression. As Kalish (1985) has noted, Kübler-Ross's stages of anger and depression may be seen as counterparts to despair and depression. However, bargaining would not appear to be a significant component of the bereavement process.

In evaluating stage theories of bereavement it should be noted that the stages described are not invariable nor necessarily adaptive. Furthermore, individuals may oscillate between stages and not everyone progresses at the same rate over time. Nevertheless, experiences associated with grief have been usefully incorporated within such frameworks by the major researchers in the area.

Experiences associated with grief involve a series of conflicts and contradictions and remarkably little is known concerning the manner in which the eventual resolution of such conflicts takes place. As Marris (1986) suggests, the process would seem to be one of 'tentative approximations' during which time the episodic pangs or waves of grief diminish in terms of both intensity and regularity. However, even after a number of years, special events, for example Christmas or birthdays, may evoke episodes of grieving.

Estimations of the average time taken to 'recover' from the experiences associated with grief vary. Smith (1982) suggests that uncomplicated grief should be expected to decline in intensity after the first six months following a bereavement. Glick, Weiss and Parkes (1974) have suggested that if no apparent steps are taken towards recovery by the end of the first year following bereavement, then this bodes ill for future adjustment. However, both Marris (1958) and Gorer (1965) indicate that apparently uncomplicated reactions to bereavement may literally take years to resolve.

Much of the confusion over the time taken to recover from the loss of a loved person would seem to stem from different indices being taken as indicative of resolution. Perhaps the loss of a loved person cannot effectively be resolved and, therefore, people never fully recover from such an experience. However, it is possible to identify the range of experiences associated with uncomplicated grief, as they are organised over time.

Uncomplicated grief

1) The initial response following the death of a loved person is usually one of shock and disbelief. This response may last for a few hours or a few days. However, despite an apparent inability to comprehend the loss, the person may occasionally suffer from outbursts of intense emotion, for example panic, sobbing or irrational anger. In retrospect, many people describe their behaviour in terms of it being an automatic response to contingencies and their perceptions of this period of time as being hazy, distant and unreal.

2) Following this period the person suffers an intense emotional, physical and cognitive reaction to the loss. This reaction may be characterised by somatic distress, deep sighing respirations, outbursts of anger and crying, general restlessness, sleep disturbances and loss of appetite. The bereaved person pines for the dead person and appears to be completely preoccupied

by his/her image. Events immediately preceding the death are obsessively reviewed in an often abortive attempt to understand what has happened. Self-reproach is common – for not having prevented the death or for causing it. Anger is frequently directed against the self, the dead person, the environment in general or specific other people who are believed, usually erroneously, to have been instrumental in either causing the death or failing to prevent it. Guilt is often experienced over minor or major imperfections in the past relationship and the grieving person may seem to others to be torturing themselves over relatively trivial issues. Dreams and vivid hallucinations about, or of, the dead person are not uncommon and may be seen as either frightening or comforting – in some cases both.

Social withdrawal frequently accompanies this intense preoccupation with the dead person. The attempts to understand the cause of the death and/or to reclaim, in whatever form, the dead person appear to coexist uneasily with an urge to escape from the intense pain which would appear to be an inevitable consequence of such activities. Such experiences may typically occur over a number of months.

3) Following, or interspersed with, the experiences described above are feelings of apathy, fatigue and despair. The grieving person appears to be uninterested in life in general and comments concerning the meaningless-ness of life are not uncommon. Difficulty in concentration is frequently reported and thoughts of suicide are often present. It would appear that the grieving person, having given up hope of reclaiming the dead person, finds life itself pointless. Intense emotional distress may occur intermittently with episodes in which the individual feels 'him/herself' again. Paradoxically, feeling better can also be a source of distress for those who have been bereaved, since feeling better may evoke feelings of guilt and disloyalty to the dead person. Eventually, episodes of relative normality occur for progressively longer periods of time and episodes of grief decrease in frequency. Again such experiences may last for a number of months and the overall consensus amongst researchers in the area would seem to indicate that the whole process takes, upon average, one to two years to progress to a point where the pangs of grief are relatively self-contained, occasional episodes.

Complicated grief

Descriptions of complicated grief are not uncommon in literature pertaining to bereavement. These descriptions may be loosely gathered under three headings: delayed grief, chronic grief and absent or distorted grief. Little is known about the incidence of complicated grief. However, Raphael (1984) has suggested that complications may occur in as many as one in three bereavements. Alternatively, Marris (1986) suggests that complications are relatively rare. However, it seems reasonable to suggest that certain types of bereavement may prove to be more difficult to come to terms with than others, thereby restricting the accuracy of estimates based upon particular populations.

Delayed grief

Delayed grief occurs when the recognition of the loss and associated expression of grief is postponed. Typically, grief is experienced with particular severity at a later date. Lindemann (1944), following his work with people who had been bereaved in tragic circumstances, believed this to be a frequent complication of the bereavement process. Volkan (1975) identified a variation of this response which he characterised in terms of an intellectual acknowledgement of the death together with an emotional denial of the reality of it. Volkan argued that such a reaction was typical of instances in which the person who has been bereaved becomes fixated in initial conflicting reactions to the death and cannot resolve these conflicts. Indeed, most descriptions of complicated grief seem to indicate that the person involved has become fixated at one point or another in the grieving process – perhaps faced with difficulties they feel unable to solve.

> A woman in her thirties who, throughout her adolescent and adult life, felt that she had been protected from her mother's vindictiveness by her father found herself unable to grieve over her father's death. Most of her energy was taken up with a panic-stricken avoidance of her mother who apparently deeply resented this behaviour. This woman felt that she could not (nine months after the death) emotionally accept that her father had died. 'I can only see him dead, I know he is dead but I remember nothing about him at all – only the fact that he is dead.'

Distorted or absent grief

Raphael (1984) has suggested that in distorted reactions to bereavement one aspect of the grief process is emphasised and others often suppressed. She further suggests that the two common patterns are extreme expressions of either anger or guilt which tend to overwhelm all other aspects of grief. Furthermore, Marris (1986) is of the opinion that young children and very elderly adults may express their grief in terms of physical ailments rather than the expected range of responses described in connection with the reactions of the adult population.

The apparent absence of grief, initially reported by Deutsch (1937), has been noted by a number of researchers in the area. Bowlby (1980) considers absent grief to be a particularly important variant in the bereavement

56

process and has argued that other difficulties related to bereavement are invariably apparent. However, Singh and Raphael (1981) have shown that some people in whom grief is apparently absent do not progress to obviously pathological outcomes in the early years following their bereavement. It would seem reasonable to suggest that under certain circumstances some individuals simply do not feel grieved over some deaths.

Chronic grief

Chronic grief has been reported and is associated with instances in which the expected range of reactions is present, but the bereaved person does not recover from them. A variant of chronic grief, 'mummification', has been identified by Gorer (1965). Mummification is a process in which the world of the bereaved individual appears to be frozen in time following the death. The grieving person often behaves as if the dead person will return at some future date. Gorer cites Queen Victoria's response to the death of Prince Albert as an example of this form of chronic grief. Marris (1986) makes a similar point in connection with loss in general, and cites an example from literature, that of Miss Haversham – a character in Dickens's *Great Expectations* who waited forever, in her tattered wedding gown, by the ruins of what should have been her marriage feast.

Determinants of complicated grief

Many factors have been cited as being associated with complicating the grief process. For example Kalish (1985) cites eleven factors and Worden (1982) cites five main areas in which problems might be expected to arise. Worden's five main areas are relational; circumstantial; historical; personality; and social; and it is within these five areas that the observations of other researchers in the area may be usefully subsumed.

1. Relationship between the bereaved and the deceased

The following types of relationship have been found to be problematic:

(a) highly ambivalent relationships (Raphael 1984);
(b) narcissistic relationships in which the deceased represents an extension of the self (Worden 1982);
(c) highly dependent relationships (Horowitz *et al.* 1980).

2. Circumstances surrounding the death

(a) when the loss is uncertain and the bereaved is unsure whether or not the deceased is alive or dead (Lazare 1979);

(b) disasters in which multiple losses occur (Raphael 1984);
(c) deaths from which no body is available (Simpson 1979);
(d) unanticipated deaths (Parkes 1972);
(e) deaths caused by suicide, murder or self-neglect (Kalish 1985).

3. Life history of the bereaved person

(a) people who have had a history of complicated grief reactions (Simos 1979);
(b) people who have experienced several losses within a short space of time (Kalish 1985).

4. The personality of the bereaved person

(a) people who avoid feelings of helplessness (Simos 1979);
(b) people who perceive themselves to be 'strong' people who do not break down (Lazare 1979).

5. Social factors

(a) the loss is socially unspeakable and a conspiracy of silence surrounds a death or a relationship which is believed to be shameful (Lazare 1979);
(b) the loss is socially negated – the bereaved person and those around them act as if the loss did not happen (Lazare 1979);
(c) the absence of social support network (Vachon et al. 1982);
(d) the presence of an unhelpful social support network (Littlewood 1983).

Therapeutic interventions and complicated grief

Both Lindemann (1944) and Raphael (1975) suggest that therapeutic interventions may be successful in altering the various patterns associated with complications of the bereavement process. Furthermore, Raphael (1977) indicates that preventive intervention in cases where people are believed to be highly vulnerable to complications arising in the grief process may, in some cases, be beneficial. The range of professional support and help available to bereaved people is discussed in detail in Chapter 5.

Throughout this chapter an attempt has been made to describe the range and order of experiences associated with both complicated and uncomplicated grief occurring in the context of contemporary Western societies. Individuals who have been bereaved experience profoundly contradictory impulses in connection with their loss and the processes associated with grief can take a very long time to resolve.

However, grief is also a social process which is experienced, understood and resolved in a particular social setting. Consequently the range of theoretical perspectives which have been used in order to understand the bereavement process is an exceptionally broad one. These theories are the subject of Chapter 4.

4

MODELS OF BEREAVEMENT: SEARCHING FOR MEANING

'I did not know how I could reach him, where I could overtake him and go on hand in hand with him once more. It is such a secret place, the land of tears.'

Saint-Exupéry (1945)
The Little Prince

INTRODUCTION

The experiences associated with grief which have been described in the previous chapter express complex, contradictory impulses. The range of theoretical perspectives used to explain these experiences is equally diverse. Some approaches have been specifically developed to account for reactions to bereavement whilst other explanations attempt to place grief within a particular theoretical framework.

The first part of this chapter looks at some of the many and varied attempts which have been made to explain the bereavement process. Inevitably these attempts are partial, explaining some aspects of grief better than others. The second part of the chapter is concerned with the issue of ethnicity and raises the question of the extent to which theoretical approaches to bereavement may be culture-bound.

ILLNESS AND DISEASE MODELS

Early research into the area of bereavement attempted to characterise grief in terms of it being a disease. For example, Lindemann (1944), in describing the reactions he observed in his sample of bereaved people, wrote in terms of the 'symptoms' and 'management' of grief. For Lindemann, grief was best seen as a syndrome of symptoms whose management might pose problems, depending upon the nature of the loss and the bereaved person's previous life experiences.

Engel (1961) found this perspective particularly helpful and pursued these points further by emphasising the usefulness of conceptualising grief as a syndrome. Engel was of the opinion that if grief could be considered to be a disease then this would facilitate scientific study into the area. In time, Engel hoped, scientific study would help improve the medical management of people who had been bereaved.

Whilst few people today would view grief in terms of it being a disease, many people who have been bereaved describe their experiences in terms of being physically injured or wounded. Expressions such as 'throbbing wound', 'torn apart' and 'broken' abound in the descriptive literature. Furthermore, in instances where bereaved people seek professional help, they usually seek such help from a doctor.

Whilst bereavement is not a physical illness in itself, it may be associated with the onset of an illness or illnesses. In terms of bereavement being seen as a mental disorder, the position is somewhat similar. For example, the *Diagnostic and Statistical Manual of the American Psychiatric Association* (DSM III, 1980) classifies reactions to bereavement under 'codes for conditions that are not attributable to mental disorder that are a focus for attention and treatment'. There are no separate classifications for complicated bereavement processes. In this manual these are accounted for in terms of the predominant problem presented for treatment, an obvious relevant example being that of depression.

BIOLOGICAL EXPLANATIONS

As Osterweis, Solomon and Green (1984) have indicated, little is known about specific aspects of the biology of grief. However, in terms of the observations and experiences of bereaved people themselves, it would seem reasonable to suggest that respiratory, autonomic and endocrine systems may all be affected by phases of acute grieving. In addition, evidence from the epidemiology of bereavement would indicate that cardiovascular and immune function may be substantially altered by grief. Furthermore, the physiological effects of certain types of bereavement have been demonstrated in a number of studies. For example, Irwin *et al.* (1988) have demonstrated that natural killer cell activity, which is important to the body's defence against tumours and viral infections, is reduced in women undergoing conjugal bereavement.

Engel (1962) viewed bereavement as a biological stressor which activated two opposing response systems. The first of these response systems is the fight–flight system which may be seen as the biological basis for anxiety. The activation of this system might account for feelings of anxiety, restlessness and irrational anger following the death of a loved person. The second of these response systems is the conservation–withdrawal system which may be seen as the biological basis for depression. This system might account for feelings of apathy, difficulty in concentrating and social withdrawal. The interaction between these two systems might

61

account for some of the apparently contradictory elements associated with the bereavement process inasmuch as the bereaved person is effectively faced with conflicting feelings.

In the case of conservation–withdrawal, Eisenbruch (1984a) has emphasised the potentially adaptive nature of this response. He refers to this response system as precipitating a valuable period of what he calls social hibernation. During this period of relative social isolation energy may be conserved, giving the person time to think through the implications of their loss in terms of their future adaptation to an essentially new environment.

An explanation of the activation of the fight–flight mechanism may be found in the work of authors who seek to place grief in an evolutionary context. Averill (1968) has concluded that the set of reactions commonly called grief is universal amongst humans and is probably present in higher primates. According to these types of explanations humans and primates are essentially social animals and grief reactions are a sub-category of reactions to separation from the group in general, i.e. reaction to separation is so painful that group cohesion is ensured. From this perspective the fight–flight system and the conservation–withdrawal system would be triggered by any separation and the intense distress involved would presumably result in, if it were possible, rejoining the group together with the elicitation of caring responses from other group members. Obviously, in the case of death, reunion with the dead person is not possible but the reaction would be triggered in any event. John Bowlby (1980) has developed these arguments further in his consideration of loss in terms of attachment theory. However, Bowlby's consideration of the area is both specific and highly influential; consequently his findings will be addressed separately.

Darwin's (1872) observations concerning the expression of grief in people and animals would support observations concerning the contradictory impulses characterising grief. Darwin observed that the facial expressions typical of adult grief are indicative of two contradictory tendencies. One tendency is the tendency to cry out and the other is the tendency to control the urge to cry out.

Biological explanations of grief would lead one to suppose that, once activated, grief runs a set biological course characterised by the complex interplay between two opposing biological response systems. However useful this perspective may be in explaining the cause of the initial reactions associated with the death of a loved person, it is of limited relevance to explaining people's need to interpret and understand their experiences.

In terms of the complications associated with the grief process identified in Chapter 3, it might be expected that uncertainty surrounding the death and inadequate social support would be particularly important factors in determining the outcome of the bereavement process.

PSYCHODYNAMIC EXPLANATIONS

Psychodynamic explanations have been extremely influential in terms of the way grief has been understood. The development of these explanations owes much to the early works of both Freud (1917) and Klein (1948). Whilst neither Freud nor Klein was interested in bereavement in itself, both offered consistent interpretations of the experiences associated with grief.

Freud (1917) saw the process of mourning as being primarily concerned with the removal of the libido from the lost object and its attachment to a new object. The reality principle forces a recognition of the loss and demands the detachment of emotional energy from the dead person. Freud believed, although he found it difficult to account for exactly why this should be the case, that this process was achieved extremely slowly and extremely painfully:

> Each one of the memories and situations of expectancy which demonstrate the libido's attachment to the lost object is met by the verdict of reality that the object no longer exists. The ego is persuaded by the sum of narcissistic satisfactions it derives from being alive to sever its attachment to the object.
>
> (Freud, 1917: 255)

Freud was of the belief that withdrawal may be accomplished by the ego's identification with the lost object. However, as Bowlby (1980) amongst others has pointed out, identification may be only one of many responses. Freud's theoretical position regarding mourning (and melancholia) would appear to rest on three main, somewhat contentious, hypotheses:

1. the hydrodynamic theory of instinct;
2. the supposition that narcissism is primary and precedes object relations;
3. an emphasis on a regression to a narcissistic oral phase in melancholia.

Freud's observations are primarily concerned with the intra-psychic processes associated with mourning rather than with the more generic aspects of the experience of bereavement. However, his description of the slow and painful way in which the loss of the loved person is acknowledged is a powerful one. As Bowlby (1977) has indicated, in some ways the processes associated with mourning would appear to be similar to those associated with falling in love – except in the case of mourning the experiences are in reverse.

In terms of complications associated with the bereavement process a Freudian perspective would focus upon the degree of ambivalence in the lost relationship. In very general terms it would be expected that a high level of ambivalence would complicate the bereavement process.

Klein's (1948) theoretical contribution to the area arose out of her study of depressive illness. She suggested that in normal mourning early, paranoid anxieties are reactivated and loss may be experienced as punishment. From this perspective a bereaved person temporarily loses their ability to maintain what Klein calls the 'depressive position' which involves tolerating the ambivalence inherent in human relationships. Consequently, the person views their situation in terms of 'all good' or 'all bad' and oscillates between the two extremes. Klein likened this experience to 'a modified and transitory manic-depressive state' which presumably is overcome by the resolution of the ambivalence experienced by the bereaved person. Again, it is the resolution of ambivalence which is seen as central to the bereavement process.

Whilst Freud and Klein were primarily concerned with the inner, intra-psychic world of bereaved people – a world perceived to be in danger of collapse, Pincus (1976) adopted a slightly different perspective. Pincus looked at patterns of actual interactions in marriage and hypothesised that bereavement following the loss of a partner would take different forms depending upon whether the past relationship was primarily characterised by identification or projection. Here, the process of mourning is seen to depend, to a certain extent, on the nature of the past relationship. For example, in the case of relationships based on identification,

> it is couples with such a strong need to identify who are in danger of finding the loss of a partner unbearable; they cannot survive the separation, die soon or collapse into paralyzing illness. Or they may find another object of identification, a son or a daughter, a close friend or a good cause.
>
> (Pincus, 1976: 34)

and in the case of relationships based on projection,

> How much greater still is the guilt likely to be in cases where the partner who has been the recipient of the other one's split-off bad, rejected feelings dies, and the projected bits can then never be withdrawn and the guilt relieved. We shall see from some of the stories which follow that these situations often lead to long and excessive mourning and grief, a grief which the bereaved cannot give up because it is his only hope for restitution.
>
> (Pincus, 1976: 36–7)

Pincus sees complicated reactions to bereavement in terms of their being exaggerations of normal responses. Furthermore, she is of the opinion that most societies encourage the idealisation of the dead person which inevitably results in the denial of real feelings and real memories of the past relationship. Again, it might be suggested that the more ambivalent the past relationship the greater the likelihood of complications arising during the bereavement process.

Whilst Pincus identifies the importance of the exact nature of the past relationship between the dead and the bereaved person, Rubin (1984) has suggested that the relationship continues, probably indefinitely, albeit in a modified intra-psychic form. Rubin proposes a 'two-track' model of bereavement in which bereavement represents the cessation of present and future interaction with the dead person in the real world and leaves the internal world to bear the weight of the continuing relationship. From this perspective the relationship between the self and the dead person is continually changed and reworked at both conscious and unconscious levels.

At a more general level, many other theorists have used bereavement as a basis from which to understand other experiences of loss from a psychodynamic perspective. For example, Parsons (1982) likened the imposed termination of psychotherapy to grief and mourning and Vachon (1987), in conducting psychotherapy with terminally ill people, has suggested that a great deal of psychiatric illness in general is an expression of pathological mourning. Furthermore, she suggests that the presence of previously unresolved grief reactions may well complicate an individual's ability to deal with current crises. Finally, Viorst (1986) adopts an extremely broad perspective and uses the concepts of loss and grief in connection with the various conflicts associated with the developmental stages of life throughout the whole life-cycle.

ATTACHMENT THEORY

The view of bereavement from the perspective of attachment theory was principally expounded by Bowlby (1980). The theory has a long history and has developed and changed significantly over time. As Bowlby has indicated, the observations of many previous researchers stemmed from their considerations of depressive illnesses rather than from observations of the bereavement process *per se*. Consequently, attachment theory may make a particularly significant contribution towards the understanding of the more uncomplicated experiences associated with bereavement. Attachment theory incorporates an evolutionary perspective along with a psychodynamic perspective. The theory rests in general upon an appreciation of instinctive attachment and response mechanisms and in particular on the hypothesis that the child's attachment to its mother is mediated by a number of instinctive response systems. Bowlby believes that all relationships of physical and emotional significance are built around the same general pattern, i.e. that of the response systems first developed in the relationship between mother and child. A mother's absence provokes certain instinctive systems such as anxiety, protest and searching on the part of the child, the presence of the mother terminates them. The mother also provides activating stimuli for other instinctive systems and goes on to reinforce these when they occur. The relationship between mother and child and later between self and significant others is mediated through these exchanges.

In terms of bereavement, when a person first experiences the loss, the anxiety evokes an instinctive response. Anger and weeping may occur as the individual attempts to recover the lost object and such experiences constitute the first phase of mourning. The second phase of mourning sees attempts at recovery slowly diminish when they repeatedly fail to achieve the desired result. Despair follows the failed attempts to recover the object and behaviour then becomes disorganised. Bowlby believes that the depression accompanying this phase of mourning represents an adaptive force in the sense that it results from the realisation that the former mode of behaving and communicating is now inappropriate. The third phase of mourning represents a reorganisation of behaviour, partly in connection with the lost object and partly in relation to new objects. As Smith (1976) has noted, attachment theory has been extremely influential in the area of bereavement and many other researchers have used the theory to explain various experiences associated with grief. For example, Parkes (1970) follows Bowlby's theoretical orientation in his consideration of a bereaved person's desire, often unconscious, to search for the lost person. Bowlby's research would suggest that this desire to search for someone who has died represents an instinctive response to the loss of an attachment object which provokes separation anxiety. The anxiety experienced following separation triggers the desire to search for the lost person. However, in the instance of separations caused by the death of a person the search is fruitless but is nevertheless undertaken. Parkes has noted that a strong desire to search for a lost object may be associated with temporarily 'finding' the object. He is of the opinion that many of the experiences associated with bereavement, e.g. hearing or seeing the dead person, feeling their presence, etc. represent the logical outcome of an intense desire to search. Parkes has also suggested that searching behaviour may become intensified if there is any uncertainty, real or imagined, over whether or not a death has occurred.

PERSONAL CONSTRUCT THEORY AND COGNITIVE MODELS

Parkes (1975) has also considered bereavement in terms of its being a 'psychosocial' transition. He suggests that certain events such as bereavement lead to major changes in people's internal assumptive worlds. These assumptive worlds are made up of a series of models which form the person's inner world and it is the interaction between a person's assumptive internal models and their external environment which determines the ways in which they experience events. From this perspective, grief involves a person relinquishing their set of assumptions about the world and developing new ones to fit the new circumstances.

Whilst these observations were derived wholly from individuals who were experiencing loss, the conclusions drawn by Parkes are remarkably similar to the observations of Kelly (1955) concerning his development of personal construct theory. Kelly was of the opinion that a person's 'self' or personality may be seen in terms of a system of interrelated constructs which inform the individual's attempt to make sense of the external world. Specifically, Kelly asserts that people look at the world

> through transparent patterns or templets which he creates and then attempts to fit over the realities of which the world is composed. . . . Let us give the name constructs to these patterns that are tried on for size. They are ways of construing the world.
>
> (Kelly, 1955: 8–9)

According to the theory, constructs are arranged in interrelated systems and the sum total of a person's construct system is that person's self. The fundamental postulate of the theory is that 'a person's processes are psychologically channelized by the ways in which they anticipate events'. From this perspective people react to the past in order to reach out to the future and engage in a process of perpetual validation which involves checking to see how much sense their 'self' has made out of the world in terms of how well they can anticipate future events.

In short, Kelly's theory indicates the importance of a person's relationship with the world in terms of that person's attempt to impose subjective meaning on the world. Thus, people develop their own view of the world (a theory concerning what it is and how it works), their own expectations concerning what is likely to happen in given situations (hypotheses based upon subjective probabilities) and constantly experiment (through their behaviour) with life.

Woodfield and Viney (1982) have proposed a model of bereavement based upon personal construct theory which shares many similarities with Parkes's observations concerning assumptive world models. According to Kelly's theory, a vitally important sub-set of personal constructs affected by bereavement is of those involved with the location and identification of the concept of the self in relation to a system of constructs relevant to self and significant others. The loss of a significant other entails a major shift in the person's construct system. The size and nature of any change will depend upon the specific constructs relevant to the relationship between the person bereaved and the person who has died. Since all relationships significant to the person who has been bereaved are involved in the person's construct system, then it follows that other relationships are likely to undergo change too.

This approach gives considerably more structure to Parkes's (1975) concept of assumptive worlds and offers a method, i.e. that of repertory grid technique, by which to analyse both the range of an individual's personal construct system and the relationship between particular constructs.

This approach also adds a slightly different dimension to the work of Rubin (1984). Specifically, if a person's construct system changes in response to their external environment then the position of the dead person will change and develop within the system. Thus, the relationship between the person bereaved and the dead person is located within a broader network of social relationships in the past, present and future.

Horowitz *et al.* (1980) have considered complicated grief from a similar perspective. Specifically, they identify four forms that depressive states following bereavement may take:

1. energy conservation, withdrawal and numbness;
2. feeling frighteningly sad, alone and needy;
3. feeling hostility and rage towards self and others;
4. feeling despair, worthlessness and defectiveness.

Whilst all of these feelings may be associated with uncomplicated grief, Horowitz *et al.* suggest that, in some cases, these states may be intensified to the point where the person feels overwhelmed by their feelings and either resorts to maladaptive behaviour or remains in the state indefinitely. It is suggested that, in the cases of complicated grief, certain 'latent self-images' are activated by the loss. These representations of the self, resulting from earlier relationships, had previously been held in check by the relationship the grieving person had with the dead person. In terms of Kelly's (1955) observations, the necessity of re-evaluating their construct systems has left these bereaved people at the mercy of extremely negative views of the self which are associated with previous relationships. The once latent images of the self believed to be particularly problematic by Horowitz *et al.* are as follows.

1. A self-image in which the self is seen as a weak helpless waif who has lost their strong caring other upon whom they relied for support and nurturance. Such a self-image was associated with a frighteningly sad response.
2. A self-image which oscillates between an image of the self as betrayed and needy and an image of the self as an evil destructive person. Such a self-image was associated with feelings of hostility and rage.
3. A self-image which oscillates between an image of the self as defective or disgusting and an image of the self as being self-sufficient. Such a self-image was associated with feelings of despair.

All of these negative self-images, once held in check by the relationship with the dead person, return or are reactivated following the death and may complicate the bereavement process.

Cognitive factors are also relevant to the bereaved person's need to come to some acceptable understanding as to why the death occurred. Kalish (1985) has identified the form this usually takes. The dead person's family and friends get together and obsessively review the available information concerning the last few hours or days before death. There would appear to be a need to develop a communal, acceptable understanding of the event. Van der Bout, de Keijser and Schut (1988) suggest that this obsession with accounting for the causes and potential preventability of the death may be necessary to the well-being of the bereaved person and explain it in terms of the more general positive relationship between 'worry work' and well-being.

Bromley (1988) has also noted this tendency and calls it 'post mortem psychology'. Bromley suggests that post-mortem psychology involves the psychological autopsy of factors surrounding the death and recommends it as a method which could be useful to professionals working in the general area of bereavement. This method has already been used in research into suicidal behaviour and presumably the aims of its general use would be to sensitise workers to the importance of this aspect of the bereavement process.

GRIEF AS A CRISIS OF COPING

Caplan (1964) devised a model of crisis intervention which has often been used to understand the bereavement process. The components of this model are as follows.

1. The person is in a state of helplessness.
2. The person's usual strategies for coping with stressful events are no longer successful.
3. Defences are weakened.
4. The person needs to turn to others for help and is particularly susceptible to their responses.
5. Current crises awaken a person's past experiences of similar crises.

This model suggests the outcome of the crisis may be dependent upon the available social support network at the time of its occurrence. Consequently, this model has been widely used by health care professionals who are in contact with people who have been bereaved (Maddison and Walker 1967; Raphael 1973, 1977, 1981). Obviously, this model may be particularly relevant to the area of professional help given after a disaster has occurred. Caplan suggests that the resolution of the crisis can result in improved adaptation if the person can learn, usually with help, to strengthen their coping capacity. Alternatively, poor adaptation may result from inadequate coping. However, coping is an extremely complex concept.

At a general level the facilitation of coping in response to environmental demands has been cited as being central to the social worker's role in caring for people who have been bereaved (Smith 1976). The term coping usually refers to the multitude of ways in which people attempt to handle a stressful situation. Coping is increasingly being viewed as a process rather than an event and usually refers to the pattern of intra-psychic, action-orientated and social strategies people habitually employ to handle threats to their physical and psychosocial well-being.

Research concerning the use of coping styles, for example, Peterman and Bode (1986), indicates that most people are highly flexible concerning the ways in which they cope with problems in general. However, one style of coping seems to be relatively fixed, i.e. that of avoidance. There would appear to be a substantial number of individuals who habitually avoid actively confronting the problems they encounter. This style of coping is so fixed that some researchers are now regarding it as a personality trait (Cronkite and Moos 1984). It seems reasonable to suggest that people who use this style of coping may experience particularly severe problems if they are bereaved. It might further be suggested that persistent attempts to avoid confronting the fact that the death has occurred may predispose them towards a complicated bereavement process.

Verbrugge (1985), in her review of the general area of coping styles, has suggested that coping styles may be gendered. Specifically, she concluded that women prefer to use social support and emotionally orientated coping styles (passive) whilst men prefer active, problem-solving and tension reducing ways of coping (active).

In the area of bereavement gender differences in coping preferences may account for the findings of several researchers. For example, Dyregrov and Matthiesen (1987). These researchers report that fathers, following the death of a young child, tended to be more critical than mothers regarding the support received from the hospital. Many fathers reported that they felt they had been 'overlooked' by the hospital staff. Barbarin and Chesler (1986) have reported that the use of passive styles of coping (a feminine preference) were associated with better supportive relationships between parents and hospital staff. Alternatively, they found that active coping styles (a masculine preference) were associated with potentially problematic parent/staff interactions. It may be possible that the greater tendency amongst men to use active styles of coping may inadvertently lead them to receive less appropriate support from hospital personnel. However, an alternative explanation may be that the hospital staff perceive the child's mother to be in greater need of support and consequently direct available resources towards her rather than her partner.

Furthermore, Mandell et al. (1980) have reported that fathers showed a marked tendency to keep busy and take on additional workloads as a way of coping with their loss and Clyman et al. (1980) found that the fathers in their study expressed a desire to move on with life when the mothers were still depressed and grieving for their child. Involvement in one's own grief may make it difficult to appreciate another person's perspective. For example, one mother in a study by DeFrain et al. (1982) reported that:

70

I was an open, throbbing wound, and he wanted to have sex. It was very hard for me to understand that he was also in pain and that he felt our closeness would be healing.

Children may find their parent's gendered responses particularly difficult to understand: For example:

Father: Yes – [his daughter] said 'I believe it doesn't make much difference to you, Daddy. I don't think you are very sad.'

Mother: 'He [father] doesn't understand' she said to me. 'I don't believe Daddy understands this very well, I haven't seen him crying once.' A child thinks you must cry when you're sad. I said: 'Well, well, Daddies don't do that very often, but you don't know if Daddy does or not. Maybe he thinks I'd better go to the garden and walk up and down when it's difficult for him. Perhaps he doesn't want to make things more difficult than they already are.' But she thought her father didn't understand it at all. But we've always encouraged the children to talk about it [their sister's death] before she died and afterwards.'

(Littlewood, Hoekstra-Weebers and Humphrey 1990)

Unfortunately, some misunderstandings about different ways of coping are not so easily dealt with and some mothers may interpret their partner's preoccupation with various activities as evidence of a certain lack of concern. Furthermore, some ways of coping may not be appropriate for all people. For example:

A man in his forties reported that he 'kept himself very busy' after his child's death from cancer. He had an ulcer 'from working so hard' and over a year after his daughter's death he still worked 'over 60 hours a week'. He felt he'd coped extremely well with his loss and that he'd helped his family to cope in a similar way. When his son's schoolwork suffered after the death, he moved his son to another school and arranged for personal tuition for him. He arranged detailed daily activities for his wife 'because it's important to keep busy'. This man's wife privately asked the interviewer if it was possible to be referred for psychiatric help. She felt she couldn't talk to her husband about her daughter's death and was beginning to fear for her sanity.

Littlewood, Hoekstra-Weebers and Humphrey (1990) have suggested that, in terms of coping with everyday events and problems, fathers regain their coping capacity more quickly than mothers following the death of a child. Osterweis, Solomon and Green (1984) indicate that a lack of synchronicity as well as differences in styles of coping may be implicated in the misunderstandings which frequently arise between bereaved parents. However, much more research concerning the concept of coping is required before any specific intervention programmes concerning the support of individual styles of coping with bereavement can be developed.

Nevertheless, several researchers have developed general models of various stressful events in order to illuminate some of the specific tasks associated with these events which have to be coped with by all individuals, irrespective of their individual coping styles. For example, Moos (1977) has developed a task-coping framework in connection with chronic illness in general and Hardiker *et al.* (1986) have developed a similar framework in connection with chronic renal failure. Worden (1982) adopts this approach in his description of the tasks which have to be coped with following the death of a loved person and Smith (1976) outlines a similar perspective concerning the tasks social workers must undertake in working with people who have been bereaved.

PHENOMENOLOGICAL AND EXISTENTIAL MODELS

Smith (1976), whilst not taking issue with other explanations of grief, has suggested that a fuller range of explanations of the meaning of bereavement might be achieved by a further appreciation of the essentially social nature of meaning and the ways in which personal identity is created, maintained and changed by a person's interaction with other people who are, for whatever reason, significant to them. Her work is of particular value in that she highlights a major omission in the available range of models put forward to account for the experiences associated with grief. Specifically, she argues that most models concentrate either upon intra-psychic processes, emphasising individuals' reactions to their bereavement or on a very broad socio-cultural level, emphasising cultural attitudes towards death and dying. Essentially, the middle range analyses have been under-represented and she suggests that an appreciation of phenomenology and existentialism might be appropriate additional perspectives upon the area. She focuses upon three levels of analysis:

1. the macro-level which looks at the relationship of the individual to the society and its institutions;
2. the intermediate level in which individuals tend to have a fairly well-bounded network of significant relationships, for example, their friends and family;
3. the micro-level in which individuals have specific personal interchanges of an intense and continuing nature, for example, with their partners.

At the macro-level, Berger and Luckmann (1967) have argued that, although the external world is socially constructed, it is subjectively experienced as existing independently of the person perceiving it. For this external world to have any meaning at an individual level people require ongoing validation of their identity and place in the world. This ongoing validation is carried out by interactions with other people at the intermediate and micro-level. People effectively construct a microcosmic social world of their own with their significant others. At the micro-level the most unique and individual aspects of a person's identity may be experienced as opposed to the more general levels of social interaction.

Natanson (1970) has argued that the 'self' is a two-fold entity. It is both past and future in that the unified history of the past and present behaviour effectively provide a platform from which to instigate new actions. These two elements of the self are termed the 'me', which represents the historical past and the 'I' which instigates new actions. Obviously, from this perspective the loss of a loved person affects both elements of the self profoundly.

Phenomenology with its depiction of the generalised typicalities of the world may give an insight into the ways in which the experience of bereavement might affect the 'me'. Extremely complex changes in social position, social status and social role frequently follow the death of a significant other. For example, the death of a husband means a movement from the social position of wife to that of widow and the death of a child may mean the loss of the role of parent. The loss of key features of past and present identity may be compounded by the loss of external social support for the 'I', i.e. the person who validated the initiation of action has been lost. This situation may be illustrated by the following comments made by a middle-aged widow. 'I just can't do without him that's all. I can't *do* anything.' In phenomenological terms, the loss of 'me' provokes a crisis of identity and in existential terms the loss of 'I' provokes existential anxieties.

From a phenomenological perspective complicated reactions to grief might be viewed in terms of the difficulties experienced in negotiating a different status and role in the intermediate world of the social network. Successful negotiation of any changes at this level would be, to a greater or lesser extent, dependent upon the availability of an appropriate social support network. Characteristics of formal and informal support networks will be discussed in detail in Chapters 5 and 6. However, irrespective of the availability or otherwise of appropriate social support, some individuals may simply avoid the required reconstruction of the self. This avoidance might take the form of the incorporation of the dead person within the self or mummification.

From a phenomenological perspective, if the person who has been bereaved simply incorporates the dead person into their selves, then the past interactions are carried on internally regardless of the dictates of external reality, i.e. the interaction with the deceased simply continues, thus sparing the bereaved person having to contemplate a future without the person who has died. It seems reasonable to suggest that elderly people who experience 'pseudo-hallucinatory thought echoes' for literally years after the death of their partner are in this position. Possibly in the absence of any real or perceived alternatives the person simply maintains the 'me' and the past in the present, thereby pre-empting any possibly painful considerations of what a different future might mean.

Alternatively mummification would be viewed from a phenomenological perspective as a suspension of the self enabling the grieving person to believe that their bereavement is a temporary phase in their lives. Such a course of action would presumably complicate the grief process in terms of its chronicity. In such a situation the bereaved person simply waits for the return of the other. Perhaps some parents who persist in keeping their dead child's room as a 'shrine' to the child might be relevant examples of such a tendency. For example a mother who desperately tried to be a 'good' mother to her eldest son who died of cancer described her situation in the following way:

> I can't describe it really, I just couldn't move. I couldn't do anything, just sat there in his room, staring at his desk and pencils. My husband tried to get me out of it——[their daughter] wanted——[their dead son]'s room. But I couldn't let him go. I kept thinking what would happen if he came back and his room wasn't the same. I just couldn't bear it, I sat there for hours.

The same woman eventually allowed her daughter to take her dead son's room some years after his death. She then experienced dreams in which she broke into the hospital where he died and searched, long into the night, in boxes where, she believed in the dream, her son would be found. Her dreams filled her with guilt and fear.

From an existential perspective even more basic anxieties are involved. The literature on existentialism is vast and, strictly speaking, it is not a philosophy in itself but a general approach to life and living. A key figure in the history of existentialism is Heidegger. Towse (1986) has argued that Heidegger's (1926) *Being and Time* reintroduced the serious study of existence and being. For Heidegger the fact of existence has to be faced in the certainty of death. Furthermore, anxiety over death has the potential to give life meaning in that death is the only certainty in life. The possibility of not existing, of non-being, was believed by Heidegger to be an anxiety central to the human condition.

Sartre, in *Being and Nothingness* (1958), took issue with Heidegger's views on death and argued that, while death may be a certain event, it occurs at an uncertain time and therefore is unlikely to give life meaning in itself. However, Sartre did consider death but considered it in terms of the loss of the self in particular rather than in terms of life's meaning in general. Sartre's conceptualisation of the self involved two aspects, i.e.

74

'being for others' and 'being for self'. For Sartre death involved the loss of 'being for self' – the 'I' in Natanson's analysis. After death it is impossible to assert the essential self; only the 'being for others' remains in the memories, accurate or otherwise, of those who survive one's death.

Towse (1986) has used Tillich's (1952) existential analysis to illustrate some of the specific crises a bereavement may provoke. Tillich saw authentic existence as being achieved through the courage to face the existential anxieties of faith and death, doubt and meaninglessness and of guilt and condemnation. Towse suggests that psychodynamic models of bereavement do not always offer a complete explanation of experiences of grief since there may be no underlying neurotic conflicts. For some people, their bereavement may be their first glimpse into the abyss of nothingness, their first experience of the possibility of non-being. From this perspective complications of the bereavement process might arise from attempts to ignore the crisis by resorting to past patterns of behaviour or by becoming transfixed by the threat of annihilation, unable to cope with the existential despair provoked by the loss. Such existential despair differs significantly from separation anxiety. Separation anxiety essentially revolves around fear of, or actual loss of, the other, whilst existential anxiety revolves around the fear of standing alone and the potential loss of the self.

Rowe (1987, 1988) suggests that this fear of the annihilation of the self is an essential part of the human condition. For example:

Waking in the early hours of the morning in a sweat of terror is an extremely common experience. It might be some comfort to her to know that, as she lies there, all across the country are people experiencing that terrible loneliness of being. They have woken suddenly to the greatest uncertainty and loneliness a human being can know. There is no shape or structure to hold them. They are falling, dissolving, totally, paralysingly helpless without recovery or rescue. Sickening powerful forces clutch at their heart and stomach. They gasp for breath as wave after wave of terror sweeps over them. . . . I went on to tell her that the terror she felt is called 'existential angst'. She laughed and laughed at this ridiculously pretentious name. 'I'll remember that next time,' she said.

(Rowe 1987: 20–2)

Rowe (1988) has argued that existential crises, if confronted, may be the key to what she calls 'the successful self'. However, she also suggests that, if such crises are denied or avoided, then a whole range of problems (panic attacks, obsessions, phobias, depression, schizophrenia) may result.

ETHNICITY: A PROBLEM FOR THEORY

As Eisenbruch (1984b) has pointed out, it is Western forms of grief and mourning which have received most attention in the relevant literature. However, recognition that individual cultural patterns need to be considered in psychiatric practice is growing. Interest in the importance of the subjective meaning of grief would suggest that a person's culture is of importance in terms of explanations of the causes and consequences for one's system of values of loss.

Whilst there are many ethnographic accounts of different mourning practices the issue of ethnicity in multi-cultural societies raises profound problems in connection with the way the grieving process has been conceptualised. Schermerhorn has defined the term ethnic group in the following way:

> a collectivity within a larger society having a real or putative common ancestry, memories of a shared historical past and a cultural focus on one or more symbolic aspects defined as the epitome of that peoplehood.
>
> (1978: 12)

A further important distinction has been drawn between behavioural ethnicity and ideological ethnicity (Stein and Hill 1977). Behavioural ethnicity refers to the extent to which a person has learned distinctive values, beliefs and norms of an ethnic group. It also refers to the extent to which these values, beliefs and norms inform that person's day to day interactions both within that group and within the broader social context. Ideological ethnicity is based upon customs and belief systems which may be adhered to on certain occasions but do not affect a person's everyday life. For example, third and fourth generation migrants may not be immersed in their culture but may still identify with their ethnic group with respect to behaviour associated with specific life events; weddings and funerals would be the obvious examples. It may also be the case that certain mourning rituals may be adhered to, not out of the beliefs of the survivors, but out of respect for the dead person.

Migration itself, as Eisenbruch (1984b) points out, is also a form of loss, particularly when the move is made out of necessity rather than choice. Over time the loss may become tolerable for the individual, but it will, nevertheless, continue. Second and third generation migrants inevitably reassess the values and belief systems of their own families and ethnic groups after having been socialised alongside groups with different values and beliefs. The following example, taken from an interview with a Polish woman in her early sixties, may illustrate the complexity of the processes involved, together with their potential to further complicate the bereavement process.

Mrs——had lived in England since shortly after the end of the Second World War. Her husband was from Poland and her mother, who had lived nearby until her death, had shared her daughter's traumatic experiences. Both had been prisoners of war. The death of her mother had left Mrs——in a state of panic and distress. She felt she had no past and that her last link with a Poland she remembered, but which in reality no longer existed, had been severed by her mother's death. Mrs——was also remembering her war-time experiences with great frequency and pain. Her father had been killed in the war and she felt that she'd been unable to mourn his death properly until after her mother had died. She was further distressed because her son had recently become engaged to 'an English woman'. Since her past caused her pain and her future caused her fear, she'd taken to hoarding jewellery in case of an unknown but frightening event which might cause her to flee again. Her jewellery, and the presence of her mother's possessions, were the only things which gave the present any degree of safety.

Because of the complexity of these issues Eisenbruch (1984b) warns against the simplistic assumption that schemes devised by Western researchers can simply be transposed onto people from different ethnic backgrounds. As he points out:

> In cross-cultural work it might be quite inappropriate to confront say, a Chinese patient who is apparently unaware of his or her psychological pain or to try to transpose notions of denial.
>
> (Eisenbruch 1984b: 324)

5

MODELS OF SOCIAL SUPPORT AND PROFESSIONAL SUPPORT NETWORKS

'Over and over again, dying and grieving persons indicate that they fear being abandoned. Thus one of the most important aspects of a caring relationship is to reduce this fear.'

Kalish (1985)
Death, Grief and Caring Relationships

INTRODUCTION

The term social support has been widely used in research concerned with both positive and negative life events. In general terms social support networks (i.e. the extent of a person's relationships with other people) are believed to play an important role in the amelioration of the stresses associated with the impact of various life events. Furthermore, the availability, or otherwise, of social support following a death has been identified by several researchers as being extremely important to the outcome of the bereavement process. Consequently, the first part of this chapter will look at four of the major models of social support which have been generated by researchers concerned with the impact of life events upon individuals and groups. Specifically, the 'Stress-Buffering', 'Stress Prevention', 'Direct Effects' and 'Social Support Deterioration' models will all be discussed.

The second part of the chapter will be concerned with the specific issues associated with social support following a bereavement and the third part will look at some programmes designed to provide social support for people who have been bereaved. The contributions preventive programmes, self-help groups and focused professional interventions may make to the area will all be discussed. However, it must be said that the majority of people who have been bereaved neither receive nor seek any focused professional help in connection with their bereavement. Consequently, the final part of the chapter will be concerned with the general observations people who have been bereaved tend to make concerning their views of support from professional sources.

MODELS OF SOCIAL SUPPORT

The stress-buffering model

Many researchers have suggested that a person's social support system may help to moderate or buffer the effects of stressful life events on psychosocial well-being (for example, Cohen and Wills 1985; Kessler, Price and Wortman 1985; Thoits 1982). The notion that social support is important in buffering the effects of such stress is fundamental to crisis intervention (Andrews *et al.* 1978). As Dohrenwend (1975) has commented, evidence from survivors of natural disasters and holocausts caused by human agency would indicate that, when stress is sufficiently prolonged and severe, nearly all of those involved will display psychiatric symptoms. Consequently, professional provision of support to 'buffer' the impact of such events might be expected to be particularly important. As Barrera (1988) has indicated, part of the popularity of the stress-buffering model lies in the recognition of the fact that the 'occurrence of many major life events could not be prevented, but social support could mitigate adverse reactions to such events' (Barrera 1988: 229).

However, despite the buffer model being widely used, its effect has not always been demonstrated. For example, Lin (1986) looked at twenty relevant studies and found that only three studies confirmed the model whilst twelve failed to demonstrate this effect. However, in a review of the area conducted by Cohen and Wills (1985) it is suggested that this model may be relevant to certain life events but not to others. These authors suggest that there is a need for greater specificity concerning the range of applications of this model.

Cassel (1976) considers the model to be particularly important since it is much easier to intervene in order to provide or strengthen social support than it is to reduce exposure to stresses. Following a similar line of argument Thoits (1982) attributes importance to the development of the model because social relationships may be more amenable to change than factors such as personality traits or preferred coping styles. Nevertheless, buffer effects need interpreting with caution. Because, whilst the model offers the attractively simple proposition that people with strong social support systems are better able to cope with various life events than are people with little or no support systems, there are major difficulties associated with the conceptualisation and operationalisation of the term social support.

There are many problems associated with the concept of social support. For example, type, source and structure of the support network may be considerably more important than the amount of support received. For example, House (1981) looked at the emotional, practical and cognitive components of relationships and identified four types of supportive behaviours:

1. emotional support involving caring, trust and empathy;
2. instrumental support involving practical help with tasks;
3. informational support involving keeping people informed about relevant developments;
4. appraisal support involving helping people to evaluate their performance, for example by encouraging and supporting the undertaking of various activities.

Also, sources of support are important dimensions. For example, family and friends may be expected to provide different types of support when compared to the types of support expected from welfare professionals.

Mueller (1980) has suggested that the actual structure of the supportive network may be relevant. Specifically, in this particular study the support systems of psychiatric patients were found to be smaller in size and more kinship reliant than those of a control group. Furthermore, the patients' networks contained more relationships which were characterised by dependency than those of controls. However, it must be said that the causal direction of these observations is not at all clear. Pre-existing psychological disturbances may determine both an individual's levels of support and their subjective experience of major life events.

Cohen and Wills (1985) have reviewed the area and suggest that if buffering is to occur:

1. the effect might only be relevant for certain types of support;
2. the support received must match the needs of the life event;
3. the model may be curvilinear rather than linear, i.e. some events may be so devastating that individuals may be overwhelmed regardless of their resources. If this is the case then it might be expected, as Murrell and Norris (1984) have indicated, that any discrepancies between low and high levels of social support and extent of distress will diminish in the case of extremely stressful events.

Obviously, any social support network is likely to have limitations.

If buffering occurs in some situations rather than others, then it might be helpful to suggest the mechanism which might underlie stress buffering. A frequently cited mechanism involves the role of perceived support in preventing adverse cognitive appraisals of life events (Wilcox and Vernberg 1985). This mechanism would be in keeping with observations concerning the role of appraisal processes in models of coping and adaptation (Lazarus and Launier 1978) and is not dissimilar to some of the observations made by cognitively orientated psychotherapists. For example, the observations of Horowitz et al. (1980), which were discussed in Chapter 4 and concern the activation of latent self-images following bereavement, might be taken to suggest that the relationship with the lost person had effectively 'buffered' the person who had been bereaved from adverse cognitive appraisals of their 'selves' that had previously developed.

Ben-Sira (1985), in looking at the relationship between coping with the demands of the environment and social support, suggests a slightly different mechanism. In this model coping is seen as a result of interactions between the following: internal resources (innate traits, previous experiences, cultural characteristics and education) and external resources (social support). If internal resources are inadequate then the external ones subsequently become more important. Ben-Sira suggests that psychosocial stress is not the demand in itself, but it is the individual's perception of the demand which determines the surmountability of it.

Ben-Sira also introduces a concept of 'potency'. Potency comprises both a feeling of confidence in personal capabilities and a feeling of confidence in the social order. Ben-Sira believes potency is enhanced by a successive series of good coping outcomes and social support. The suggestion here is that 'learned success', possibly the other side of the coin to 'learned helplessness' (Seligman 1975), plays a key role in successful coping.

Rowe (1988) has suggested that people under stress effectively amplify their preferred ways of being in the world, i.e. their internal resources in Ben Sira's terms, in order to cope with its demands. Using the concepts of extraversion and introversion she suggests that introverts will respond to stress by taking refuge by withdrawing into their internal world and extraverts take refuge in social activities and their social network. These previously held preferences may have implications for network size and, hence, range of availability of social support. It seems reasonable to suggest that an introverted person would tend to have a smaller social support network than an extrovert. However, the quality of the network, i.e. a few intense contacts as opposed to many diffuse ones, may also play a part in determining the usefulness of available support in terms of the support system's relevance to the particular life event.

Overall, the stress-buffering model clearly has value but much more needs to be known about the nature of the life event itself and the personal and social characteristics of those involved. Bereavement presents particular difficulties since bereavement effectively causes a disruption of a person's social support network. The situation is one in which a major stressful life event has occurred which results in the potential loss of the 'buffering' previously provided by the lost relationship. Furthermore, insofar as social support following bereavement tends to be kinship related, then many members of a given individual's support network will also be experiencing a major life event. Specifically, the social support system may break under the strain of rather than buffer against this particular source of stress.

81

The stress prevention model

The stress prevention model was designed to demonstrate the ways in which social support might have a more direct influence on the prevention or reduction of distress (e.g. Gottlieb 1981, 1983; Gore 1981). This model suggests that stress processes themselves can be altered by social support. The two basic premises associated with this model are as follows:

1. Supportive exchanges involving information giving, environmental manipulation and behavioural assistance operate to avert or stop the consequences of stressors.
2. The availability of this type of support decreases the cognitively appraised stress value of the life event and its consequences.

For example, controlled studies have shown that preventive programmes for people who have been bereaved (Parkes 1980; Raphael 1984) can reduce post-bereavement distress and morbidity.

The direct effects model

This model depicts a negative relationship between social support and distress which is independent of any life stressor. The assumption underlying the model is that people have a basic need for attachment to others and social support simply contributes on an ongoing basis to psychological well-being and the reduction of distress by meeting this basic need for contact. The obvious example of research which would support such an approach would be Bowlby's (1969) work on attachment behaviour. However, in the case of bereavement it might be suggested that the loss of a member of one's social support network might elicit a greater degree of caring responses from other people in the network in an attempt to 'buffer' or protect the bereaved person from the full impact of the loss.

Barrera (1986) in his review of the area concluded that what he called measures of social embeddedness, such as social support network size and social participation, were more likely, in general, to conform to a direct effect rather than a buffering model. Furthermore, Cohen et al. (1986) and Bell et al. (1982) have made similiar observations. Also, Cohen and Wills (1985) suggest that structural measures of support, i.e. those that appear to assess a concept comparable to social embeddedness, were likely to show direct effects rather than interaction effects.

However, whilst it must be said that this model may display better fit to the life event of bereavement, it is not necessarily the case that attempts to provide social support for a bereaved person will have no effect on bereavement outcome.

The social support deterioration model

Several studies have questioned the view that the relationship between social support and stressful life events is a positive one. Specifically, some have suggested that certain life events precipitate a deterioration in social support at the very time when it could be most helpful. These results are particularly common in studies where the measure of social support used is an individual's perception of the social support they received (Barrera 1986).

One plausible explanation for support deterioration would be that certain stressful life events inevitably lead to a depletion of available social support. Social exit events (death or divorce) are obvious examples (Dean and Ensel 1982; Lin and Dean 1984). In the case of divorce Leslie and Grady (1985) have suggested that in-laws and friends connected primarily with the previous partner may fall out of the support network, thereby inevitably further depleting it. Their work emphasises the importance of the contextual nature of social ties and the importance of the qualities of relationships which link people to each other. This emphasis may be particularly important in connection with bereavement. For example, if the survivors of the death had difficult relationships with each other, what might have, for years, been an uneasy acceptance of the support network because of the relationships everyone enjoyed with the person who died may rapidly deteriorate into mutual recriminations and/or avoidance. Furthermore the work of Lehman et al. (1986), Littlewood (1983) and Wellman (1981) can be taken to indicate that not all social relationships an individual has are necessarily seen in a positive light by that person. Furthermore, it must be said that not all attempts at supportive interventions will necessarily be perceived by their recipients as helpful.

Another way in which social support might deteriorate following a traumatic life event involves a tendency towards the shunning or avoidance of those who have either experienced it or have been associated with it. Evidence from various areas, including chronic renal failure (Hardiker et al. 1984), cancer (Wortman 1984) and dying (Kalish 1985), indicates that there is a tendency for people to avoid individuals who are experiencing these particular problems. Furthermore, avoidance would seem to be a problem commonly experienced by bereaved people (Gorer 1965; Littlewood 1983). It has been suggested that avoidance may be particularly associated with certain causes of death, for example, Barraclough (1987) suggests that deaths from suicide may cause particular problems in this respect and Kastenbaum (1988) has indicated that deaths from AIDS may provoke this reaction.

Lehman et al. (1986) have considered some of the mechanisms which might underlie avoidance or shunning. They found that, whilst potential supporters knew what sorts of behaviours and patterns of communication would be helpful to people who had been bereaved, they were unable, in practice, to engage in helpful communication. These researchers suggested that anxiety and uncertainty concerning attempts at help resulted in supporters, literally against their better judgements, falling back on stereotypical responses which were likely to be seen as unhelpful. For example, 'you'll soon get over it' or 'you can always have another baby'. Other examples of the failure of good intentions resulted in potential supporters avoiding open communication about the death or avoiding the person who had been bereaved. It seems reasonable to suggest that more traumatic deaths may result in greater levels of anxiety in would-be supporters, thereby, paradoxically, leading to higher levels of support deterioration in these cases.

It might further be suggested that anxiety amongst would-be helpers may stem from uncertainties regarding exactly how distressed a given person who has been bereaved is likely to be. Again, the closer the relationship between the person who has died and the person who has been bereaved, the more likely it might be that people on the periphery of the bereaved person's social support network may resort to avoidance or shunning. However, given the contemporary cultural context surrounding death which has been described in Chapter 1, avoidance of people who have been bereaved is likely to be a common response of people who have not been affected by a particular death. The situation may be further complicated by the contradictory rights and obligations associated with ritual transitions. For example, it may not be immediately clear exactly who in a given situation may be expected, and therefore allowed, to give support and who may be expected to withdraw, leaving the bereaved person's right to privacy intact.

For people who have a social role, e.g. befriender or bereavement counsellor, the approach may be much more straightforward. However, since the bereaved person's social network may be undergoing rapid change, anyone who does approach the person is tacitly inviting a change in their relationship with that person and this may be a source of anxiety in itself. Smith (1976) points out that whilst social workers clearly have a role to play in offering social support to a bereaved person care must be taken over the relationship to avoid a straightforward substitution effect which might inhibit the process of adjustment to the loss.

SOCIAL SUPPORT AND BEREAVEMENT

The available evidence from studies of life events and social support would seem to indicate that the support deterioration model would seem likely, outside exceptionally good social support networks, to occur after a death.

However, it might still be the case that professional interventions may serve to either buffer or prevent stress associated with bereavement given that many bereaved people must experience a need for social support which is unlikely to be met from informal sources of help.

It must be said that there is some evidence that stress buffering prior to a death may occur and this, in turn, may lessen the distress associated with the subsequent bereavement. For example, Marris (1958) found that following a death practical help from relatives halved while more emotional sources of support stayed constant. It may well be the case that social support, particularly in cases where the death has been preceded by a terminal illness, might effectively buffer the impact of distress. Indeed, stress buffering might partly account for the observation that expected deaths tend to be less distressing than unexpected deaths.

Magni et al. (1986) investigated the relationship between psychological distress and social support in parents of children with acute lymphocytic leukaemia during the diagnostic phase of the child's illness. These researchers found that parents were experiencing moderately high levels of distress and that social support had a buffering effect on the impact of the stress occasioned by the diagnosis. This effect held for all experienced symptoms with the exception of sleep disturbances.

Walker et al. (1977) in their review of the area have suggested that different types of social support may be required. These researchers found that, immediately following bereavement, small dense social support networks are particularly supportive in connection with the early experiences of grief. However, later on in the process needs shift towards reorganising an active social life and at this point a larger heterogeneous network might provide more assistance. Bankoff (1983) makes a similar point in a study of widows. Despite the measure of social support correlating with distress, the correlation only held for women whose husbands had died between eighteen months and thirty-six months previously, what Bankoff called 'the transition phase'. Social support did not influence women who had been bereaved for less than 18 months (called the crisis-loss phase). Bankoff suggested that the timing of support may be particularly important. Specifically, in the 'crisis-loss' phase only emotional support may be important. In the transition phase a broader range of support may be helpful. Bankoff further suggested that sources of support also varied. In the crisis-loss phase parental support was particularly important whilst in the transition phase the support of friends and acquaintances contributed towards the well-being of the person. Bankoff found that support from outside these two sources was of considerably less importance in alleviating distress. It would certainly seem to be the case that, following the death of a loved person, people expect support of a certain kind to come from a particular source. For example: Mr——felt that he could

85

say little about the social support he'd received after his daughter's death because different people helped him in different ways. He felt he'd been helped by his employer and co-workers because they'd 'left him alone'. He was unsure whether this would count as support since he was also supported by his family who 'didn't leave him alone to mope'.

Maddison *et al.* (1969) add a different dimension to the discussion. In making a comparison between good and bad outcomes following the first year of bereavement they found no significant overall differences between the groups in perceptions of the helpfulness of social support. However, they did find that the receipt of specific types of social support was associated with the good outcome group. Specifically support which facilitated the expression of feeling and the revision of the past and encouraged orientation towards the future was associated with the more positive bereavement outcomes. This result is not surprising since it indicates that supporting the needs of the person who has been bereaved directly is more helpful than support which does not encourage confronting these issues. However, it is interesting to note that failure to receive appropriate support in this respect was associated with a relatively poor bereavement outcome.

In a prospective study Vachon *et al.* (1982) interviewed a group of widows for a maximum of four times in the two-year period which followed their bereavement. Variables which might predict high distress were identified at two years. A high distress group and a low distress group were thus identified and compared. The high distress group showed, along with other differences, significantly more deficits in social support when compared to the low distress group. However, a high level of distress in itself may strain a social support network and contribute to others avoiding the person who has been bereaved in a way that lower levels of distress may not.

Alternatively, Dimond *et al.* (1987) found the role of social support to be modest in terms of its impact on bereavement outcome. However, it must be said that this piece of research was concerned with the adjustments made in the first year of their bereavement by elderly people who, in all probability, may not have as much access to the range of relevant support available to those in the younger age ranges. It might also be the case that some elderly people neither want nor need to make the same range of changes in their internal and external environments that younger people feel compelled to undergo.

Gauthier and Marshall (1977) make the point that grief reactions can sometimes be prolonged or exacerbated if the bereaved person's social support network continues to reinforce grief-related behaviour. They indicate that if people in the bereaved person's social environment do not change their focus, i.e. away from emotional support towards encouraging more outgoing behaviour, then they may effectively discourage the bereaved person's attempts at adaptation.

I made similar observations concerning a minority of participants in my research (Littlewood 1983). In this study many people identified and valued the support given to them, after a period of time, to re-engage in social activities. However, 40 per cent of those interviewed were of the belief that the withdrawal of emotional support was somewhat premature. For example:

> My family were very nice for about six weeks – very understanding but I was terrible for months afterwards, I used to forget things – I was living in another world, it takes me a long time to get over things. Anyway, in the end they just lost patience. My husband was really nasty about it, he said: 'For God's sake woman what's the matter with you, I was never like that when my mother died – it's been *months.*'

Alternatively, 18 per cent of those interviewed felt that the emotional support they received was of a prolonged duration. In extreme cases, individuals reported feeling trapped by their relatives into an unwanted perpetuation of their grief.

Raphael (1984) has also suggested that the response of the family and social network to the bereavement may be implicated in poor bereavement outcomes. Specifically, she cites: failure to share or allow for expressions of grief; failure to facilitate the review process of mourning; chaos in the family; and family members failing to support each other as being associated with relatively poor outcomes of the grieving process.

PROFESSIONAL INTERVENTION PROGRAMMES FOLLOWING BEREAVEMENT

The helpful role professionally provided support may play following bereavement is possibly most clear when there are deficits in the support systems which leave the bereaved person with an insufficient range of possibilities to make the necessary adjustments to their situation. This assertion may be supported by the work of Parkes (1980) in the area of bereavement counselling. Parkes found that those people with deficits in social support who received support from either professional or self-help services had a reduced risk of post-bereavement morbidity. Further support may be drawn from the work of Raphael (1984). Raphael studied the effectiveness of an intervention programme in improving the health status of widows. A group of widows believed to be 'high risk' (traumatic death, ambivalent marital relationship, life crises, lack of support) were identified and a treatment group and control group established. The group which received treatment was found to have a better outcome at thirteen months than the control group. A good outcome was predicted most accurately by perceptions of (non-) supportiveness. Raphael, like Parkes, concludes that the provision of social support plays an important role in the minimisation of post-bereavement morbidity.

Some researchers have offered more general models of supportive interventions for professional groups whose work frequently brings them into contact with bereaved people. For example, Worden (1982) offers a comprehensive guide for bereavement counsellors and Smith (1976, 1982) has focused upon the social worker's role in helping both dying and bereaved people. Furthermore, Wright (1987) has published a citizen's advice guide on how to deal with the practicalities associated with a death.

Outside professional assistance, volunteers or self-help groups often function as sources of social support for people who have been bereaved. Whilst volunteers may be used to implement various programmes which have been planned and developed by professional workers, self-help groups usually function more or less autonomously. Whilst there are many different kinds of groups, research concerned with groups for widows and groups for parents who have lost children would appear to indicate that these groups offer valuable and appropriate support to their members.

Barrett (1978) investigated the outcome of a programme designed for widows. Seventy widows entered the programme and were randomly assigned to one of three groups: a self-help group; a confidante (widow to widow) group or a consciousness-raising group. After the programme, the women assigned to the groups were compared to a control group. This comparison found that group members had higher self-esteem, a greater ability to feel and express the intensity of their grief and more optimism concerning their physical health than members of the control group. Interestingly enough, group members were also less likely to be predisposed to remarry than were members of the control group. It seems reasonable to suggest that remarriage may be an indication of avoidance in some cases and an indication of recovery in others, a situation not dissimilar from findings regarding both the positive and negative implications of pregnancy and childbirth following a previous child death in the family. A follow-up study of the widows involved with this programme indicated that the differences between the groups endured over time. Similar results, which might be taken to indicate the value of these programmes, were reported by Vachon (1983).

Lieberman et al. (1979) conducted extensive work on the role of self-help groups in coping with crisis. In their consideration of Compassionate Friends (a self-help group for bereaved parents) they found that most people who contacted the group did so for what they called 'process goals', i.e. to utilise various forms of help in order to facilitate the process of grief. Lieberman *et al.* further identified six sub-categories of these process goals:

1. similarity goals of sharing;
2. cognitive-informational goals of learning;
3. modelling upon those who have had similar experiences;
4. emotional support;
5. safety goals, seeking a safe environment in which to express emotions;
6. linkages with others.

Edelstein (1984) points out that this particular self-help group's own belief systems and goals closely matched the goals and needs of those who sought to join it. Furthermore, Videka-Sherman (1982) found that involvement in this organisation offered some degree of prevention against the development of emotional problems. In this study parents whose children had died in the previous 18 months who were more active in the group were less likely to be depressed a year after the death than a similar group of parents who were also group members but who were not as active in terms of group participation and helping other group members. However, once again, it must be said that the causal direction of these observations is not at all clear, i.e. those who were less affected by the death in the first instance may be more inclined to higher levels of participation and vice versa.

Klass (1982) has suggested that the support received from those who have had similar experiences may be more helpful than the interventions of professionals. However, Kalish warns against an overly optimistic approach:

> This does not mean that participation in death-related self-help groups never leads to serious disturbance or even to pathology. We know that participation in group therapy or individual therapy with the most astute of psychotherapists will occasionally create serious emotional disturbances. The findings do suggest, however, that such participation [self-help group] is extremely low risk and the potential rewards are substantial. Caution, of course, is necessary in the selection of the group, especially if it has a designated leader.
>
> (Kalish 1985: 313)

Professional interventions following the onset of complications to the grieving process

Unfortunately, the prevention of complications arising from the bereavement process is not always possible. In many cases, professional intervention is not requested until the person is already experiencing a painful, complicated reaction associated with their bereavement. In recent years several specific techniques which are believed to be helpful have been described in the literature, an early example of which is the work of Volkan (1970). Volkan was concerned with the tendency of some bereaved people to obscure the distinction between the bereaved person's 'self' and the dead person. Volkan *et al.* (1975) found that in some cases this identification with the dead person was achieved and maintained by the bereaved individual keeping a possession or object associated with the deceased to form a linkage (a linking object). Volkan has developed a particular form of therapy, 're-grief therapy' in order to work with certain people who cannot complete the grief process unaided. The use of linking objects to provoke an emotional realisation of the reality of the death may form part of the therapeutic process. However, Volkan (1981) has stressed that re-grief therapy is only one of many therapeutic options which may be used in connection with the process of grief, and further suggests (Volkan 1985) that it may not be suitable for all cases in which grief has taken a complicated course, for example:

> The clinical picture of established pathological mourning may appear in persons of different personality make-up. A person with low-level character organization who presents characteristics of established pathological mourning is probably not a good candidate for re-grief therapy or for psychoanalysis proper. This sort of person may, however, benefit from long-term treatment with modified psychoanalytic techniques . . . the evaluation of internal considerations is more important. Do the underlying pathologies need resolution now? Can the patient's ego adaptively contain the underlying pathologies once the complicated mourning is resolved?
>
> (Volkan 1985: 291)

From Volkan's perspective the last two questions are of key importance. For example, if the underlying problems do not require immediate resolution then psychoanalysis proper may be the preferred treatment option. Any answer to the second question would presumably depend upon a detailed assessment of the individual case. Volkan is of the opinion that some complications of the bereavement process are caused by the person who has been bereaved becoming 'stuck' in the bereavement process because to resolve it would mean confronting other, potentially serious, underlying pathologies. Obviously, from this perspective re-grief therapy should only be undertaken after a careful assessment of the individual case has been made.

Lieberman (1978) is also cautious about the benefits of what he calls 'forced mourning'. From this perspective forced mourning may have negative consequences in terms of heightening distress levels without necessarily facilitating any insight into their cause. He also stressed the importance of accurately assessing, rather than simply assuming, that present syptoms are associated with past loss. The process of 'forced mourning' involves three stages.

1. An explanation of the normal processes associated with grief and their importance for emotional well-being.
2. A focus upon emotions the bereaved person has in all probability been previously intent on avoiding. Lieberman stresses, although this may be something of an understatment, that the therapist must have the ability to tolerate any strong emotional display which may be elicited during this stage of the process.
3. The facilitation of a review of the relationship between the person who has died and the person who has been bereaved. This review should acknowledge both the positive and negative aspects of the relationship.

For 'forced mourning' to be successful Lieberman emphasises the need for warm, empathic confrontation together with the need to legitimise any strong feelings the bereaved person may display. During this process old losses may also be reviewed and its completion involves the understanding that the loss of the therapeutic relationship is, itself, a loss that needs to be acknowledged.

Hodgkinson (1982) identifies a somewhat similar approach from work with hospitalised patients who were denying the loss of a loved person. Again a three-phase treatment plan was utilised.

1. The first treatment phase concentrated upon releasing an emotional response to the death together with an acknowledgement of the death's reality. Linking objects were used to stimulate cathartic outbursts in this phase.
2. The second step involved the 'third chair' exercise – a Gestalt technique of externalising conflict by talking to the 'third chair' as if one was conversing with the dead person.
3. The final stage in the treatment was designed to facilitate 'letting go' of the dead person by beginning to say goodbye to them.

Mawson et al. (1981) undertook a controlled study of what they called 'guided mourning' amongst people who were experiencing problems related to grief. Having established that no improvements occurred in the group whilst they were waiting for treatment, group members were assigned to one of two treatment groups. One group was encouraged to face painful cues associated with their bereavement (guided mourning) whilst the other group was encouraged to avoid such painful experiences. At one month, the guided mourning group had improved significantly in terms of their ability to approach bereavement cues when compared to the other group. However, whilst phobic-obsessive problems appeared to respond relatively well to these guided mourning techniques, bereavement-related depression did not respond as well to the techniques.

Sireling *et al.* (1988) conducted a replication study of Mawson's work and obtained results in accordance with the previous study. However, despite this range of promising results, it must be stressed that all of the short-term interventions designed to alleviate complications of the bereavement process guide mourning rather than complete it. Furthermore, it might be suggested that some interventions may be more suited to certain problems than others.

Overall, the evidence would seem to indicate that social support from outside the bereaved person's immediate network of family and friends would appear to be extremely helpful to those who have the opportunity and need to utilise such support. Whilst it might be argued that future research would benefit from the consideration of which types of support are particularly helpful to certain individuals, it should not be forgotten that the vast majority of people who have been bereaved, despite the probability of a deterioration in their social support network, do not have the opportunity to enter any programme of support at all.

Perceptions of sources of general professional support

As Kalish (1985) has noted, there is very little research evidence concerning bereaved people's perceptions concerning the helpfulness or otherwise of social support received from professional sources. However, three studies have addressed this area directly and their findings are similar in certain respects (Littlewood, Hoekstra-Weebers and Humphrey 1990; Edelstein 1984; Littlewood 1983).

Edelstein (1984) investigated the social support available to mothers following the death of their child. She noted that, whilst most of the mothers in her study used support from professional sources, very few of them actively sought out professional help. Most mothers cited doctors and clergy, two groups of professionals who would inevitably be involved following a death, as sources of support. A surprisingly small percentage (18.6) actively sought out support from other professional groups.

These mothers' assessments of the help they received was often extremely ambivalent. Doctors were frequently criticised for not doing their job properly and interfering whilst clergy were criticised for not really knowing the child. It seems reasonable to suggest that some mothers may have resented the interventions of professionals they came into contact with because the individuals involved were not known particularly well by the mother prior to the death. Alternatively, some mothers reported actively resenting what they saw as unwanted professional interference in a highly personal matter. Edelstein summarised her findings in the following way:

> Most women had contact with doctors, clergy or therapists during mourning, but the results were often unsatisfactory. Interactions with professionals were intensely personalized. Doctors and nurses were often seen not as doing their jobs, but as interfering with the family. Clergy were sometimes dismissed as 'not understanding death', or not really knowing the child. Some therapists were experienced as unempathic. On the positive side, many hospital personnel were singled out as helping the family through the nightmare, clergy as providing comfort and answers, and therapists as aiding an understanding of the powerful and overwhelming feelings that tormented some mothers. Professionals were amongst the first people contacted, but use of these individuals declined after the first year. The relationships that were most often maintained were those that had been established before the child's death. In some instances it is easy to see where professional responsibilities or needs clashed with the needs and wishes of women during their bereavement. They wanted somebody to 'be there', to listen and to understand. But they also wanted answers and to have their dependency needs met, and in this area, professional help can be less satisfying than that of family and friends.
>
> (Edelstein 1984: 104)

Edelstein's results contrast sharply with those of our study, i.e: Littlewood, Hoekstra-Weebers and Humphrey (1990). The latter study was concerned with parents' evaluations of the social support they received from hospital personnel following their child's death from cancer. The vast majority of these parents reported that the support they received was either 'good' or 'very good'. However differences in the original samples could well account for the differing evaluations of social support. In Edelstein's sample anticipated and unanticipated deaths from a variety of causes were associated with the mothers she interviewed. It may be the case that professional support is perceived to be valuable only if it represents a continuation of support received from professional sources prior to the death. Not unreasonably, bereavement is seen to be an intensely personal experience and comfort derived from professional sources may be dependent, at least in part, upon the availability and quality of support received prior to the death. In these cases support after the death might appear to be the logical conclusion of a relationship rather than the imposition of expert guidance. In our research, most of the deaths followed relatively long periods of contact with members of particular hospital departments and this may go some way to explaining the relatively positive parental assessments of professional support following their child's death.

In my earlier study (Littlewood 1983), in looking at perceptions of support received from various sources following the death of a husband, wife, brother or sister, child or parent, I found that the following issues were believed to be particularly relevant in connection with professional sources of support:

1. practical help prior to and immediately after the death;
2. the continuation of wanted emotional support from valued professionals involved prior to the death;
3. a need for support from professional sources together with a recognition of its unavailability.

Practical help prior to and after the death

The support from professional sources which was most valued was practical support concentrated in the immediate period following the death. This support frequently took the form of expert guidance. As Silverman has indicated, in the course of life most problems are handled by 'cook book' knowledge which:

allows us to take their sting away with a label (a dream, an hallu-cination) or with a recognition that while we may not be able to understand the experience, nevertheless there are experts (doctors, scientists, priests) with the knowledge to transform the problematic into the routine.

(Silverman 1972: 167)

The professional provision of a framework which informed and guided people concerning the appropriate steps to take following a death was particularly highly valued.

Also valued was advice given which explained some of the more dis-tressing aspects of terminal illnesses and the provision of adequate pain control prior to death; such advice was universally praised. However, the group as a whole tended to focus upon purely practical aspects of professional support and periods of hospitalisation prior to death were frequently cited as being particularly distressing for bereaved people. Professional interventions tended to be highly valued only if the person who was bereaved believed that some specific function could be performed by the relevant professional which they themselves could not perform. If the care the dying person received in hospital was diffuse then it tended to be less highly valued since many bereaved people felt themselves to be capable of providing such support.

For example:

they didn't look after him properly you know. They weren't doing anything I hadn't been doing or couldn't have done better. I used to feed him because he couldn't manage himself, they wouldn't do that – hadn't got the time. I wanted him home when I felt better but they said I wasn't well enough . . . Then he got a cold which turned into pneumonia and that was that.

(comments of a 72-year-old woman concerning her husband whom she had nursed for fifteen years prior to his death)

Valued emotional support from professional sources

Whilst relatively few people associated professional support with emotional support, those who did so tended to have been relatives of someone who had experienced a long terminal illness prior to their death. During the illness many people became involved in relationships with hospital personnel, GPs and nursing staff who attended their relative. Support following the relative's death from these sources was seen to be particularly valuable if it was received. However, many people felt that, after the death, support from professional sources deteriorated since they were no longer in contact with the personnel who had been associated with the terminal illness. One woman described her feelings on this issue in terms of being 'abandoned by the nurses'.

However, it must be said that not all people in this situation would appreciate bereavement visits as a matter of course. In some cases, those in attendance at a death were believed to have caused it, and on those grounds could be distinctly unwelcome, for example:

Oh it's [reaction to the death of her husband] as bad as it ever was. I'll never get over it. The doctor still comes round but I've told him he's wasting his time. He killed my husband you know – ineptitude rather than negligence I reckon. He comes around because he still feels guilty. I tell him he needn't bother – I'm having none of it. He once said to me: 'You know, Mrs — there are two types of widows, those who remarry again and those who never get over it.' Yes, I thought, and I'm the last sort, so you needn't bother coming round here telling me to get out more often.

(comments of a 68-year-old concerning her doctor's intervention after the death of her husband)

The need for professional help following bereavement

Many people reported feeling a need for help following their bereavement but did not act on their feelings in terms of seeking help from professional sources which may have provided valuable social support. The main reason for this would appear to be confusion over the status of bereavement itself. As a problem, bereavement is difficult to define, i.e. on one level people tended to account for their experiences, however disturbing, in terms of being inevitable responses to the loss and therefore were of the opinion that little could be done to help them and on another level the lack of availability of services for bereavement deterred many people from seeking help. Clearly, if services are not specifically made available, then this, in itself, acts as a deterrent to any potential demand for them. The major problems people felt they might have liked more help with were as follows:

1. fear concerning the experiences associated with grief;
2. distressing interactions with friends and relatives following a death;
3. loneliness resulting from a death;
4. depression following a death.

At a very general level the provision of more informational support from caring agencies would meet some of these needs. However, it might be argued that many people would benefit from the provision of more focused supportive help following their bereavement. Unfortunately, such help, despite being proven to be beneficial in most cases, is not available for many people or is available, but not known to be so amongst people who have been bereaved. Under these circumstances many bereaved people are heavily reliant upon the social support available from their families, friends and acquaintances and given the prevailing context in which bereavement occurs these support networks may not be enough, in themselves, to prevent complications arising during the grieving process. Chapter 6 will be concerned with the general range of conditions under which both helpful and unhelpful supportive attempts are made outside the context of professional interventions.

6

INFORMAL
SUPPORT NETWORKS

'The chief mourner does not always attend the funeral.'
Emerson (1832)
Journals

INTRODUCTION

The term informal support network is used to refer to the range of social support available to a person from his/her family, friends or neighbours. Since this type of support is often the only long-term support available to people who have been bereaved it is of considerable importance to their well-being. The first part of this chapter is concerned with the role informal support networks play in alleviating psychological distress in general. The second part considers the importance of the concepts of roles and status in connection with bereavement, while the third part looks at the relationships between roles, status and the distribution and evaluation of informal social support following a death. The final part of the chapter is concerned with some of the common problems associated with the distribution of informal social support following a death.

INFORMAL SUPPORT NETWORKS AND THE ALLEVIATION OF PSYCHOLOGICAL DISTRESS

In general, psychological and emotional problems would appear to be widespread in the community. In a review of the area Goldberg and Huxley (1980) found that in any given year the prevalence rate is as high as 25 per cent of the general population. However, Levine and Perkins (1987) are of the opinion that if levels of emotional distress other than those associated with formal psychiatric definitions of mental illness were taken into account, the prevalence rate would be much higher.

Several studies have been conducted concerning help-seeking behaviour in the general population (e.g. de Paulo, Nadler and Fisher 1983; Veroff *et al.* 1981). These studies indicate that most people prefer to take their problems to their partners, close friends or neighbours. It would appear to be relatively rare for people to contact any of the various mental health agencies. Indeed, there is general agreement that initial help-seeking patterns tend to be directed towards informal rather than professional support networks.

Whilst most of the relevant studies have been conducted in the USA, some cross-cultural evidence has suggested that, at least in the case of British and French people, those from other cultures may be even less likely to seek help from professional sources than Americans (de Barbot 1977; Tod and Shapira 1974). Given this situation, Barker and Lemle (1987) have suggested that there is a need for looking closely at the ways in which informal help is distributed in close relationships. It could be argued that it might be easier to improve the quality of help received from a preferred source of support rather than try to impose help from a non-preferred source of assistance.

The situation specific to distress following bereavement may well be one in which these general tendencies are exaggerated. Firstly, the lack of acknowledgement of bereavement in the broader community may in itself cause people who have been bereaved to withdraw into a relatively close network of mourners. Secondly, the contemporary tendency to see dying and bereavement as the province of a limited range of experts as described in Chapter 1 may result in an inclination amongst bereaved people to limit their range of support-seeking behaviour to those groups.

Edelstein describes the situation amongst bereaved mothers in the USA in the following way:

> Women used psychological resources the least of all professional help. This is explained, in part, by the fact that doctors and clergy were very often a part of the illness and burial process whereas therapy had to be actively sought by the mother and still conveys, for many, a stigma of mental illness.
>
> (Edelstein 1984: 105)

Finally, the bereavement process itself would seem to necessitate a preference for help to be sought from people who actually knew the dead person reasonably well. Again, Edelstein, amongst others, makes the following points in connection with this issue.

1. Only those who had an established relationship with the dead person would be in a position to immediately facilitate a review of events surrounding the death.
2. Bereavement is experienced as a uniquely personal trauma. Possibly this in itself leads to a lack of appreciation amongst bereaved people of the role those who did not have a prior relationship with either themselves or the person who has died could play.

The experience of bereavement, in the contemporary context, would seem to be one which requires the receipt of social support primarily from close family members, relatives and friends. It must be said that the terms 'family' and 'relatives' are being used in a broad sense here and should be taken to refer to the group of people most affected by a particular death. Obviously, such people need not necessarily be related to each other through birth or marriage.

Whilst several researchers in the area of bereavement have noted that a bereaved person's perceptions of social support are important determinants of both the course of grief and the likelihood of the person being able to return to effective functioning (Raphael 1984; Reid 1979; Vachon *et al.* 1982), research in this area is primarily speculative and fraught with difficulties and questions. For example, in heterogeneous societies the negotiation of group norms concerning the meaning of a bereavement is essentially left to be handled in specific local contexts which may vary considerably. Alternatively, both Kaplan (1975) and Rosenblatt *et al.* (1977) indicate that there would appear to be a very limited number of ways in which bereavement experiences are, in fact, socially organised. Consequently, there would appear to be the potential for both continuity and variation in this area.

The situation may be further complicated by variance in whom the group or individual regards as being the locus of responsibility for coping with bereavement, e.g. individual, nuclear family, extended family or friends. Obviously, there may be many different sources of help and support available in a given person's informal support network but preferences concerning exactly what constitutes legitimate support, how such support might appropriately be elicited, who can elicit it and how it is evaluated might vary considerably.

Lasch (1977) and Lifton (1979) have identified the key problems as being as follows:

1. the culture of individualism;
2. the loss of looser social networks precipitated by the focus on close nuclear families;
3. the weakening of rituals.

These three problems combined have been argued to place people who have been bereaved in a particularly disadvantageous position in the contemporary cultural context of Western societies.

However, the key question remains the same, i.e. if informal support is the main source of help a bereaved person can and does expect and if bereavement in particular and the culture in general leads to a weakening of informal support networks, then exactly who expects what from whom. Marris acknowledged the importance of this point in the following way:

99

A person learns from his culture where he or she is expected to commit themselves most and their life will be built around these commitments. So, for instance, in modern societies the death of a husband, wife, child, parent, brother or sister or friend roughly represents a declining order in the severity of bereavement.

(Marris 1986: 38)

Some bereavements are adjudged, albeit implicitly and purely in social rather than personal terms, to be more significant than others.

Leming and Dickinson (1985) take this point further and note that in the USA people are exempted from normal responsibilities following a death dependent upon the society's perception of the nature and degree of relationship between the bereaved person and the person who has died. They suggest that it is generally accepted that a period of absence of up to a week may be required in connection with the loss of a husband or wife. However, they also note that for other types of loss the only concession may be time off to attend the funeral. Clearly, certain types of loss are given more recognition and informal support than are others. However, equally clearly, an individual's perceptions regarding the meaning of a lost relationship need not necessarily coincide with that relationship's social value.

Researchers looking for concepts which might mediate between the broader social assessments of personal relationships and individual assessments of the given meaning of a specific relationship have used the concepts of role and status widely. The next part of this chapter is concerned with an investigation of these concepts.

ROLES, STATUS AND SOCIAL RELATIONSHIPS

Roles

Leming and Dickinson (1985) define role as 'the specified behaviour expected for persons occupying specific social positions'. Two issues associated with the concept of social role have been identified in connection with the bereavement process. The first issue is concerned with the extent to which particular roles are lost following a death and the second is concerned with whether or not it is possible to identify particular roles specifically associated with bereavement. The 'hierarchy' of loss suggested by Marris (1986) and referred to in the previous section of this chapter represents a culturally ordered hierarchy of social roles. To a certain extent, the death of a person for whom one played a social role entails the potential loss of the role as well as the loss of the person for whom the role was played. For example, the death of an only child for a mother entails the loss, temporarily or permanently, of the role of mother as well as the loss of the child and the loss of a spouse entails the loss of the social role of husband or wife. Some

100

people's sense of identity itself may be tied to their ability to play particular roles. For example, a woman whose major source of self-esteem is derived from her role as mother, with all the care, time and nurturance which such a role implies, may fare particularly badly following the death of an only child. Furthermore, Marris indicates that the impact of bereavement may be particularly severe upon women who have occupied the traditional role of wife. Specifically:

> Think of a married woman of about forty: her life is centred on her home, and its pattern is largely determined by her relationship to her husband. Most of her purposes, her important anxieties, resentments, satisfactions, involve that relationship. The meaning of her life is constructed about it. When a widow says life has no meaning any more, she is expressing a literal truth, for the relationship which principally defined who she was and what she had to do is gone.
>
> (Marris 1986: 33)

Other researchers have used the concept of role in a slightly different way and have attempted to identify the norms and cultural patterns in Western societies specific to bereavement roles. For example, Robson (1977) suggests that the bereavement role shares certain similarities with the sickness role (Parsons 1951). According to Parsons, the sickness role consists of two rights and their associated obligations. The first right effectively exempts the sick person from their normal range of social responsibilities – the extent to which they are exempted depends upon the nature and severity of the relevant illness. The second right relates to the right to be taken care of and, as an adult, the right to become dependent upon others in order to attempt to return to normal social functioning as soon as possible. In exchange for these rights the person who is sick has two social obligations. The first obligation involves an expression, verbally or otherwise, of the desire to get better and the second obligation involves seeking technically competent help in order to effect a full recovery as soon as possible. Robson suggests that the rights and obligations of people who have been bereaved are quite similar to those associated with the sick role. Specifically, immediately following a death, people who are socially acknowledged as having been bereaved are exempted from normal social responsibilities depending upon the nature and degree of their past social relationship with the person who has died. Those occupying the bereavement role are also allowed to, as adults, become dependent upon others for practical and emotional support.

However, obligations are also associated with the bereavement role which, like the sick role upon which it is based, is temporary. Consequently, the bereaved person is obligated to make an effort to return to normal life as soon as possible and, if it is believed to be necessary or desirable, to seek appropriate technical help in order to achieve this end.

Robson also suggests that in certain instances bereaved people may be unwilling to play the role appropriately and therefore risk being seen as deviant. Three examples of potential areas of difficulty are cited:

1. where the person who has been bereaved is seen by others to be malingering in the bereavement role or is not perceived by others to be taking the necessary courses of action towards social reintegration;
2. where the bereaved person is seen to be rejecting social support believed to have the potential to facilitate their eventual recovery;
3. where the bereaved person rejects public acknowledgement of the death and, albeit indirectly, of the social value of the relationship.

According to Robson, avoidance, ostracism and criticism may be invited by anyone who chooses, for whatever reason, to reject the obligations or rights associated with this role.

However, it must be said that the sickness role, upon which Robson's consideration of the bereavement role is based, is not quite as clear as Parsons would have us believe. Hardiker and Tod (1982) have suggested that Parson's model applies only to acute illnesses and does not fit chronic illness well. Furthermore, in the specific instance of chronic illness, Littlewood *et al.* (1990) have identified five roles associated with coping with chronic renal failure, including one which involved a degree of resistance expressed towards adopting any role at all. Rodabough (1981–2), in looking at people's behaviour at funerals, identified a range of roles available to people. Examples of these roles are as follows:

1. coping griever
2. bewildered novice
3. hysterical performer
4. stoic spartan.

Whilst the naming of these roles might be construed as being unsympathetic to their players it must be stressed that the roles themselves involved certain specific behaviour patterns and the point being made here is that there may be a series of alternatives, rather than one fixed way of behaving which may be acceptable to people.

Status

In general terms the concept of status refers to a person's position in relation to other people – to a person's standing or rank within a given community. Leming and Dickinson (1985) use the concept of 'master status' which they define as a status position which dominates all other statuses in the mind of the individual. In a discussion concerning terminal illness the following points are made:

When an individual's condition has been defined by self and others as terminal, all other self meanings take on less importance. While a given patient may be a lawyer, Republican, mother, wife, Episcopalian, etc., she tends to think of herself primarily as a terminal patient. The terminal label, in this instance, is what sociologists refer to as a master status, because it dominates all other status indicators.

(Leming and Dickinson 1985: 55)

As indicated in Chapter 1, it has long been known that perceptions of the social status (in general terms) of people who are dying may influence the social support those people are likely to receive from professional sources. However, there is little information available concerning possible relationships between the perceptions of the status of a bereaved person and the support they are likely to receive from informal sources. Nevertheless, as has previously been noted, some relationships tend to be seen to be more important than others and Marris (1986) has suggested that role loss may be viewed hierarchically.

One possible source of information concerning the importance of status positions following bereavement is the work of Pincus (1976) who used the concept of 'chief mourner' to identify the person who is socially acknowledged to be the most affected by the death. For Pincus, the status of chief mourner was one of relative power. Although she does not analyse the implications of the position in depth, she cites two interesting cases.

In her first case a daughter was extremely distressed by the fact that her mother was making complex arrangements concerning the estate of her father. The daughter felt that she was being kept in the background by her mother and doubted her mother's ability to cope with the complexity of the task so soon after the death (this was not, perhaps, seen to be her mother's appropriate role). Pincus also cites another case in which an adult daughter felt that her stepmother was behaving as if she were the only person to have been bereaved. This daughter felt that her stepmother's behaviour implied that her own and her brother's grief was insignificant. Pincus describes the situation in the following way:

She [the stepmother] would not let them have any share in the bereavement, nor in anything that had belonged to the father, even refusing to give the brother a wallet which he had given his father and which the father had particularly cherished. She constantly talked about money, although the father's will was quite clear and left everything to his wife. Worst of all, the stepmother now demanded the support, compassion, and affection due to a mother, which made Mrs Cooper feel hateful. We spent the first individual session talking about her reactivated feelings about giving, taking, and being cheated, and her anguish about not being recognized as the chief mourner.

(Pincus 1976: 224–5)

Perhaps, in Leming and Dickinson's terms, 'chief mourner' is a master status following the death of a loved person. In my own study, Littlewood (1983), two key status positions were identified, one was that of chief mourner and the other was that of helper. The rights and obligations attendant upon these positions were clearly identified by those who participated in this study, and were particularly important in connection with the distribution of social support.

Chief mourner

This position tended to be held by the person who stood in the closest social relationship to the person who had died. The chief mourner was seen to have, in the first part of the bereavement process, few obligations other than to mourn the dead person. This person, when required, also acted as an agent for the dead person, speaking, as it were, on their behalf.

Generally speaking, it was not seen to be appropriate to question this person's interpretation of the dead person's wishes. For example:

The doctor asked my mother if they could do a post mortem to examine my father's heart – he said it might help other people. My mother said no because my father wouldn't have wanted it. I knew that wasn't true because I'd talked to him about things like that and he used to say: 'they can have anything that's any use', but I didn't say anything – it was my mother's place to decide.

The majority of offers of support, condolences and practical help were directed towards chief mourners – presumably in the belief that this person would require the most support. It was not expected, except in cases where a person had small children, that they should offer condolences or practical help to other people, and in fact, they rarely did so. After a certain period of time, which varied considerably, this status position was slowly withdrawn as issues other than the death took on greater importance.

Helper

Helpers had many more obligations than those holding the status of chief mourner and fewer rights in connection with the dead person. Most of the obligations tended to revolve around providing and channelling support for the chief mourner. Although people who held this position often referred to the dead person, these references tended to focus upon the dead person's expectations in connection with themselves as providers of care. For example: 'I couldn't leave him on his own, in that lonely old house – my mother wouldn't have wanted that. I had him to live with me.' Helpers tended to see themselves as giving rather than receiving support and this could cause problems in terms of the ways in which these roles and status positions tended to be distributed.

In general, the role of chief mourner tended to be taken by the dead person's next of kin, and helpers tended to be the chief mourner's next of kin. Consequently, this type of distribution of roles and statuses tended to result in bereaved people helping other bereaved people. The situation was particularly difficult for helpers, since many of them had experienced a major bereavement themselves and were not always in a position where it was easy for them to acknowledge their loss. Furthermore, helpers tended to need two, potentially contradictory, types of support which they did not always receive.

Honorary experts

Outside chief mourners and their helpers there was considerably more flexibility, but possibly less social acknowledgement, experienced in connection with bereavement. However, there was one other role which was fairly constant and that was that of honorary expert. Honorary experts were people who had undergone a similar bereavement who contacted and offered support to other bereaved people on this basis. As a matter of interest, bereavement itself did not qualify people for this role but, rather, specific role loss, i.e. widows would tend only to contact other widows and parents who had lost children contacted other parents who had lost children.

ROLES, STATUS AND
THE DISTRIBUTION OF SOCIAL SUPPORT

Those who held the status of chief mourner tended to be the focus of all available support networks. Holders of this position were far more likely, when compared to helpers, to expect and receive support they perceived to be helpful. The general pattern of supportive interchanges would appear to be as follows:

1. Immediately following the bereavement supportive gestures usually involved practical help. Most people who had been bereaved were particularly grateful for help which involved the funeral arrangements and the distribution or disposal of the dead person's possessions. However, practical help seemed to cover a very broad range of day to day activities which, it was generally believed, bereaved people should not undertake. People also reported receiving emotional support which tended to take the form of agreeing and elaborating upon the chief mourner's interpretation of the death and subsequent events. Helpful

emotional support often took the form of encouragement, i.e. telling the chief mourner that they were coping relatively well.

2. After a certain period of time, which often varied, the supportive interchanges changed from support which encouraged withdrawal from all but a few people to support which encouraged re-engaging in social activities. The commonest problems people experienced tended to be associated with the premature withdrawal of emotional support which encouraged expressions of grief. This withdrawal was associated with premature encouragement to re-engage in normal activities. Over time the support network of chief mourner tended to change from reliance on a few, usually closely related, support networks to a broader network which involved friends and acquaintances.

Those occupying the position of helper tended to be remarkably ambivalent concerning the support they were offered and the support they wanted. At one level helpers found interactions which confirmed the value of their position helpful, but on another level the support they were offering to the chief mourner often effectively involved a degree of social denial concerning their own feelings. The need to receive support to help tended to conflict with the need to receive support to grieve and, given general cultural pressures, the need to grieve was often, at best, unacknowledged or, at worst, actively discouraged. For example, one woman reported her husband's reaction to her crying over her father's death in the following way:

> My husband said, 'Don't you think you're rather indulging yourself? There's your mother to look after, you know. She's suffering more than you are and she's maintaining a fair degree of control over herself. You should be supporting her rather than making such a pathetic exhibition of yourself.'

Paradoxically, many helpers, despite making strenuous efforts to facilitate another's grief, reported feeling distressed when the person responded to their support. Many helpers seemed to doubt the depth of distress suffered by the chief mourner, possibly because they themselves continued to experience relatively high, often socially unacknowledged, levels of distress.

Honorary experts offered valuable loss-specific support in many instances. As a person who had undergone a similar experience they were often in a unique position to offer advice, understanding and relevant information. They also tended to be valued as 'living proof' that the experiences associated with the loss could be more or less successfully negotiated. However, it is my impression, and it is only an impression, that some of the people who adopted such a role tended to be overly prescriptive in terms of the advice they offered.

As Dalley (1988) has pointed out, the organisation of social support described here reflects the family model of caring. Dalley, in her discussion of the distribution of care in society in general, has suggested that this form of care is not necessarily the best option available and that there may be more viable alternatives. Specifically:

> By the collectivity taking on responsibility for the provision of care, the tensions, burden and obligation inherent in one-to-one caring relationships which are the product of the family mode of care are overcome. Particular individuals are not forced into particular caring and cared-for roles dictated by their social and biological relatedness; for it is in those relationships that dependence becomes a warped and unhealthy pressure on the actors involved. In collectively shared relationships of caring the burdens are dispersed and fewer pressures arise.
>
> (Dalley 1988: 115)

Perhaps what is normal in this context is not necessarily helpful for anyone. However, given the situation in which the family model of care predominates it is not surprising to find that many people perceived the social support they received following the death of a loved person as less than helpful. In some instances a person's informal support network proved profoundly problematic. Some examples of these problems will be discussed in the next part of this chapter.

PROBLEMS ASSOCIATED WITH INFORMAL SUPPORT NETWORKS

There is a good deal of evidence from research in the area which indicates that bereavement does not necessarily result in greater family cohesion. Parkes (1972), in considering how best to help the bereaved, identified a number of these cases. For example, he mentioned a tendency for some widows to control the expression of feeling because they believed their in-laws to be insincerely expressing grief. In one instance a widow reported being accused by her mother-in-law of being responsible for her husband's death. He also identified a situation in which a widow constantly bickered with her teenage daughter who had enjoyed a particularly close relationship with her father prior to his death.

The work of Maddison and his colleagues (Maddison and Walker 1967; Maddison and Viola 1968; and Maddison, Viola and Walker 1969) also suggests that mothers-in-law often caused distress to widows. Claims concerning the widow's loss being of less consequence than their own and allegations concerning the widow's lack of care for her dead husband were cited as being particularly upsetting. Furthermore, Smith (1982) makes the general observation that people who have been bereaved often have inappropriate expectations of their families which may cause considerable distress and resentment if the expectations are not met. In short, there is evidence which suggests that family discord and distress may follow bereavement.

There is also evidence to suggest that discord in the family may be associated with unfavourable outcomes of the bereavement process. As Bowlby (1980) has indicated, the importance of family, friends and others, in terms of either helping the process of grief or hindering it, has long been noted by clinicians.

Gorer (1965) made the tentative observation that the perception of the lack of supportiveness of others appeared to be associated with relatively complicated grief reactions. However, he was uncertain whether or not such perceptions accurately reflected the quality of support. This line of enquiry has been pursued more rigorously by Maddison and his colleagues in the previously cited studies, and expanded upon by Raphael (1975, 1977). These studies concluded, at least with respect to widows, that women who reported few or no unhelpful interactions proceeded to adjust relatively well, whilst those who reported frequent unhelpful interchanges tended to make a poor adjustment to bereavement. Obviously, there are many ways in which these observations might be interpreted but Maddison was of the opinion that the reported experiences were both accurate and influential in determining the eventual outcome of the process of grief.

In my own study, Littlewood (1983), particular problems seemed to be associated with the following:

1. lack of availability, and therefore, access to informal or professional support;
2. family disputes over the social position of chief mourner;
3. lack of social acknowledgement of the relationship between the person who had died and the person who was bereaved;
4. the social position of helper.

All of these problems, to a greater or lesser extent, tended to be associated with both complications arising from the process of grieving and certain types of loss.

Lack of available support

Whilst it is relatively rare for people in the younger age ranges to be totally unsupported, in social terms, following a death, many elderly people find themselves in this position.

Changes in social demography have left numerous elderly people isolated from their families, and, obviously, not everyone either marries or has children. In some ways, old age may be viewed as a time of multiple losses, with bereavement being one amongst many losses which have to be coped with.

Specifically, many people over 75 years of age experience problems with mobility and, as Marris (1986) has pointed out, bereavement may be a different experience for elderly people because the context of their life has shrunk. However, it must be said that the changes associated with advancing age often result in elderly couples investing most of their time and energy in each other. Consequently, the loss of a partner could be a devastating blow from which, given few alternatives, it may be difficult to recover.

It is within this context that the tendency of many widowed elderly people living in the community to simply carry on as if their partner were still alive must be evaluated. In my own study (Littlewood 1983) the majority of widowed elderly people were found to have adjusted to their loss in this way. Although the fact of physical death was accepted, people frequently reported holding 'conversations' with their dead partner and feeling their continual 'presence' for literally years after the death. Many elderly people strongly believed that they would be reunited with their partner and, consequently, their bereavement was simply a short-term separation.

Elderly people who did not report maintaining contact with their dead partner were far more likely to report feeling lonely and isolated. For example, one woman felt so desperately lonely that she often took her elderly pet dog out for a walk, often against her pet's will, in the hope that she might see someone 'to say hello to'. However, it must be said that beliefs concerning being reunited with the dead person operated independently of social support networks in that elderly people who were not socially isolated also tended to report these beliefs.

It might be suggested that, for many elderly people, the processes normally associated with grief are circumvented by their beliefs concerning death. The following two examples illustrate the complexity of grief amongst elderly people, together with the tendency amongst this group actively to maintain their relationship with the person who has died.

Example 1

Mr L was a retired machine operator in his seventies whose wife had died of lung cancer seven months prior to his agreeing to discuss her death. Four months after his wife's death one of his stepdaughters also died from lung cancer. Mr L's wife died at home and he cared for her during her terminal illness.

Mr L lost weight following his wife's death and reported difficulties with sleeping. He continued to receive visits from a large number of relatives and friends following the death of his wife but particularly missed her if he himself went out socially. Consequently, Mr L continued to wear a dark suit and a black tie (the same ones he had worn to both cremations) whenever he left the house.

Informal support

Mr L had been married twice. He and his first wife had been divorced many years ago and he had no wish to discuss her. However, he had two daughters from this marriage, one of whom lived locally and visited him regularly. His second wife had seven children from her first marriage, five of whom lived locally and visited him frequently. He had lived at the same address for thirty years and, although the neighbourhood had changed, he remained on good terms with both old and new neighbours.

At the time of his wife's death Mr L believed his greatest support to have come from his wife's family. He found helping to care for his stepdaughter during her terminal illness to be particularly comforting. He also valued talking to his stepchildren at length about his wife and his bereavement. He had experienced many bereavements in the past. He clearly remembered both of his parents dying and nine out of ten of his brothers and sisters had died.

Professional help

Mr L felt that his wife's GP had been particularly understanding. He had visited daily and often made calls in the evening. Mr L's wife was always pleased with her contact with the GP and Mr L expressed gratitude over this concern which also extended to Mr L himself. Apparently this GP frequently asked how he was coping and checked whether he needed any sleeping tablets or not. Mr L declined this help before and after his wife's death and expressed considerable fear about becoming dependent upon drugs. Mr L was particularly moved by the fact that his wife's GP called the day after she died and wept with him.

Various district nurses attended Mrs L during her relatively short terminal illness. Mr L found them all very caring and helpful. He particularly valued their specificity over the help they could provide.

After Mrs L's death one of the nurses visited Mr L and he felt comforted by her presence and the fact that she cried, too.

Mr L's experiences with the funeral director and the minister at the crematorium were also described as good. Mr L considered the service to be a celebration of his wife's life and took comfort from the thought that she was now in a better place.

Mrs L had been diagnosed as having lung cancer three months before her death. Mr L thought that the cancer 'spread to her liver very quickly'. Mrs L knew she was dying and discussed her death and funeral arrangements frequently. One of her daughters was suffering from the same disease and had been told she may have only eighteen months to live. Mr L felt that this 'coincidence' compounded his own and his wife's shock on learning of her illness.

On the night Mrs L died several members of her family had visited her. In the early evening one of her stepsons came to visit and when Mr L went upstairs to see if his wife needed anything, he found that she was dead. Although he knew her death to be imminent he was still deeply shocked. Very soon afterwards the district nurse called and together they called the doctor.

Mr L remembered feeling dazed and trying to deny to himself that his wife was 'really' dead. He did not return to the room in which she died and was grateful to his stepson for spending the night with him. For several days after the death Mr L felt very anxious and could neither eat nor sleep. However, he was of the belief that his wife would want him to look after himself and so forced himself to eat and devised strategies to tire himself in order to sleep more easily. At the time of interview he was focusing upon maintaining his house exactly as his wife would want it and managing to sleep relatively well. Mr L still imagined himself to be 'living in a house full of people' and was paradoxically quite surprised when 'real people turned up'.

Mr L took comfort from the fact that he had cared for his wife up to her dying moments. This was particularly important to him because he was of the belief that her first husband had made life difficult for her and prided himself on his ability to provide comfort for her. He felt that despite her considerable weight loss she had looked quite well before her death and he took particular comfort from the trouble he'd taken to try and ensure that she ate some food when her appetite had gone.

He and his wife had discussed death at great length and, according to him, neither had any fear of dying but both were sad at what they saw as a short-term separation. Mr L believed that he would be reunited with his wife following his own death. They both held strong beliefs in an afterlife and Mr L found his wife's organisational skills concerning the practical matters associated with her death to be both supportive and impressive. Mrs L had arranged that her savings be divided among her grandchildren and had discussed the practicalities of housekeeping at some length. She told Mr L that she wanted him to keep the rings she wore after her death, so he asked the undertaker to remove them and wore them on a chain around his neck. Mrs L even wrote and delivered her Christmas cards by the middle of December since she was of the belief that she would die before Christmas.

Mr L strongly believed that his wife still actively communicated with him. When he needed advice he felt that he heard her voice giving it to him. He also felt that she was with him constantly and took comfort from this. However, he still felt a deep sense of loss.

Mr L was quite close to his stepdaughter who survived her mother for just over three months. However, he did not appear to be close to his stepson-in-law who, according to Mr L, left his wife's funeral service and went straight to a public house. Mr L had no great wish to see his stepson-in-law again, and in fact rarely did so.

Mr L was of the belief that his past experiences of death had made the loss of his wife easier to accept. Mr L felt that death invariably caused him great sadness and a feeling of emptiness and loss, but that there were 'different degrees of it'. Mr L's mother had died unexpectedly as a result of a fall when he was 7 years old and his father had died of lung disease when Mr L was in his early thirties. Mr L thought that familiarity with death from an early age made bereavement and the inevitability of loss easier for him to accept.

Example 2

Mrs B was a retired machinist in her eighties when her husband died suddenly of a heart attack three years prior to her discussing the death. Mr B died at home with a doctor in attendance. Mrs B lost weight following her husband's death although she regained it during the following year. She suffered, and continues to suffer, from sleeplessness for which she was prescribed Valium. Mrs B has relatives who continue to visit fairly regularly and many friends at her local church. Mrs B did not wear any clothes to signify her bereavement after the day of her husband's cremation because she believed that her husband would not have wanted this.

Informal support

Mr and Mrs B had been married for over sixty years and Mrs B described their relationship as being very close. There were no children of the marriage so Mrs B was dependent largely upon one neighbour who herself was widowed. This neighbour was Mrs B's main support following her bereavement. Mrs B's neighbour was also helpful during Mr B's illness because she was alone when her own husband died and did not wish to leave Mrs B without support in that way.

Mrs B was active in her local church and had many friends and acquaintances who visited her socially and kept an eye on her well-being. Mrs B also had a sister who was disabled whom she helped as much as possible both before and after Mr B's death.

112

However, due to mobility problems she and her sister did not see each other often. Mrs B's only other surviving family member was her husband's brother who was cited as being particularly helpful because he stayed with her for a few weeks after her bereavement.

Professional help

Mrs B did not find their GP particularly helpful at the time of her husband's death. However, her GP did make a bereavement visit and told her to approach him if she needed help. After a few weeks she consulted him and was prescribed Valium which she continued to take occasionally. Mrs B found the funeral directors to be very sympathetic and helpful, but described her main support as being the church and her faith. Her local minister visited her daily for a considerable time after her bereavement and was a great comfort to her. Mrs B believes that she will be reunited with her husband and this belief sustains her.

On the day of Mr B's death he and his wife had been out shopping and had returned home for tea. Mr B said he didn't feel hungry and that he had a pain in his chest. Mr B decided to go to bed and Mrs B, after consulting with her neighbour, telephoned the doctor. The doctor came immediately and informed Mrs B that her husband had had a serious heart attack and was dying. Mrs B was distraught and wanted to stay with her husband. However, to the best of her recall she thought the doctor called her neighbour who had stayed with her and her neighbour persuaded her to go downstairs. She stayed downstairs for a few minutes and became very agitated. Then the doctor came downstairs and told her 'it's all over'.

Mrs B remembers feeling absolutely shattered. She just kept saying 'No, oh no', over and over again. She couldn't believe that her husband had really died despite the warning she'd had. She continues to be terribly upset not to have been with him at the last minute, and felt that in some way she had failed him. She has wished since 'a thousand times' that she had stayed upstairs. She couldn't eat for a week after the death but was eventually persuaded to do so by her friends and relatives.

Mrs B derived immediate comfort from the support of her church, her religious beliefs and the closeness of her past relationship with her husband. Following his death Mrs B became afraid of taking over the practical tasks that her husband used to perform. However, she described several experiences where she heard her husband's voice telling her what to do. She believed her father had helped her in similar ways previously. She said that she frequently asked for her husband's help and always got a response from him.

Mrs B still thinks of her husband constantly and often talks to him as

113

if he was in the room with her. She points out things in the newspaper which she knows would interest him and watches TV programmes which she knows he would like. She remains totally convinced that he is alive somewhere else. She feels that she has recovered from her bereavement and sees her communication with her husband as an indication of her ability to accept the fact of his death.

However, Mrs B felt in some way responsible for her husband's death. About six months before the death she had apparently fainted whilst out shopping. She had an out of body experience during which she experienced herself floating above her body and the people who were trying to help her. She felt she returned to her body out of concern for her husband who was apparently distraught by her accident. Mrs B felt that this distress may have contributed to her husband's eventual death.

Mr B's death was unexpected. However, the couple, having discussed death between themselves, were of the opinion that Mr B would die first. Mrs B does not fear dying and actively looks forward to being reunited after death with her husband.

Mrs B felt that her past experiences of bereavement had been very different to her reaction to her husband's death. Specifically, Mrs B reported feeling angry over the death of her only son. As a young couple, Mr and Mrs B had a baby son who died a few hours after his birth. The couple were advised not to try to have any more children and took this advice. Mrs B still feels that had she been moved to hospital during labour then her baby might have survived. Mrs B was advised by her doctor not to see her son after his death and she continues to regret this bitterly.

Mrs B also described her reaction to her mother's death as being different in that she remembered feeling exceptionally guilty over her mother's death. Mrs B's mother was an invalid and Mrs B had cared for her for some years prior to her death. However, Mrs B worked full-time as a machinist and, consequently, was not with her mother when she died. Mrs B remembered feeling extremely guilty about this and feels that neither anger nor guilt were particularly strong components following the death of her husband (despite her feelings that worry over her health might have contributed towards his death and her regret at not being with him when he died). Mrs B felt that her previous experiences of bereavement were all so different that they did not in themselves ease subsequent experiences.

Family disputes over the position of chief mourner

By far the commonest category of problems reported in the literature regarding bereavement may be usefully considered as disputes over the

114

position of chief mourner. These disputes were serious in nature since they frequently either further depleted the range of informal support available to people who had been bereaved or so distorted the provision of support that the interactions were regarded as unhelpful. In my own study, Littlewood (1983), these disputes were frequently associated with the following kinds of social relationships:

1. brothers and/or sisters following the death of a single or sole surviving parent;
2. children and a dead parent's second or subsequent partner;
3. parents and partners following the death of an adult child.

However, despite these problems being reported over a range of relationships, the form the unhelpful interactions took was remarkably uniform and involved one or both of the following allegations:

1. that the person who occupied the position of chief mourner had no right to the position because they had behaved in a less than caring way towards the person who had died;
2. that the person who occupied the position of chief mourner had by act or omission been somehow responsible for the death.

Whilst on the surface such disputes might appear to be petty and ungenerous in spirit they undoubtedly reflected deeper and more central preoccupations amongst the relevant parties, i.e. that of exclusive possession of the memory of the dead person. Unfortunately, many people saw their relationships in such terms, and, consequently, the position of chief mourner became vitally important in terms of the access it gave to the holder effectively to speak on behalf of the dead person, i.e. it gave them literally, as well as figuratively, the last word. Perhaps this is the darker, more unacknowledged, aspect of the process of monotropic bonding described by Bowlby (1980). Bowlby reminds us that the word bereaved stems from the same root as to rob and it would seem that in certain instances some people are left with nothing. Specifically, if access to the memory of the deceased is either denied or violated by unwanted disclosures then the process of grieving may be significantly impeded by such actions. Consequently, the review of the death becomes critical and evaluative, frequently opening old and possibly causing new wounds and losses for people.

Brothers and sisters

Sibling rivalry is not uncommon and may take many forms following the death of a parent. For example, one woman reported amusement over the fact that throughout her adult life she'd always believed herself to be her mother's favourite child – her 'best girl'. At her mother's funeral the four sisters discussed this matter openly for the first time and realised that they had all been their mother's 'best girl' – although for different reasons.

However, the death of a sole-surviving parent was not always handled amicably. In the case of brothers and sisters, disputes over the position of chief mourner usually reflected the anguish of one of the siblings believing themselves to have been wrongly judged to have been 'second best' by the parent. For example:

> She'd got a cheek. She hadn't been near him [her father] for years and then she just moved back and thought she could take over – it was like the return of the prodigal for me Dad – he thought the sun shone out of her. After he died the rest of the family were saying 'Poor——'. I never went near her and I haven't been since, if she was so bloody fond of him it's a pity she didn't do more for him when he was alive.

Obviously, this particular brother neither gave support to nor received any from his sister. However, even if the remaining family didn't actively avoid each other problems could still occur. One woman described a situation in which she was the youngest daughter in a family of three. Her eldest sister had cared for the family following the death of their mother which had occurred when the woman was still a child. When she was in her mid-teens her father died suddenly of a heart attack. Her sister, by that time, had married but lived near her father providing him with meals and companionship. Following his death both sisters were distraught. The younger sister looked to the older for support only to find that her older sister blamed her adolescent rebelliousness for contributing to her father's heart attack: 'He always said you'd break his heart carrying on like that.' The older sister insisted that she was receiving messages from her father telling her what to do. The dead father was constantly invoked every time the younger sister tried to regain what she saw as a normal life. On the eve of her wedding, two years after the death, her sister tried to persuade her to see a medium. Her sister told her that her dead father was unhappy with the arrangements and wanted the wedding cancelled. The woman observed that her relationship with her sister felt 'almost like a competition'.

This woman's mother had died from a brain haemorrhage when she was 8 years old and she was of the belief that her older sister blamed her brother for the death which had occurred soon after an argument between mother and son. She was also of the opinion that her sister blamed her for her father's death and was trying to punish her for this:

116

Every time I went there it was always the same: 'How could you have done this, and you shouldn't have done that.' I don't know why I kept going and putting up with it really, but I just couldn't help it. I had to see her, I just had to, but she wasn't helping me really; in fact, I think she was making me worse.

Adult children and the parent's partners

As Pincus (1976) has pointed out, some adult children resent a parent's new partner and can be particularly upset over the social arrangements made when their parent dies. For some people their parent's remarriage was enough in itself, seen in terms of disloyalty to the deceased, to result in a termination of contact between parent and child. One woman who had been widowed for twenty years before her eventual remarriage put it thus:

She hasn't been near me since I got married again. She didn't approve of it at all. You only marry once was all she said. When I rang her and told her that my second husband had died she just didn't want to know. There's not a lot I can do about it really. She's 53 and old enough to make her own mind up about things.

Usually, expressions of dissatisfaction following a death entail a refusal to be helpful to the step-parent or extremely grudging offers of support. For many people, the representation of their dead parent offered by their step-parent often bore little resemblance to their own image of their parent which was usually formed when the original family was intact. Consequently, contact was often broken off following the parent's death. For example:

My stepmother didn't get on with my wife although my Dad quite liked her. After he died my stepmother said Jean wasn't really family as far as she was concerned and couldn't come to the funeral. Well, that was it, she wasn't my mother and I wasn't going to have her tell me what to do and what not to do. So neither of us went to the funeral and we haven't seen [stepmother] since.

Some adult children felt that either their own relationship with their parent was being devalued or that someone who was not entitled to have authority over them was trying to exercise it following the parent's death. Given the current social changes in the rates of divorce and remarriage it might be suggested that these problems are likely to increase in future years.

Partners and parents following the death of an adult child

A review of the literature in the area would seem to suggest that problems often occur between mothers and daughters-in-law. However, it must be

117

born in mind that this literature has primarily focused upon widows so the position of sons-in-law must remain unclear. However, the social position of parents who lose a child in adulthood is an unenviable one. Gorer (1965) has suggested that this may be one of the most difficult types of loss to come to terms with due to the fact of the commonly held expectation that children will outlive their parents. However, it must also be said that this is a loss which quite often remains socially unacknowledged, particularly in instances where the parents are elderly and their adult children have families of their own.

In my own study (Littlewood 1983), parents who lost adult children frequently blamed their child's partner for the death. For example: 'if she'd been doing what she was supposed to instead of going out to work none of this would have happened.'

Equally frequently, widows and widowers reported receiving such allegations and often countered them by alleging that neglect or abuse in childhood had been partially responsible for their partner's death. Unfortunately, relationships rarely improved after such exchanges.

It must be said that there was considerable confusion in these cases over who had a right to expect support from whom. Many parents of adult children strongly believed that their dead child's partner should be supportive towards them. Furthermore, widows and widowers often reported that their dead partner's parents were making unreasonable demands upon them. In short, there seemed to be genuine social confusion regarding appropriate expectations in these instances. Clearly, if relationships prior to death had been strained then this social confusion could effectively serve to sever the relationship on the basis of a series of misunderstandings. Furthermore, in many instances attempts which may have been made to protect elderly relatives were misinterpreted as neglect. For example:

> We never had a say in anything. We only found things out after everything had been sorted out. . . . She never even told us that she was going to get a headstone, said she didn't want to upset us any more than she had to.– but she did though.

Lack of social acknowledgement of relationships

Some people's personal relationships do not mirror cultural expectations and they may feel particularly attached to a relationship which may be socially unacknowledged or unacknowledgeable. For instance: 'He was the best friend I ever had. I'd never had a brother you see, only eight sisters. He was like a brother to me.' This man was distraught over the death of his close friend and went on to say of his friend's wife: 'I don't think she was that bothered myself. They were never really close.'

The lack of social acknowledgement associated with these losses can be a devastating experience and one which may be associated with the receipt of inadequate social support. For example, a woman in her eighties made the following observations:

> I lived with her for twenty years since my parents died. I know she was only an aunt but she was like a mother to me. I didn't know what to do with myself after she'd died. It was almost as if people thought it didn't matter.

One woman whose son was fostered felt distraught over his death but felt unable to acknowledge her feelings because she believed she had given up her 'right' to him when she'd agreed that he should be temporarily fostered. Consequently, she turned down offers of support from her son's foster parents on the grounds that 'it wouldn't be fair on them'.

This general position is considerably more difficult when the relationship which has been lost is one which is difficult to acknowledge for various reasons. For example, one woman whose lover had died reported her horror at the thought of her lover's wife making his funeral arrangements. Obviously, if a relationship is secret in this way it may be difficult or impossible for the bereaved person to receive any social support following the death, particularly if the bereaved person shared a similar social support network to the deceased. Unfortunately, for many people only the socially legitimate relationships take priority after a death. One woman who had cohabited with her lover for ten years reported how her partner's daughters had virtually evicted her from the home she had shared with their father. Both daughters were believed by this woman to be ashamed that their father had taken a new partner in his sixties, consequently: 'I couldn't say they treated me badly, it was more like I didn't exist.'

Homosexual couples may experience particularly difficult problems in this respect. The relationship itself may not always be socially acknowledged and, consequently, its loss may go largely unsupported. One woman who had lived with her partner for a number of years prior to her unexpected death in a road traffic accident made the following comments:

> Well, we had several friends in the local gay community who were very supportive. But no-one knew about the relationship at work, so there was no help from there. ——'s family didn't know about the relationship either. I found that very difficult to cope with personally because I felt our relationship was being undermined all the time. ——'s parents kept introducing me as ——'s friend from London. I found that very hurtful. I don't suppose that's very rational is it?

The situation was considerably worse for gay men who could find themselves totally excluded from their dead partner's family on the grounds that they simply 'shared a house' or were 'flatmates' with their partner.

One man whose partner had died a year previously from AIDS and who was HIV positive himself made the following observations:

> I suppose it would have been easier for us if we'd lived in London where there must be more of a community. We were fairly well organised about practical matters and had both made wills. I'd recommend that to anybody who's gay, you can get into all sorts of problems if you don't. ——'s family knew about the relationship, but after the death they simply denied the relationship and avoided me. I felt very hurt by that. I know that they weren't perhaps particularly well-educated, but I still feel that they caused me a lot of unnecessary pain. I couldn't even go to his funeral. His father told me I wouldn't be welcome.

Clearly, the presence or absence of informal support from friends or the availability of professional or voluntary support may be particularly important to bereavement outcome when a relationship is either difficult to acknowledge or is denied social legitimation for whatever reason.

Helpers

As previously noted, helpers were in a difficult social position following a bereavement and many experienced difficulties concerning resentment over the chief mourner's rate of adjustment to the loss or the lack of social support they received in connection with their bereavement. For example, a 28-year-old woman made the following observations about her relationship with her mother.

> I did absolutely everything for my mother, all the practical things. I even mended her blasted fence and all she kept saying was: 'I need a man to do this or that . . .'. Not a word of thanks. Well, my father hadn't been dead for six months when she got herself one. I never said anything about it, but I thought it was a bit off. I don't have much to do with her now, I don't know whether she knows why or not – I don't much care to be honest.

Many people were disappointed over their lack of opportunity to discuss their feelings associated with the loss. For example, 'Oh, I don't know what I expected – for him to throw his arms around me or something, some comfort I suppose. Anyway, there was none of that. It finished the relationship' and 'I can't describe it really. I just felt he let me down that's all.' When helpers did receive support it tended to be in the opposite direction: 'He said "Come on now, pull yourself together; you've done really well so far, don't break down now." I couldn't even cry at home after that.'

Many people were particularly hurt to find that their efforts to control

120

the expression of emotion in public, which were often considerable, were sometimes interpreted by other people as insensitivity or lack of caring. For some helpers their bereavement led to loss of other close relationships. However, it must be said that helpers themselves expressed a high degree of ambivalence about what might constitute appropriate social support. Many helpers actively avoided or shunned people or situations which they felt might provoke a period of active grieving. In general, helpers were highly dependent upon the sensitivity of their own informal support network and were essentially reliant upon others being able to interpret what were undoubtedly mixed messages. Unfortunately, this type of ability was highly variable and for the most part the effective support of helpers was arbitrarily distributed.

It would appear from the previous discussion that what Dalley (1988) has called 'the family model of caring' might be less than adequate for some people. Specifically, at a time when social support in general is likely to deteriorate a great deal of strain is placed upon one or two people rather than the community as a whole. In instances where family relationships were not particularly good prior to the death, the strain of bereavement may lead to a further deterioration in a person's access to social support. This support is seen as particularly important if cognitive and social explanations of the bereavement process are considered. Support deterioration in the informal network may significantly disrupt the more communal elements of the grieving process by effectively denying or inhibiting the grieving person's attempts to reassess the most important elements of their relationship.

Perhaps, under the circumstances, access to professional help immediately following a death in cases where inadequate informal support, for whatever reason, is likely would prove to be particularly beneficial.

However, whilst professional and informal sources of social support are undoubtedly important to the outcome of the grieving process, other factors inevitably play a part. Consequently, the chapter which follows is concerned with a loss which is almost universally cited as being particularly painful, i.e. the loss of a child during childhood, adolescence or adulthood. In this chapter the influence of specific causes of death and of the events surrounding the death will be considered in terms of their potential to facilitate or inhibit the process of grieving.

7

THE DEATHS OF CHILDREN
IN CHILDHOOD, ADOLESCENCE
AND ADULTHOOD

'What greater pain could mortals have than this
To see their children dead before their eyes?'

Euripides (c.421 BC)
The Suppliant Women
(tr. F. W. Jones)

INTRODUCTION

Whilst grieving is universally acknowledged as painful, many researchers have argued that the loss of a child is a uniquely devastating experience for the child's parents. In contemporary Western societies such deaths are almost always viewed as untimely because they conflict with people's taken-for-granted assumptions and life-cycle expectations. It is now reasonable to suppose that children will outlive their parents. Whilst the loss of a child or children was exceptionally common in earlier years the contemporary situation is one in which deaths in childhood and early adulthood are relatively rare occurrences. Consequently, few parents actively anticipate the deaths of their children and, fortunately, relatively few will experience this type of bereavement.

The range of experiences following the death of a child tend to vary with the age of the child, the cause and context of the death and the personalities and experiences of the parents – both having and losing a child can mean different things to different people. However, in general terms, the age of the child and the cause and context of the death are important factors. Consequently, this chapter will be concerned with issues associated with the developmental age of the child and the common causes of death associated with various age groups.

The first part of the chapter looks at parental reactions to the deaths of younger children, whilst the second part focuses upon the particular problems associated with the deaths of adolescents. The third part of the chapter is concerned with the experiences of older parents whose children have died in adulthood, and the final part considers the similarities and differences between the ways in which mothers and fathers express their grief.

THE DEATHS OF YOUNG CHILDREN

Miscarriages and induced abortions

Miscarriages and induced abortions may be difficult losses to cope with, because, in most cases, there is no body to mark the fact that a death has occurred. Furthermore, in social terms, these deaths tend to be treated as non-events – the deaths of non-persons. However, for the mother, and to a greater or lesser extent depending upon his degree of involvement the father, the unborn child may, indeed, have achieved the status of personhood. As Raphael (1984) has pointed out, parents, often from a very early stage in the woman's pregnancy, actively fantasise, together or alone, about what sort of person their baby is or will be. Consequently, lack of social acknowledgement of the bereavement and the parent's sense of loss can make these kinds of deaths painful experiences to cope with.

Stillbirths

Stillbirths may cause particular problems for parents. In these cases an anticipated joyful event turns into a tragedy, often leaving the parents with little or no time in which to anticipate that the death may occur. Kirkley-Best and Kellner (1982), in their review of the area, have suggested that the commonest situation is one in which the baby was viable until labour. However, in some cases there may be forewarning before delivery, but, according to Kirkley-Best and Kellner, such forewarning tends to be met by denial on the part of the parents. Consequently, the emotional reaction to a stillbirth is similar in both cases. For example:

> They'd told me he was dead but I just didn't believe it. The midwife said that I could have strong pain relief during labour because nothing I did would hurt the baby. I didn't have any pain relief, I wanted it to hurt because I thought that if it hurt he would be all right when he was born, all I can remember thinking was please, please, don't let him be dead.

The above-mentioned comments illustrate a general tendency amongst parents of stillborn children to experience their child's birth as a birth followed by a death.

Most births in Western societies now tend to take place in the hospital rather than the home. Hospitals as organisations are clearly geared, given low child mortality rates, to the reception of live babies rather than dead ones. Consequently, the whole atmosphere surrounding a stillbirth may be painfully inappropriate for the child's parents. The parents almost certainly would have assumed, prior to their child's death, that most people produce healthy children. Unfortunately, they may be surrounded, after the death, by people who have done just that. Furthermore, hospital staff often feel a painful sense of failure and helplessness following the birth of a dead child.

Under these circumstances a conspiracy of silence frequently follows such a death. In the past many women were not allowed to see their babies, were heavily sedated and dissuaded by well-meaning hospital staff from speaking about their experiences. Stringham *et al.* (1982) have noted that the silence following a stillbirth often confirms the mother's feelings of terrible guilt that the death was 'unspeakable'. Wolff *et al.* (1970) have also noted that lack of discussion with parents actually exacerbates the negative feelings experienced by many parents.

This lack of inclination to acknowledge the child may extend into the community. Bourne (1968) has shown that general practitioners are apparently reluctant to know or remember anything about a woman who has had a stillbirth. Family and friends may also act as if the birth and death had simply never happened in the first instance. Lewis (1979), in arguing for a change in professional practice in this area, summarises the potential impact of this 'conspiracy of silence' in the following way:

> This avoidance by the helping professionals extends into neglect of the study of the effect of stillbirth on the mother and the family. There is a conspiracy of silence. We seem unwilling to come to terms with the fact that it is a tragedy which can seriously affect the mental health of the bereaved mother and her family. After the failure to mourn, mothers can have psychotic breakdowns or there can be severe mental difficulties. Children born before or after a stillbirth where there has been a failure to mourn a stillbirth can have severe emotional difficulties.
>
> (Lewis 1979: 303)

Morris has argued that over the past fifteen years practice has changed radically in this area. Specifically, many self-help groups have been established to help parents whose children have died prior to or at birth. Furthermore, it is now seen as appropriate to permit the parents to see and hold their dead baby:

> The routine photography of all stillborns, and now even miscarriages and practices such as giving parents the baby's name tag, lock of hair or other memento shows how much progress has been made.
>
> (Morris 1988: 871)

The range of practices described by Morrin are similar to those advocated earlier by Lewis (1979) which included encouraging rather than discouraging parents from the following:

THE DEATHS OF CHILDREN

1. laying out their dead baby
2. receiving a photograph of the child
3. certifying the death
4. naming the baby
5. making the funeral as memorable as possible.

Presumably, the purpose of these actions is to make the child and his/her subsequent death appear to be as socially real as possible for his/her parents. Acknowledging the reality of the loss may facilitate the grieving process. Alternatively, failure to acknowledge the death may well inhibit or complicate grief.

Perinatal deaths

In many ways perinatal deaths share similarities with stillbirths insofar as lack of social acknowledgement, an untimely death and parental feelings of guilt or failure may all contribute towards complicating the grieving process. However, it must be said that, even if the child lives for only a few days, the medical staff are likely to be more involved with the care of the child, and, therefore, more likely to acknowledge and be supportive of the parents after the death. Nevertheless, Benfield *et al.* (1978) have noted that medical staff still show a marked tendency to avoid the implications of the death and point out that this tendency is associated with considerable parental distress. Furthermore, these researchers indicate that mothers are inclined actively to blame themselves for the death – usually because of perceived acts or omissions which may have been damaging to the child during the mother's pregnancy. Kennell *et al.* (1970) and Wilson *et al.* (1982) all point to the terrible sense of loss parents feel following the death of their child during the first few days of life. What follows is an example concerning a baby boy who lived for six days following his birth. This boy's mother clearly articulates the couple's need for, and insistence upon, what they saw as a proper social acknowledgement of their loss.

Ms W was 28 years old when her first child died in hospital. He was 6 1/2 days old. Ms W's son had suffered severe asphyxiation at birth and she was with him in the special care unit when he died. Although Ms W felt that she'd slept considerably better following the death of her son, she felt devastated by his death and, eighteen months after the experience, still openly grieved for him. Following her child's death, Ms W gave up most of her leisure activities and reported that she lost some friends as a direct result of the death. Apparently, some people felt that they were unable to discuss the death with her or, in fact, face her at all.

Informal support

Ms W felt that her husband and her sister were her greatest support throughout her distress. Her husband and sister both took turns in staying with her and the baby whilst he was dying and she found this to be particularly helpful. Ms W's mother offered to help, but Ms W felt that her mother's presence would be too overwhelming. No other relatives were cited as being helpful. Ms W was somewhat critical of her husband's behaviour on the day her son died because he went home and only just returned in time for the baby's death. If he hadn't come back in time Ms W felt that she would never have forgiven him despite the fact that she knew it was impossible to be certain exactly when their baby would die.

Professional help

Ms W had no contact with funeral directors but wished the child to be buried quickly in a marked grave. A friend made the relevant arrangements for the couple. The profession with whom Ms W had the most contact over her bereavement was the medical profession. She had nothing but praise for them, saying that she valued their honesty. She was told before her Caesarean section that her baby might not survive and that if he or she were alive he or she might not be healthy. She felt that she had some preparation for what was to happen.

Once the child had been born and it was clear that he had been severely brain-damaged, people continued to be honest with her. She had access to her baby and the paediatricians were open about their prognosis. The paediatrician who attended the baby wept with the parents when the child died.

The only reservations Ms W had about the support she was given concerned what she considered to be an unwillingness to tell her what happened to babies' bodies after death. Apparently, it was policy to bury them in a mass grave, so Ms W and her husband asked for their baby's body to be returned to them.

The only other source of professional support Ms W mentioned was the stonemason who carved their son's headstone. She and her husband visited his workshop and found that the radio was playing and people were chatting away happily as they carved memorial stones. In retrospect, Ms W viewed her shock with amusement on the grounds that this job was presumably as routine as any other.

At the birth of her child Ms W felt that if he were going to have to be kept alive artificially, then it was better that he should die. However, when she saw her son he looked better than she expected and efforts

126

were made. By the third day of his life Ms W felt differently and desperately hoped her son would survive. However, she was told that there was no hope of his recovering and that the machines were to be switched off. Ms W felt that the fact that her son had struggled to survive made his personality seem that much stronger, so the decision to let him die was much harder to take.

Once the decision had been made Ms W stayed with her son, held him and cradled him in her arms. One thing she regretted was that she was unable to hug him because he had a drip in his stomach. She was told that once the machines were switched off, he would take about fifteen or twenty minutes to die, in fact, it took nearly three days. Ms W remembers being told that the baby could be injected to hurry up the process of dying, but that most people felt uncomfortable with this – she did not agree to it. Despite having full knowledge of her son's impending death, Ms W remembered feeling shattered when the death finally occurred.

Ms W stressed throughout the interview that she and her husband both fought to have the child recognised as belonging to both of them and both felt the death of their son must be socially acknowledged. Consequently, they claimed the death grant for the burial of their child despite it being a very small amount of money which they didn't, in financial terms, need. Interestingly enough, Ms W remembered it took them about eight attempts before they received the money.

Whilst Ms W clearly accepted her son's prognosis, Waller *et al.* (1979) have suggested that this may not always be the case. In connection with deaths occurring in paediatric intensive care units, Waller *et al.* argue that hostile denial of a poor prognosis is a particularly common parental response:

> when physicians gave parents an honest appraisal of poor prognosis, they were met with what seemed to the physicians to be a hostile denial of the realities of the situation. It was in the context of the doctor–parent relationship that parental denial seemed most extreme and the consequences most severe. Parents viewed physicians with frustration and suspicion since they were seen as possessing the ability to effect a cure if they really wanted to. One father said, 'I want to believe that you're doing all that you can, but I just can't.'
>
> (Waller *et al.* 1979: 1122)

Perhaps, within the context of intensive care units, the denial which so often accompanies a child's death is exacerbated by the application of advanced technology. It must be difficult, given what must appear to the parents to be heroic attempts to save the life of their child, to accept that these attempts are likely to fail. For example, one woman in my own study (Littlewood 1983) remained convinced, three years after the death of her baby son, that staff on the intensive care unit hadn't really tried hard to save her child because they believed that her negligence had contributed to his condition. Also, parents frequently feel helpless and unable to protect and care for their child in the face of complex medical procedures. What follows is the discussion between two parents whose son died unexpectedly of cancer following five days' hospital treatment.

Mother: And that's another thing I'm not happy about. At least, I don't know how he [her husband] thinks about it but this is how I feel. On Sunday, first we said 'we'll stop all this and just take him home', but later he went under the scanner after all, because it had been talked over with us. There we were sitting in the corridor and I heard the monitor running down and I said 'this is wrong' and then a nurse came running from another corridor, and she saw us sitting there and she suddenly stopped and went into another room. Then you think this is crazy, just to sneak into another room when the monitor is running down and then stopping. Well, someone else came out and I said 'I have already heard, this is going wrong'. 'Things are not going the way they should' is what I was told. And then later, a doctor, or someone like that . . .

Father: A surgeon I think.

Mother: Well, anyway, he came running out with a big syringe, really unbelievable. . . . A huge syringe, he went to get something and when he came back I said 'things are not going right'. Well, he said nothing, and then a paediatrician came out and said he [their son] had had a cardiac arrest, so what would we like to do? Well, then he said he [her son] could be mentally retarded or stay in a coma. So we said, well, stop this, so he was going to talk it over with the anaesthetist but then I thought 'Well, he did come to discuss this', but then he went back right away, so it had already happened.

Father: Well, I think it was a sort of formality to ask us.

Mother: Yes, but I also think that . . . Why at a time like that don't they let you in until . . . he is really gone . . .

Father: Yes.

Mother: I don't know.

Father: One thing you really know, that you are never going to forget this.

128

Mother: But you're left with a rotten memory. They tried resuscitation and so on. Well, I mean, like we were there when he was anaesthetised and he went under crying. Then he said: 'Mama, I have such an awful taste in my throat . . .' and then he was injected and we couldn't say anything . . . so he went off crying with those words.

Father: So then I thought look this is really awful. Why didn't they let him be, those last few minutes. That would have been all right. And I also thought why don't they tell the truth when I ask a question. It was not going right because the monitor stopped twice and all they said is 'It is not going as it should.' They didn't say anything else when I could hear myself, they could have tried to tell us honestly, I think . . .

Grief following the adoption or fostering of children

Whilst people caring for a woman who has suffered the death of her newborn child are increasingly recognising her need to grieve for the child and the problems which may follow attempts to repress or deny sorrow, Morris suggests that this is not the case for women whose babies are fostered or adopted at birth. In the case of adoption Morrin suggests that it:

> May be because adoption is a voluntary act on the woman's behalf it somehow appears different. And the need to mourn her child may therefore go unrecognised by those who care for her.
>
> (Morrin 1983: 33)

Fostering may present even greater difficulties for the woman involved. For example:

> Mrs G was 42 years old and separated from her husband when she had her third child. Unfortunately, her baby son suffered from Down's Syndrome. Mrs G was of the opinion that she hadn't been informed of this at the hospital where the birth took place and was consequently extremely shocked when her GP, on a routine visit, casually mentioned this to her. Her family persuaded her to have her son fostered for a while and she reluctantly agreed to do so. The couple who fostered Mrs G's son had lost their own son, who also suffered from Down's Syndrome, some years previously. This couple's affluence contrasted sharply with Mrs G's poverty, and, although she wished for her son's return, she felt unable to articulate this desire. However, Mrs G constantly fantasised that when she 'got everything sorted out' her son would be returned to her. Mrs G's son died at his foster-parents' home when he was

2 years old. Two years, and several psychiatric in-patient admissions following the death, Mrs G remained inconsolable and ridden with guilt. She felt that she had no right to grieve for her son because 'I rejected him and it was all my own fault for giving him away in the first place'.

The death of a handicapped child

Emde and Brown (1978) have suggested that the birth of a handicapped child is, in itself, a cause of intense grief for the child's parents. This grief is associated with the loss of the healthy child the parents expected to have and is complicated by the failure of the child to reach the various developmental milestones healthy children achieve as a matter of course. Raphael suggests that:

> The grief for this lost child is complicated further by ambivalence, guilt and sometimes lack of support. It is difficult for the parents to relinquish the fantasy and attach to a baby so far from their ideal. And both the grief and the attachment are likely to be inhibited and complicated as a consequence.
>
> (Raphael 1984: 254)

The situation is further complicated by the death of the child. My own impression, from a small number of people, would be that strong religious beliefs which are often developed after the death of the child are particularly supportive to the child's parents. For example, one couple were of the belief that 'We could think of him in a far nicer state this way. In spirit – completely free of pain.' It might be suggested that beliefs concerning the spirit of the child are particularly helpful to the parents of handicapped children who die.

However, it must be said that the situation would appear to be complicated by the ways in which parents come to terms with their child's handicap. One couple described, at great length, the understanding they came to following the birth of their daughter, when both parents were in their early forties, who suffered from Down's Syndrome. Apparently, the couple, particularly the father, interpreted their daughter's handicap in a positive way. They were of the opinion that, whilst their other children would develop normally and leave home, they would 'always have a little girl'. The father described his reaction to his daughter's death from leukaemia in the following way:

> It's been seven months now, and I just can't accept this at all. It's so unfair, she was never well, her little heart wasn't normal and then this happened. My wife had seen a television programme and suspected that [their daughter] might have leukaemia because

she was so tired all of the time. I said 'No it couldn't be, not on top of everything else, we couldn't be that unlucky'. Then, of course, it was leukaemia and she died of it. She was such a happy little girl, always laughing. She used to like to help me in the garden. I often go there now, half-expecting to see her, there – in the garden. What upset me most of all was my father, a blessing in disguise, he said. A lot of other people said that too, you know, because of her handicap. Her life was a blessing to me, her death was a curse. I keep thinking that all of this is a bad dream and I'll go down the garden one day and there she'll be.

Sudden Infant Death Syndrome (SIDS)

SIDS is the most common cause of death during the first year of life. These deaths usually occur between one week and one year of age and peak amongst the two to four months' age group. The cause of SIDS remains unknown and it is impossible to predict those babies who are likely to be at risk. Most infants appear to be entirely healthy prior to the death which usually occurs without warning, often when the child is asleep. The sheer suddenness of the death may, in itself, be associated with complications in the grieving process. However, unfortunately for the parents, many other factors associated with a SIDS death also contribute to putting the parents of these children at risk from a complicated reaction to their loss.

The absence of any immediately obvious cause of death may lead others, including the police, to suspect child abuse. Guilt is especially intense following a death from SIDS. Donnelly (1982) has found that clarification of the fact that neither parent was responsible for the death is both necessary and helpful to the parents following the death of their child. Raphael (1984) reports that the unexplainable nature of the death may lead to a relentlessly obsessive review of events preceding the death. This review may be complicated by family members persistently questioning the parents about what it was they may have done differently immediately before the death of the child.

Paradoxically, even if the inexplicable nature of the death is accepted, then this, in itself, may leave the parents feeling particularly vulnerable and helpless – it seems that nothing they could have done would have prevented the tragedy. Lowman (1979) indicates that many SIDS babies are firstborn children and it might be expected that parents who have lost a child from SIDS would be particularly vulnerable to anxiety over any subsequent children they might have.

Social support networks are frequently perceived to be unsupportive by these parents. Cornwell, Nurcombe and Stevens (1977) have indicated that over 50 per cent of doctors experienced problems in communicating with parents whose children have died from SIDS and informal support may be perceived to, or may actually be, concerned with the allocation of blame for the death. Consequently, self-help organisations may be particularly helpful to parents following a child's death from SIDS.

Given the social circumstances surrounding the death, it should not be too surprising to note that many parents have difficulty in accepting that the death has occurred. Longing for, and searching for, the dead child are frequently particularly intense components of the process of grieving in these instances.

Deaths in childhood from accidents or malignancy

The accidental deaths of children during the childhood years are far more common than those resulting from malignancies. Accidental deaths are sudden, unexpected and often involve some degree of responsibility, parental or otherwise, for the death. Anger is a commonly reported reaction following deaths from accidents. As Raphael has indicated:

Extreme anger about the accident – a hatred of the driver of the car, for example, a desire to hit out and get revenge – may dominate the parent's response. This may be directed towards other agencies or towards the husband or wife. A traumatic neurosis effect is common if the parent was present at the death or in any way involved.

(Raphael 1984: 270)

In my own study (Littlewood 1983) one man reported that he blamed his wife for neglect, following his 3-year-old daughter's drowning accident. However, upon attending meetings of Compassionate Friends he found that many fathers whose children had died tended to do this, and made a conscious effort to see the death as an unfortunate, unforeseeable accident. Nevertheless, he was further annoyed at what he saw as his wife's irrational behaviour. She had been present when her daughter's body had been found in a neighbour's pond and was phobic about the sight of anything floating in water.

Whilst the loss of a child from childhood malignancy is rare, few would doubt the severity of the impact such a death has on the child's parents. Sanders (1979–80), in an empirical study comparing the loss of spouses, parents and children, concluded that those who had lost a child experienced the highest intensity of grief as well as the widest range of reactions. It might be suggested that different circumstances surrounding the deaths of children might account for the wide range of reactions Sanders reported.

Most children who die from malignancy in childhood have a relatively

132

long period of illness which may give their parents some time to anticipate the death. Also, the parents will be in contact with potential sources of support from professional sources prior to the death and would, therefore, be more likely to find the use of such support, following the death, acceptable.

Nevertheless, it must be said that available research concerning the loss of a child from malignancy illustrates the potential severity of the impact of such a loss. Early research in the area tended to focus upon the terminal aspects of the disease. This research tended to focus upon preparing the parents for the death of their child and their subsequent bereavement. However, recent medical advances have led to considerably better chances of survival and childhood malignancy is now viewed as a chronic life-threatening disease rather than a terminal illness. Consequently, parents are being increasingly encouraged to prepare themselves for long periods of uncertainty preceding the distinct possibility of long-term remission or cure (Kalnins, Churchill and Terry 1980; Gogan, O'Malley and Foster 1977; Lansdown and Goldman 1988).

In an early study, prior to these improvements in treatment outcome, Kaplan, Grobstein and Smith (1976) found that at least 80 per cent of families who had lost a child from malignancy had at least one member who experienced relatively severe psychosocial problems. Later studies by Binger (1984) and Mulhern, Lauer and Hoffmann (1983) found that at least 50 per cent of the parents they studied required psychiatric help. Furthermore, Mann (1987) reported that 8 per cent of bereaved mothers in her study attempted or committed suicide following the death of their child.

Spinetta (1982) has hypothesised that prolonged periods of uncertainty of outcome, together with the distressing side-effects of treatment, may have led to an increase rather than a decrease in the psychological problems faced by parents of children with malignancies. Difficult decisions have to be made regarding, for example, whether to stop curative therapy, and parents, whatever they decide, may later regret their choice.

However, Spinetta et al. (1981) have also suggested that effective parental coping following a child's death is, at least in part, related to variables occurring during the life of the child. Specifically, Spinetta and his colleagues found that parents who adjusted relatively well to their child's death shared the following characteristics:

1. a consistent philosophy of life during the course of the illness;
2. a viable ongoing support person to whom they could turn to for help during the course of their child's illness;
3. open and honest information and support given to the child throughout the illness.

Spinetta et al. conclude that:

The parents have shown us that families can adjust to life without their child. Pathology and maladjustment are not inevitable. We have demonstrated the generally beneficial effects on the ultimate adjustment of the family members of such variables as a viable support system, open and responsive communication with the child during the course of the illness and a commitment to one's basic life view. What is called for in the light of the present results is to help strengthen the adaptive capabilities and coping styles specific to each family and to each member of the family, to help the family members struggle forward as best they can in a commitment to the value of the remaining months or years of their child's life and to give them access to the intrafamilial sources of support they most need to help them in that struggle.

(Spinetta *et al.* 1981: 261)

Obviously, if parents can be actively helped to cope with the implications of their child's illness, then this may reduce the possibility of complications to the bereavement process arising for them.

Lauer *et al.* (1983) have suggested that family participation in the care of a dying child reduces feelings of helplessness and anxiety, particularly in the case of the child's parents. Consequently, they suggest that high levels of parental involvement in care should be encouraged. In their study, which looked at reactions to bereavement following the death of a child from cancer, they compared home care deaths to deaths occurring in hospital. They suggested that home care of a dying child had a major impact upon parental adaptation following a child's death. Parents who cared for their child at home experienced relatively rapid attainment of previous levels of social interaction and experienced a relatively low incidence of overt complications to the grieving process. Alternatively, non-home care parents showed relatively high levels of guilt during their child's terminal care and experienced relatively high levels of complications to the grieving process.

Lauer *et al.* suggest that these results might be explained in terms of high levels of parental participation in care being associated with low levels of guilt, i.e. the parents felt that they had done all that they could for their child, and low levels of denial, i.e. the parents found it difficult to deny their child's terminal illness when they were actively coping with it on a day-to-day basis.

Five years following their first study Lauer *et al.* (1989) conducted a long-term follow-up of these parents and found that home care parents still report stronger social relationships, more adequate coping capabilities and less residual guilt when compared to non-home care parents. Overall, they conclude that home care of a dying child is significantly associated with relatively good outcomes to bereavement for the child's parents. However,

134

it must be said that the home care parents in these studies were in receipt of a specific professional care programme which may in itself have had an impact on parental reactions to the death of their child. Also, although the two groups of parents were closely matched on sociodemographic variables, home vs. hospital care was a result of parental choice. It may be possible that parents who opted for hospital care were more likely to wish to deny the implications of their child's illness in the first instance, despite feeling guilt over their denial.

Nevertheless, it must be said that improvements in the support of parents prior to their child's death would appear to be highly significant in terms of a reduction in the likelihood of parents experiencing complications arising from the process of grieving.

DEATHS OCCURRING DURING ADOLESCENCE

Deaths occurring during adolescence may be particularly difficult for parents to cope with because of the heightened ambivalence associated with struggles for independence which may occur at this time. Deaths of adolescent children in accidents provoke a similar reaction to the deaths of younger children from similar causes. Typically, road traffic accidents are particularly common causes of death amongst this age group. These deaths are sudden, unexpected and frequently result in a parental tendency to try and allocate blame. My own impression, from a small number of instances, tends to be that the reaction to the death frequently becomes distorted if the parent believes that their child in some way contributed to their own death or was engaged in activities which were judged, by the parents, to be wrong.

Unfortunately, as Raphael (1984) has indicated, suicides are becoming an increasingly common cause of death in this age range. Barraclough has indicated that:

> Bereavement resulting from suicide, in contrast to bereavement from natural causes, has unique consequences for the surviving relatives for the following reasons. . . . The shock of the event, the trauma of the police inquiry and the inquest, gossip and disapproval among friends and neighbours, publicity in the local newspaper and sometimes radio and television all add to the relatives' short-term distress. Self-blame for failing to prevent the death and a sense of stigma may be longer lasting.
> (Barraclough 1987: 134)

Whilst Barraclough emphasises that not all deaths from suicide result in complications to the bereavement process, Raphael has suggested, in connection with adolescents, that suicide:

> occurs on a family background high in ambivalence, with open hostility and unresolved dependence. The death itself brings shame,

135

stigma and guilt. Complicated, maybe pathological bereavements seem a likely outcome for the survivors.

(Raphael 1984: 280)

The deaths of adolescents from malignancy have also been cited as being particularly problematic. For example, Jurk, Ekert and Jones (1981) found that approximately half of their sample of bereaved parents were showing disturbances outside the range they considered to be normal following the death of their child from cancer. These researchers suggested that abnormal reactions tended to be concentrated amongst the parents of adolescent children. Specifically, they suggested that loss of an adolescent daughter seemed particularly likely to cause problems for the parents. Jurk *et al.* also considered parents who did not agree to take part in their study:

> Although the reason for non-compliance is unknown, a review of the records revealed that ten were adolescents and a further six were the only child in the family at the time of death. Although not assessed by the interviewer, there is strong reason to believe from contacts who know these families that disturbances in family function were still present.

(Jurk *et al.* 1981: 87)

Clarke and Williams (1979) and Cooper (1980) also suggest that non-response rates are associated with parents finding their bereavement particularly distressing. In our own study (Littlewood, Hoekstra-Weebers and Humphrey 1990), we found that the parents of adolescents, particularly the parents of adolescent boys, were far less likely to agree to be interviewed about their experiences of bereavement than were the parents of younger children. Details of response rates are given in Table 7.

Table 7 Percentages (and numbers) of parents agreeing and refusing to discuss their bereavement according to age and sex of child

| | Agreed | | Refused | |
	%	(n)	%	(n)
Younger girls	83	5	17	1
Younger boys	78	7	22	2
Adolescent girls	75	3	25	1
Adolescent boys	40	4	60	6

Carr-Gregg and Hampson (1986) report that parents of adolescents face particularly severe psychosocial stress during the treatment of their child and this in itself may complicate the bereavement process. Stresses concerning treatment compliance, and/or confusion over adolescent dependence vs. autonomy may both contribute to an adverse reaction to the death.

Tebbi *et al.* (1989) have noted that non-compliance with the medical

136

regimen amongst adolescent cancer patients is reported to range from 47–59 per cent.

Little is known about the relationship between medication compliance and developmental processes in critical periods such as adolescence. The diagnosis of a severe illness, such as cancer, may, for example, delay the expected decreased reliance on parents as children move from dependence in pre-adolescence to self-reliance in late adolescence. Such a delay may have a significant effect on the adolescent's engagement in subsequent treatment.

(Tebbi *et al.* 1989: 135)

It seems reasonable to suggest that an adolescent's decision to refuse to comply with or to withdraw completely from a treatment programme might be perceived by their parents to be misguided and, in this sense, wrong. In these instances, parental guilt may well complicate the bereavement process.

However, Schowalter, Ferholt and Mann have discussed an adolescent patient's decision to die, which was supported by her parents (although not necessarily by the medical staff) and report that:

Karen died on June 2 with both parents at her bedside. The relative speed and peacefulness of her dying were unusual for a uraemic death. Shortly prior to her death she thanked the staff for what she said she knew had been a hard time for them and she told her parents she hoped they would be happy . . . In the final days she supported her parents as they faltered in their decision. She told her father, 'Daddy, I will be happier there (in the ground) if there is no machine and they don't work on me any more'. Six months later the family is proceeding through quite a normal grief sequence with a minimum amount of psychiatric and pastoral assistance.

(Schowalter, Ferholt and Mann 1973: 98)

However, family agreement on such a proposed course of action may not always be as clear or the young person as supportive of others as in this case. It is unclear whether all adolescents wishing to die would handle the situation as well as this young woman apparently did.

Confusion concerning autonomy vs. dependence may also cause problems. What follow are two case studies in which the mothers of two adolescents who were terminally ill with cancer intensified their relationship with their child. Both children experienced a long terminal phase to their illness and both mothers believed that their emotional presence kept their children alive. Three and five years after the deaths both mothers remained locked in a pattern of chronic grief.

Mrs R was in her early thirties when her youngest son was diagnosed as having leukaemia. She described a situation in which she and her son 'went through everything together'. Following two courses of active treatment her son elected to undertake a third course despite the knowledge that the outcome was uncertain. He became ill and was hospitalised. His mother stayed with him in the hospital, becoming increasingly anxious and refusing to leave his side because she was afraid that if she left him he would die. He died, nevertheless. Three years following his death his room remained the same as the day he went into hospital for the last time. Mrs R was in the process of separating from her husband but did not think that this was an important issue since her son was all that mattered to her. Mrs R did not fully believe that her son was dead, preferring instead to believe that the hospital had stolen him. She literally, as well as figuratively, believed that she had been robbed.

Mrs S was in her early forties when her only daughter was diagnosed as having bone cancer. During her daughter's long terminal illness she was determined to care for her at home. On the night her daughter died she was admitted to hospital and Mrs S was of the belief that her daughter gave up and died the moment she herself left the hospital to get some rest. Mrs S's husband left her shortly after her daughter's death, although Mrs S felt that her husband had abandoned the family in emotional terms long before the death of his daughter. Five years after her daughter's death Mrs S maintains an intense attachment to her. She does things her daughter used to like to do and often feels her daughter's presence or hears her voice. Mrs S has few friends and feels that she does not need the ones she has. She still has her daughter to think about.

In terms of patterns of coping after a child's death has occurred, it has been suggested that conceiving another child is associated with a more positive bereavement outcome for parents (Videka-Sherman 1982). Parents of adolescent children may (because they tend to be older themselves) be unable or (because of family composition) be unwilling to take such a course of action. Furthermore, Littlewood et al. (1991b) suggest that, in terms of coping with everyday problems and events, the parents of adolescents fare less well when compared to the parents of younger children whose child has died from malignancy. Specifically, the parents of older children were less likely than the parents of younger children to use active, problem-focused ways of coping following their child's death. Parents of older children were also less likely to cope with problems by using comforting thoughts or trying to make themselves feel better.

Kerner, Harvey and Lewiston (1979) report that the parents of children who died from a fatal genetic disease (cystic fibrosis) reported different responses to their child's death when compared to parents of children who died from leukaemia. These researchers speculate that this was due, in part, to the long duration of cystic fibrosis giving the parents time to prepare for what was an inevitable loss.

However, these researchers report relatively high levels of incomplete mourning in their study. Furthermore, although they do not comment upon the implications of their findings, all of the parents they identified as experiencing incomplete mourning were the parents of adolescents. None of the parents of younger children they interviewed were affected in this way by their child's death. Specifically, out of sixteen families:

1. seven suffered from incomplete mourning exemplified by maintaining the child's room as a shrine and/or visiting the child's grave at least once a week;
2. in three one or both parents sought psychiatric care to help them cope with their grief.

Twelve out of these sixteen families had received genetic counselling and nine parents had decided to have no more children. Kerner, Harvey and Lewiston account for their findings in the following way:

> they [the parents of children who died from cystic fibrosis] appear more ready to prepare for their child's ultimate death and to be more accepting of death when it occurs, yet also more reluctant to surrender the child by completing the mourning process.
> (Kerner, Harvey and Lewiston 1979: 225)

Witte (1985) interviewed the parents of terminally ill adolescent boys who were suffering from a progressive, fatal genetic disorder (Duchenne muscular dystrophy) and suggests that parental guilt and adolescent fear combine to create severe problems of communication in these families. Whilst the adolescents tended to raise death related issues with their parents, the parents experienced great difficult in responding to them – resulting in the boys feeling isolated and the parents feeling guilty. Witte describes the situation in the following way:

> As these boys and their parents face death, they experience an intense urge to make empathic contact. However, because of the family injunction to avoid acknowledgement with each other of feelings about the disease process and prognosis each remains existentially alone in facing death . . . Not to address their grief with each other in order to ensure normal family functioning condemns each family member to live a guilt-related, yet alienated and affect-deadened life in and outside the family. Addressing their grief, it is proposed, allows the dystrophic boy to approach death with less terror and guiltless completion, and will allow his parents release from having to repeat, in future life situations, the depressive anhedonia which enmeshes the family.
> (Witte 1985: 185)

It would seem likely that complications to the bereavement process will occur in these circumstances.

DEATH OF AN ADULT CHILD

The commonest causes of death among adult children are accidents and cancers. Shanfield *et al.* (1986–7) have compared parents who have been bereaved in these ways and have found significant differences between the groups they studied. Specifically, parents whose children had died in accidents felt more depressed and guilty after the death, found the loss of their child more painful and developed more health complaints than did the parents whose children had died from cancer.

Shanfield *et al.* suggest that the age of the child at death accounts for these differences. However, the age of the child was also linked to the type of death and the level of parental involvement with their child. Sudden deaths from traffic accidents tend to be associated with young adults and the more anticipated deaths from cancers tend to affect middle-aged adults.

The suddenness of the loss from accidents and the probability that younger adults tend to have closer ties to their parents may account for the tendency of parents who have lost children in accidents to display more psychiatric symptoms and to suffer from more health complaints when compared to parents who have lost children from malignancies.

The same authors (Shanfield *et al.* 1984) have looked in more depth at a group of parents whose adult child died in a hospice from cancer. In this case it might be suggested that parent–child involvement would be relatively high since most parents were actively involved in the terminal care of their child. Shanfield *et al.* found the following factors to be important in shaping parental response two years after the death of their child:

1. the prolonged and debilitating nature of the illness;
2. the sex of the parents and children;
3. aspects of the parent–child relationship.

The prolonged and debilitating nature of the illness was associated with more difficulties experienced by parents after the death of their child. A particularly protracted terminal phase was associated with greater parental difficulties in coming to terms with the loss. This finding is similar to the responses of parents of younger children who have died of cancer, reported by Rando (1983). She suggests that there may be an optimum time during which to anticipate a death, with particularly long terminal illnesses being associated with an increase in parental difficulties related to their bereavement. Whilst in general terms expected deaths are associated with fewer bereavement-related problems than unexpected deaths, it could be the case that a long-expected death may, paradoxically, fuel parental

140

denial. Both of the mothers of adolescent children who died of cancer, who have been previously discussed in this chapter, had children who had survived much longer than had been anticipated. This greater than expected survival time was associated, in the minds of the mothers, with a belief that, if care continued to be given, then the child might not, after all, die. Consequently, neither mother, after a certain period of time, really anticipated what for everyone else was an expected death. Furthermore, both of these mothers became intensely attached to their dying children and this resulted in a depletion in their social support networks prior to the death occurring.

Mothers, more often than fathers, reported feeling that the loss of their child in adulthood was the most painful experience of their lives and, two years after the death, mothers tended to think of their dead child more frequently than did fathers. The loss of a daughter in adulthood was associated with particular problems for mothers, who reported relatively more anger and guilt following the death. Also, mothers whose daughters had died of cancer tended to report having a sense of unfinished business with the deceased child. In terms of aspects of the parent–child relationship intense grief was associated with greater closeness to the child. However, parents who felt closer to their children, despite reporting a relatively intense reaction to the death, also reported relatively less guilt. According to Shanfield et al.:

> relationship between parent and child characterized by negative feelings portends increased psychiatric symptoms during the bereavement period. This last finding is in keeping with observation that the loss of an ambivalent relationship is a forerunner of problems in the bereavement period.
>
> (Shanfield et al. 1984: 295)

Orbach and Eichenbaum (1980) have made some general observations concerning mother–daughter relationships and loss which may contribute towards an understanding of the mother's responses concerning unfinished business in Shanfield et al.'s study. Orbach and Eichenbaum characterise mother–daughter relationships in terms of a push–pull dynamic. From this perspective mothers tend to socialise their sons into achieving independence, 'pushing', and their daughters in a similar way. However, the mother, in using her daughter to meet her own unmet needs for nurturance, also 'pulls' her daughter into a close relationship with her, at the same time as encouraging independence; 'push–pull'. These researchers suggest that many women, in their social role as carers, have unmet needs to be cared for themselves, hence a sense of vague loss. From this perspective, 'business' between mother and daughter is never really 'finished'. Furthermore, the underlying dynamic of the mother–daughter relationship suggested here might predispose a certain degree of ambivalence in the relationship. Both

141

of these factors could account for the findings of Shanfield *et al.* concerning mothers' reactions to the deaths of their daughters.

One feature strongly associated with deaths of adult children from accidents, rather than cancer, which may affect the bereavement process, is a request for organ donation from the dead child. Typically, the adult child will be in the intensive care unit of a hospital following a road traffic accident or a sub-arachnoid haemorrhage. Both causes of death tend to be unexpected and the tendency of parents of younger children to deny the implications of a poor prognosis in intensive care units has already been discussed in this chapter. Requests for organs are typically made following a diagnosis of brain death (Bodenham, Berridge and Park 1989). Whilst the concept of brain death has undoubted medical validity (Pallis 1984), it may have limited social validity for parents who may see a largely (externally) undamaged child who is apparently 'breathing'. It might be particularly important for parents of adult children who have donated organs to see their child's body after death, since this may help them to accept that the death has occurred. Another problem which might be expected to arise in terms of the grieving process is that of searching. Parts of the child may still be perceived to be 'alive' in some way, and the recipients of donated organs may become the objects of the parental search. Little is known about the effect of organ donation on the process of grieving, but it might be anticipated that many people would interpret the donation in the spirit of reparation which has been described as helpful to the bereavement process (Raphael 1984). However, the context in which the death occurs is undoubtedly traumatic, and it seems likely that at least some people will experience complications in connection with their bereavement, irrespective of the sensitivity with which requests for organ donations are undoubtedly made.

Other situations in which parents may lose adult children are those which arise from wars or disasters. The impact of war deaths upon parents has been briefly mentioned in Chapter 2 and is undoubtedly devastating. Levav, in a review of the area, considers the position of bereaved parents in Israel and notes that:

> Israel has suffered a relatively high toll of deaths since its independence, and even prior to the existence of the State. It is, therefore, puzzling to note that very little research has been done on the subject of parental bereavement. This is in contrast with the highly developed system of care and rehabilitation available to them.
>
> (Levav 1982: 31)

However, Levav goes on to suggest that whatever evidence there is would indicate that parental adjustment is poor, with the death of a male son in war causing particular problems for the father. Palgi has noted that the:

Death of a male son may lead to severe feelings of deprivation and premature ageing because in some way the father's future has been cut short. In Jewish religion, the Kaddish prayer recited by a son at the death of the father symbolizes the fulfilment of the father's life and deeds through their perpetuation by his son. Where a son precedes his father in death this sense of continuity is thwarted. In Jewish folklore there is a belief that a soul will not come to rest unless he has a son to say Kaddish after him.

(Palgi 1973: 309)

In my own study (Littlewood 1983), when asked about previous losses, many elderly people reported the loss of sons, during the World War II, as the most painful loss of their lives, and one that they could not, many years after the event, come to terms with. For instance:

A man, in his eighties, felt that he would never fully accept the death of his only son during the war. Immediately after the death he had, as he put it, 'turned to drink', and he believed that he had caused major difficulties for his wife. Following his wife's death, in her eighties, he found himself feeling guilty over the impact that his son's death had upon him, feeling that he'd 'ruined the best years of her life' with his grief.

Many of the older people in my study found that bereavement was related to recalling the losses of various relationships as a result of war and all of them appeared to have been traumatised by their war-time experiences. Clearly, the impact of war deaths is extremely long-lasting and never completely overcome.

Bereavement by disaster seems to intensify the features of grief associated with unexpected violent deaths in general, and, under these circumstances, it would be expected that there would be an increased risk of poor outcome following such bereavements. Proactive support programmes do much to help people bereaved by disaster. In terms of the deaths of adult children, anger over the death would appear to be a particularly common reaction to bereavement. It seems likely that all parents view the deaths of their children as untimely events which have occurred outside the 'natural' order of things, and bereavement by disaster may be a double blow to parents in that disasters are also events which are outside their everyday expectations. Furthermore, following a man-made disaster many people have a target to focus their anger upon. As Hodgkinson (1989) has pointed out:

Following the Zeebrugge disaster, parents who had lost adult children, for whom no compensation was indicated in British law, banded together to form the Herald Families Association. They were enraged that they were symbolically denied recognition that they had been bereaved. Their avowed aim was to see the prosecution of the ferry operator for negligence and the institution of safer ferry standards. It remains to be seen whether this channelling of anger will prove an aid or a block to resolution.

(Hodgkinson 1989: 353-4)

Clearly, the lack of social recognition routinely experienced by the parents of adult children following their child's death (discussed in Chapter 6) was felt particularly keenly by these parents, who obviously and understandably have a great desire for their loss to be seen as legitimate.

THE GRIEF OF MOTHERS AND FATHERS

Nixon and Pearn (1977), Lowman (1979) and DeFrain and Ernst (1978) have all indicated that the majority of information concerning parental reactions to the loss of a child tends to come from mothers rather than fathers. Consequently, care must be taken when generalising from studies concerned with parents. However, some research has actively compared mothers' and fathers' reactions to the death of their child and the general consensus would appear to be that mothers and fathers grieve in different ways. Benfield, Leib and Volman (1978) found that fathers showed significantly lower grief scores than mothers, while Wilson *et al.* (1982) found that fathers showed fewer symptoms of depression than mothers following their child's death. Furthermore, Berg *et al.* (1978) reported that fathers experienced the loss of a child less deeply than mothers, and Helmrath and Steintz (1978), Forrest (1983) and Raphael (1984) have all suggested that fathers have a shorter grief period than mothers following the death of their child.

However, considerable controversy exists about parental grief reactions. Kennel, Slyter and Klaus (1970) found that the fathers in their study tended to deny the fact that they were grieving, despite grieving in fact for as long or longer than their partners. Wilson *et al.* (1982) have found that fathers were more unwilling than mothers to agree to discuss their dead child. Obviously, a disinclination to report aspects of grief could account for some of the apparent differences between maternal and paternal grief.

Dyregrov and Matthiesen (1987), in looking at the reactions (following the death of an infant) of fathers and mothers, found that fathers tended to be more critical of the hospital staff than mothers. Specifically, many fathers felt that they had been overlooked by the hospital staff, who tended to concentrate their supportive efforts on the mothers. However, fathers are also reported to feel an obligation to 'stay strong' and support their partners (Berg *et al.* 1978; Standish 1982). Perhaps this gave the impression that they did not require any help from the hospital staff.

144

Dyregrov and Matthiesen's study indicated that mothers report significantly more anxiety, self-reproach, sadness, intrusive thoughts about the child and disturbance than do fathers. They also found that, in terms of long-term adaptation, mothers experienced lasting emotional and physical problems following their child's death. Mothers also felt that they had recovered less from their loss than fathers. The death of a child continues to have an impact on the child's parents for several years after the death. Rando (1983) has suggested that parental grief may actually worsen over time and women would appear to have more adaptation problems than men. However, the reasons for this are unclear. Some suggestions are as follows:

1. there may be a difference in the nature of the parent–child relationship;
2. men may under-report or fail to acknowledge the patterns of disruption they nevertheless undergo;
3. there may be different reactions to stress and different coping patterns in men and women;
4. the differences may reflect the different social contexts in which men and women find themselves both before and after the death of their child.

In terms of the nature of the relationship between parents and children, it must be said that many of the studies which report differing reactions between mothers and fathers have been conducted concerning the loss of very young infants. It may be the case that the mother feels she has known the child (in physical reality and fantasy) for longer than the father and, consequently, feels more distressed by the loss. Hoekstra-Weebers et al. (1989), in looking at parental reaction to the loss of older children from childhood malignancy, found that if high levels of distress were present they tended to occur in both parents, rather than just the mothers in their sample. Consequently, it might be suggested that grief arising from the deaths of older children is more likely to have a similar impact on both parents.

Given that men tend to feel obliged to 'stay strong' after a death, in particular, and are discouraged from overt displays of sadness, in general, it would seem likely that men would be more disinclined to admit to aspects of the grieving process than women. However, it may be the case that the suppression of emotion is more or less successful. Nevertheless, any direct measurement concerning the impact of the death is likely to be affected. Littlewood et al. (1991a) have addressed this question indirectly by looking at the ways in which fathers and mothers coped with everyday problems and events following the death of their child. However, we found that fathers did, in fact, revert more quickly to normal patterns of coping than did mothers. Our results suggested that not only did fathers suffer less general reduction in coping capabilities than mothers, they also showed a tendency to keep busy and take on additional workloads in order to cope with their loss.

Different coping patterns between men and women have been reported by several researchers in the area and the possibility that coping styles may be gendered has already been discussed in Chapter 4. For example, Mandell, McAnulty and Reece (1980), report that fathers use activity-based coping styles in connection with the loss of a child. Furthermore, Clyman *et al.* (1980) report that the fathers in their study expressed a desire to get on with life when the mothers were still depressed and preoccupied with thoughts of the dead child. These differences in duration and patterns of coping with grief following the death of a child have led Osterweis, Solomon and Green (1984) to suggest that 'synchronicity' may be a problem for parents following the death of their child. Specifically, if fathers move back to more normal patterns of behaviour more quickly than mothers, then this may cause problems for the couple and put considerable strain upon their relationship. Marital tension and separation are not uncommon following a child's death, and different ways of expressing grief might contribute towards relationships failing to be supportive.

Men and women often lead very different kinds of lives and this, too, may affect the different experiences of mothers and fathers following the death of a child. Jurk *et al.* have indicated that 'The involvement of the father at the emotional and practical levels with the child's illness was significantly associated with absence of family dysfunction' (1981: 87).

Obviously, any emotional withdrawal on the part of the father would be likely to put more strain on the mother's emotional resources. Furthermore, if a child is ill it is usually his/her mother who takes the responsibility for caring for the child. In our study (Littlewood, Hoekstra-Weebers and Humphrey (1990)), many of the men interviewed identified the buffering effect of the social support they received from their employment, whilst most of the women had either given up paid employment to care for their child or worked in the home. Furthermore, it tended to be mothers rather than fathers who, during their child's terminal illness, increasingly focused their attention on the dying child. Some women reported being concerned that, at times, this resulted in the neglect of other children. For instance:

> Mother [having just told her son that her daughter 'wasn't going to make it']: 'And I told him, I choose for your sister now. I know you need time, too, but you have the rest of your life . . . I thought, he'll just have to live with it.'

Furthermore, the mothers in this study tended to be sensitive to the needs of the father and actively tried to support their partners. For example:

One mother reported that her first reaction on hearing her son's prognosis was that her son was always more her husband's boy than hers, and she thought only of how terrible the loss would be for her husband. She resolved, at that time, to try and make it [her son's death] up to him [her husband] as best she could.

On reflection, it seems highly unlikely that any two people, whatever their relationship or gender, will react to the same traumatic event in exactly the same way at the same time. However, the overall situation would seem to be one in which many fathers do tend, for whatever reason, to express and recover from their grief, associated with the death of their child, in different ways to mothers. Nevertheless, for most parents the loss of a child results in what Raphael (1984) has called 'shadow grief'. Parents tend to remember their dead child at certain times during their lives because of the developmental milestones the child would have passed if s/he had survived. For example:

I was really upset at John's [her son's friend] wedding. I had to go home early, weddings are supposed to be happy occasions and all I could think about was —— [her dead son]. You see, if he'd been alive he could have been the one getting married. But he wasn't and he never would.

In this sense parents of either sex rarely, if ever, fully come to terms with the death of their child.

This chapter has been concerned with the impact that the circumstances surrounding an untimely death may have upon the grieving process. The next chapter looks in more depth at the ways in which certain kinds of relationships are associated with both complicated and uncomplicated reactions to bereavement

8

THE DEATHS OF PARTNERS AND PARENTS

'The intensity of grief is related to the intensity of involvement, rather than of love.'

Marris (1986)
Loss and Change

INTRODUCTION

As Bowlby (1980) has pointed out, there is a great deal of available evidence concerning adult reactions to the loss of a partner. Also, the general range of experiences associated with grief and the theoretical frameworks which have been forwarded to explain them have already been discussed in Chapters 3 and 4. Consequently, in terms of the loss of partners, this chapter will focus upon particular aspects of relationships between partners which have been associated with either complicated or uncomplicated grief.

Relatively little is known, however, about the impact the death of a parent has upon adult children. Consequently, the second part of this final chapter looks at the range of reactions to this type of loss and documents certain aspects of parent–adult child relationships which may, in some cases, make the loss of a parent in adulthood particularly difficult to adjust to.

THE DEATH OF A PARTNER

The loss of a partner represents a multiple loss, in that loss of confidante, sexual partner and social role are all involved to a greater or lesser extent, depending upon the particular relationship. These personal losses may be accompanied by economic deprivation resulting from the loss of earning-power and/or the necessity of making alternative child-rearing arrangements following the death of a partner. In terms of the global differences associated with particular kinds of reactions to the loss of different kinds of relationships, those who have lost partners are far more likely to experience loneliness than are those who have lost parents or children.

Whilst the experiences associated with grief over the loss of a partner have been discussed in general terms most of the evidence upon which the discussions are based tends to be derived from the experiences of widows. However, Raphael makes the generally accepted point that:

> Patterns of 'normal' bereavement for widows and widowers are essentially the same. The external manifestations, however, may differ because of sex role differences in behaviour. The widow may more readily express her feelings openly and elicit care – her tears and sorrow are easily accepted as womanly. The widower may be expected to control his distress – tears and need are seen as unmanly in many Western societies.
>
> (Raphael 1984: 190)

What follows is an example in which a widow, Mrs O, discusses her reaction to a relatively common loss in middle age, i.e. the unexpected loss of a partner from a heart attack.

> Mrs O's husband died nine months before she was interviewed, and he was cremated following his unexpected and premature death from a heart attack. At the time of his death, he was in hospital recovering from a previous heart attack. The fatal attack occurred unexpectedly following an apparently good recovery.
>
> After her husband's death, Mrs O saw a great deal of her relatives and friends and went out socially more often than she would have done under more ordinary circumstances. However, she lost weight, suffered from great difficulty with sleeping and was being treated for depression by her GP. This treatment had started three months after the death of her husband.

Informal support

At the time of her bereavement both Mrs O's parents were dead and she had not had any contact with her only sister following their father's death. Her main source of support was her only daughter, who was married with a young child. Her daughter lived locally, but Mrs O was less than positive about the support she received from her. Mrs O believed her daughter to be trying to ignore her father's death, and to be acting as if her father had never existed. However, Mrs O said that her daughter visited often and had been 'extremely close' to her father prior to his death. Mrs O had a neighbour who called to chat to her and was planning to join a local club for single people. She particularly wanted to meet some widows and widowers whom she assumed would be supportive of her. Mrs O felt that her employers and workmates had been extremely unhelpful following her husband's death. She felt that she had to return to work quickly because of financial insecurity but was tearful, depressed, and her work was full of errors. Apparently her employer had told her that 'he would have to get someone else' if she didn't improve. This had contributed towards Mrs O's feelings of insecurity because she was of the belief that she would be unable to get another job with bad references. Nevertheless, Mrs O wanted to leave her employment, but didn't feel well enough to do so.

Professional help

Mrs O was unhappy with the GP who first treated her husband for chest pains. She was very worried by her husband's pain because a friend's husband had recently died of a heart attack. However, Mr O's pain was diagnosed as stress and he was advised to take time off work and rest. Mrs O's husband continued to have pain and another GP was called who diagnosed a heart attack, and Mr O was immediately admitted to hospital. Mrs O found the hospital staff to be very helpful, despite most of the communication she received being concerned with her husband's recovery. Mrs O was completely unprepared for her husband's death and wondered if the hospital staff had lied to her. However, she discounted this possibility. 'No-one would be so cruel – would they?' Mrs O also wonders if her husband would have survived had he been in the intensive care unit when he had his fatal heart attack, and resented a request made by the hospital for a post-mortem. She refused the request.

Mr O had progressed well following his first heart attack and Mr and Mrs O were planning a holiday at the time of his death. Mrs O saw her husband the night before he died and she remembered him as being cheerful and looking forward to his return home. However, she received a telephone call the next morning asking her to go to the hospital immediately. Mrs O went to the hospital with her daughter, where they were told of Mr O's death by a ward sister and a doctor, in the ward sister's office. Mrs O remembered the ward sister saying what a pleasant man her husband had been and it was only then that she began to realise that her husband had died. She remembered feeling very shocked but wishing to see her husband's body. She felt that seeing her husband's body was helpful, although upsetting. But she deeply regretted not being with him when he died, and, consequently, felt she had not said 'goodbye properly'. She could remember little about the period of time between the death and the cremation and nothing of the cremation service itself.

Mrs O constantly reviewed the events surrounding her husband's death. She described this as 'self-torture', but could not stop herself. She was obsessed with the idea that her husband knew he was going to die and was particularly pained by the thought that her husband had suffered and/or was frightened before he died.

Mrs O felt very insecure and vulnerable and reported losing all confidence in her ability to do anything. She described her husband as 'a companion and a friend' and the couple, according to Mrs O, did everything and talked about everything together. Mrs O described herself as being lonely, but not seeing any real point in going anywhere or talking to anyone. She remained convinced that she was coping badly with her loss and was equally convinced that things would not improve. She was afraid that her memory and powers of concentration had been permanently affected by her bereavement because she experienced great difficulty in concentrating on anything for any length of time.

Mrs O described her feelings in terms of 'anguish' and found it difficult to accept that her husband had died and that she 'would never see him again'. She found memories of her husband very painful and was often tearful. Mrs O believed that 'nobody cared' about her. At the time of the interview Mrs O had been treated for six months for 'depression'. She found her GP to be quite sympathetic, but doubted that the treatment would work.

She had particular difficulty remembering what her husband actually looked like and was afraid that she would never remember him accurately again. Furthermore, she bitterly regretted all the arguments they had together over the years, and felt extremely guilty because she 'should have done more' for her husband. Overall, she felt vulnerable and expressed the opinion that she 'couldn't trust' anyone. In recalling her reaction to previous bereavements Mrs O was of the opinion that she had reacted in a somewhat similar way to her mother's death. However, she felt that she had been less distressed over the death of her father. Her father's death was her second experience of parental bereavement and Mrs O felt that guilt was one of the most important similarities between her feelings about the deaths of her mother and her husband. She didn't recall feeling any guilt in connection with her father's death.

Mrs O's experiences reflect the pain associated with the grieving process as well as the more general feelings concerning ontological insecurity which frequently follow a death. Experiences of feelings of helplessness, isolation and a lack of capacity to initiate meaningful interactions with others, together with a lack of a basic feeling of trust in the world, are all strongly associated with grief following the death of a partner.

Marris (1986) suggested that the degree of involvement with a particular relationship is associated with the intensity of felt grief following its loss. Possibly, relationships which tend to be exclusive, i.e. those in which both partners 'do everything together' and are the only mutual source of self-esteem for each other, may be particularly difficult to come to terms with. However, as Marris has also indicated, these relationships tend to be associated with the more traditional patterns of interaction between men and women. Furthermore, it is often the woman's sense of identity which is more closely tied, in exclusive terms, into the relationship than it is the man's. It is perhaps, in these instances, unsurprising that researchers (Raphael 1984; Littlewood 1983; Glick *et al.* 1974) have noted a greater tendency amongst widows to express a general sense of irritability and hostility following the death of their partners. It is also, perhaps, understandable that people who put 'everything' into a relationship may be more likely than people who have other sources of social esteem and value to interpret their bereavement in terms of 'abandonment' and to feel angry about their loss.

In contrast to Mrs O's case, we can now turn to the reactions of Mrs F, who had also lost her partner, through a heart attack, in middle age. Mrs F's situation was similar to Mrs O's, apart from Mrs F's greater general sense of irritation and futility following the loss of an extremely significant relationship. Unfortunately, a sense of hostility following a death may lead to deterioration in informal support networks if the feelings of irritation are diffuse and long-lasting.

Mrs F's husband died thirteen months before she was interviewed and he was cremated following his unexpected death at home from a heart attack. Mr F had already had one heart attack and recovered from it.

Following her husband's death, she saw less of her relatives, reported having few friends and lost weight. Mrs F had considerable difficulty with sleeping and felt that she 'doesn't really sleep through the night at all'. She felt 'weak and tired all of the time' and was of the belief that she 'had lost interest in everything'.

Informal support

Mrs F had two sisters and one brother living in the area, but only saw one sister occasionally following the death of her husband. Mrs F felt bitter that her sister didn't want to talk about Mr F's death. Mr F's relatives were also criticised for lack of support. Mrs F felt that they turned up for the funeral and then simply abandoned her afterwards. Mr and Mrs F had three children, two of whom were the target of Mrs F's criticism. The remaining child, a teenage daughter, who was still living with her parents at the time of the

152

time of the death, was seen to be helpful in terms of practical support.

Mrs F was also of the belief that her neighbours had made many offers of help immediately following her husband's death, but had 'let me down'. Mrs F particularly resented her husband's family's attitude towards her and felt them to be critical of her. 'They don't offer to help, they just tell me what to do, they tell me to get on with cleaning the house and to pull myself together, they say you just have to get on with life and forget about it.'

Professional help

Mrs F was also critical of the help from professional sources she received following her husband's death. She felt she had been told very abruptly of her husband's death, and that her GP was hiding the severity of her own illness from her. Shortly after her husband's death she said she'd developed 'angina pectoris', and her GP had told her eldest daughter, although not her, that she'd already had one slight heart attack. Mrs F said she was afraid to question her GP further about her health. However, she did report deriving some comfort from the knowledge that her husband had known the funeral director and so 'strangers wouldn't be handling his body'.

Mr F had been told four years prior to his death that he was suffering from angina pectoris and diabetes. The latter was hereditary. For three years his health remained relatively stable and then he had a slight heart attack. However, with rest he recovered from this. On the day of his death he returned home from work early with chest pains which rapidly worsened. Mrs F sent for a doctor, who arrived quickly and immediately summoned an ambulance. Mrs F remembered the ambulancemen giving Mr F heart massage, but did not realise that he was dead. Mrs F went to the hospital with her husband in the ambulance and remembers feeling sure that he would be resuscitated. She was convinced that he would survive and remembers shouting 'No, no, no, it can't be true' when she was told of his death.

Mrs F was critical of the hospital staff in general. She felt that they should have tried harder to save her husband's life, and that they should have broken the news of his death to her more gently. She realised, retrospectively, that her husband had probably died at home, but at the time 'it didn't sink in'. A friend was called to take Mrs F back home and she remembered sitting up all night with her daughters and sister-in-law.

Mrs F believes that she has never recovered from the shock of the death and will never do so. She described her relationship with her husband as 'extremely close'. Apart from shopping they 'did everything together'. They consulted with each other over absolutely everything, shared all the decisions and 'he taught me all of his ways and I followed them'.

Mrs F felt herself to be in a daze following the death and gave up work for a number of months. She has little memory of the funeral or the arrangements she made, but remembers her youngest daughter's distress when she saw her father's body. Mrs F recalled being puzzled by her husband's appearance because, as she found herself repeatedly saying at the time, 'he looked very much like his father, very, very different from how I remembered him'. Mrs F remembered feeling bemused at her husband's funeral service and 'not really knowing who to turn to'.

Shortly after her husband's death Mrs F began to develop the same symptoms as her husband, and, since she is of the belief that she may have already had one heart attack, is very worried that her next attack might be the last, as her husband only survived one.

Mrs F could not sleep because she constantly thought of her husband and, consequently, only dozed for short periods of time. Shortly after his death she had a dream in which he told her he was going for a short walk and left but did not return. She often sensed her husband was in the room with her, although she strongly believed that the dead do not 'reappear'. Despite her heart condition Mrs F was a heavy smoker (as her husband had been). She had been advised to give up smoking cigarettes but claimed not to be concerned about the risk she may be taking because, if she died, she believed she would be reunited with her husband. Mrs F spent a lot of time cuddling her daughter and talking about their loss in the months following the death, and continues to feel a strong desire for physical contact and affection. She feels that it is impossible to recover from the loss of a relationship as close as the one she enjoyed with her husband. She believed that marriage 'was forever' and that couples should never, under any circumstances, part. She recalled that her wedding ring, which had always been loose prior to her husband's death, had become impossible to remove after it.

Mrs F felt that all of her interest in life had died with her husband. She felt rejected by her relatives, had no close friends and felt disinclined to make any. She said she did not wish to go anywhere on her own because she had always gone places with her husband and did not wish to do anything without him.

Glick *et al.* (1974) have considered the differences and similarities of the experiences of grief amongst widows and widowers and, despite concluding that the overall differences were small, identified the following tendencies:

1. Widowers tended to be more likely to attempt to control the expression of emotion following the death of their partner.
2. Widowers were more likely to report a sense of sexual deprivation following the loss of their partners and, when compared to widows, their thoughts turned more quickly towards remarriage.

Also, slightly more widowers than widows reported 'feeling themselves again' immediately following the first year of bereavement in this study. The tendency of the fathers of children who have died to regain their normal patterns of behaviour more quickly than mothers has been noted in the previous chapter.

That men in Western societies try to control the overt expression of emotion is perhaps an unsurprising finding. Broverman *et al.* (1972) have suggested that sex-determined role expectations for men tend to emphasise the importance of appearing competent, independent, under control and unemotional. Given such expectations it would seem reasonable to suggest that the expressions associated with grief might be suppressed in men.

However, the age of the man might affect his tendency to conform or otherwise to these role expectations. Glick *et al.* were looking at men who were under 45 years of age at the time of their bereavement, and it may well be the case that differences between men's and women's responses to the loss of a partner lessen with advancing age. For example, in my own study (Littlewood 1983), there would appear to be very little difference in the reactions of very elderly men and women, i.e. 75 years or over, concerning the expression of emotion following the loss of their partner. Furthermore, many elderly men identified a tendency in themselves, as younger men, to try, sometimes successfully, to repress emotion following an experience of bereavement. For example:

A retired headmaster, in his late sixties, looked back over his life and recalled his reaction, as a young man in his early thirties, to the loss of his wife. He described his reaction as being one in which he 'tried to pretend as if nothing had happened'. He was of the opinion that 'at one level' the pretence had worked since he'd managed to keep himself busy and avoid thoughts of his wife. At 'another level', however, he was uncertain of his strategy. He recalled that his mother-in-law 'for no reason at all' lost her temper with him a few months after his wife had died and had said to him 'Don't you *know* your wife's dead. Don't you understand anything?' He thought that he must have acknowledged the loss 'at one level or another' because he burst into a fit of uncontrollable sobbing following his mother-in-law's comments. Retrospectively, this man felt that advancing age had been associated, at least for him, with a greater understanding of 'the more emotional aspects of life'.

Given these observations, it might be suggested that young men, rather than older men and women, might be particularly at risk from a complicated reaction to a partner's death if they successfully suppress emotion.

What follow are the recollections of Mr N, concerning the death of his wife (brain haemorrhage) in middle age.

It is possible that Mr N's reaction to his wife's death was complicated by the fact that his mother had died when he was 8 years old. His father had died in Mr N's infancy and he had no memory of him. Mr N had been brought up by an aunt and he left home to join the Army at the earliest opportunity. It was whilst he was serving in the Army that he met, and later married, his wife.

Mr N's wife died four years before he was interviewed, and she was cremated following her unexpected death at home. Following his wife's death, he saw more of his relatives, particularly his adult children, and considerably less of his friends (due to taking time off work to look after the couple's younger children). Mr N's weight remained constant after his bereavement, but he continued to have difficulty sleeping and felt that his mental health was considerably worsened, 'and it wasn't so good before', following his wife's death. He said he felt 'frightened of committing myself again' and was of the belief that 'it's better not to care about anything these days'.

Informal support

Mr N had four children, two adult and two dependents, at the time of his wife's death. His wife had a sister with whom the couple maintained occasional contact, but apart from these relatives, Mr and Mrs N had no other family. Mr N felt that his greatest source of support came from his eldest daughter, who made the funeral arrangements and took the youngest child to live with her following Mrs N's death. Mrs N's sister took care of Mr N's second youngest child for a short period of time but, because of behavioural difficulties, returned the child (a son) to his father, shortly after the death. Mr N didn't know his neighbours well, 'I worked long hours', and had limited contact with his workmates following his wife's death because he took time off to care for his children.

Professional help

Mr N had no recollection of help from professional sources following the death of his wife. He felt the ambulancemen had done 'everything possible' to try and resuscitate his wife, but was of the belief that she was dead before they arrived. His eldest daughter made 'all of the arrangements', and he had no contact with any other source of professional assistance at the time of, or following, his wife's death.

Mrs N had apparently been in good health and her death was completely unexpected. Mr N recalls returning from work one day to find his wife saying that she felt 'faint'. She fell to the floor and Mr N took her in his arms and carried her to the couch. He telephoned for an ambulance and alerted his elder son and daughter. However, 'when I picked her up I knew she was dead'. Mr N can recall little of what followed his wife's death. Apparently, his daughter went to the hospital leaving Mr N caring for the younger children at home. However, Mr N 'wandered off' and he was found the following morning, by his eldest daughter, sitting by a disused railway line. He told his daughter that he 'had to get away'.

Mr N can remember little or nothing about his reaction to his wife's death. He apparently accepted her death almost immediately after its occurrence, but had no clear memory of his reactions after that point in time. The only feeling he remembered was a desire to 'get on with it and get back to work'. 'I didn't want to be stuck at home looking after the kids all day.' Nevertheless, Mr N can still 'see' clearly the events surrounding his wife's death and is still plagued by nightmares in which he dreams that his wife is alive and trying to attack him with a kitchen knife she is intent upon using as a weapon.

Mr N was of the opinion that his past experiences of death, particularly two accidental deaths he had witnessed during his Army service, had left him relatively 'immune' to the impact of bereavement. He said it was 'just one of those things' that 'had to be lived with'. Mr N felt that he'd recovered quite quickly from his wife's death because his eldest daughter had taken the responsibility for his youngest child and 'did the shopping and the cleaning for me'. Mr N said that 'one or two' women had tried to offer him practical and emotional support following the death of his wife, but he 'preferred to be on my own'. 'I couldn't be bothered with that sort of thing any more.' However, Mr N was also of the opinion that bereavements were accumulative in their effects upon people and despite, on the one hand, reporting immunity, on the other, he reported that his wife's death was 'the last straw'. 'That one [i.e. his wife's death] really finished me off.' Overall, Mr N was of the opinion that he'd 'coped quite well under the circumstances'.

Raphael (1984) has pointed out the difficulties associated with the expression of sexuality amongst people who have been bereaved. In general terms, it is still more socially acceptable for men to openly acknowledge having sexual desires than it is for women. Furthermore, there are many stereotypes of 'merry' or 'wise' widows that women who have been recently bereaved may wish to avoid. In general terms the death of a partner would appear to either heighten sexual desire or inhibit it, and both situations may prove problematic for people who have been bereaved. It may be particularly difficult for some women to appreciate the legitimacy of their need for sexual contact following the death of their partner. Alternatively some of the widows in my own study (Littlewood 1983) reported experiences of unwanted sexual advances or innuendoes as being particularly upsetting occurrences following the death of their partner. Specifically:

What I can't get over is that he was ——'s best friend. It started two nights after —— died. He came round and left some money with my daughter. I was lying down at the time and she didn't want to disturb me. Anyway, he started waiting for me when I'd finished work. It was funny, he didn't do anything, he just kept asking me if I'd like to go out for a drink some time . . ., but I was terrified of him and told him to go away and leave me alone.

I've been dead from the neck down ever since it [her husband's death] happened. It didn't take his brother that way though. He was round fairly sharpish saying, 'if ever you're lonely', and the rest of it. I showed him the door and I haven't spoken to him since.

In this particular study, none of the men who were interviewed described having these kinds of experiences. Overall, it must be said that the situation remains unclear and, given the potential for two diametrically opposed sexual responses to occur following a bereavement, the potential for misunderstanding between people would appear to be almost limitless.

In terms of other aspects of relationships between partners which might be associated with complications arising from the process of bereavement, ambivalence would appear, as ever, to be inevitably problematic. Also, the work of Horowitz et al. (1980) might be taken to suggest that the death of a partner may leave people whose earlier relationships have been problematic without the protection of a relationship which guards against the activation of negative self-images.

It might be the case that the observations of Pincus (1976) concerning relationships in which the dead partner was seen to be the source of all good in the relationship may be examples of what Horowitz et al. (1980) would presume to be a defence against a previously generated self-image in which the self was seen as weak and helpless. Having lost their good, strong supportive other, the reaction to the death would appear to be, initially, frighteningly sad and, latterly, characterised by intense depression. For example:

> I can't really explain it . . . it's just that all the lights went out when he died and whoever I thought I was got lost in the darkness. I couldn't honestly say that I think things will get better, because they won't, everything's faded to grey somehow and I haven't really got anything to look forward to any more.

In contrast, relationships in which the dead partner was seen to be the source of all conflict in the relationship might be taken to be examples of defences against an image of the self which is seen to be defective or disgusting. In this instance the defence might to be locate all that was believed to be defective in the other person, thereby relieving the self of the burden. It may be that it is these kinds of relationships which result in the surviving partner oscillating between feelings of euphoria and self-sufficiency, and despair and self-hatred. This situation would appear to be somewhat similar, albeit in an exaggerated form, to Klein's (1948) observations concerning a tendency amongst people who have been bereaved to see the world in terms of 'all bad' or 'all good', for a certain period of time. Unfortunately, other defences against such latent self-images are possible, for example, 'I could just see it in him, that's all. He was just the same as his father and he got more like him as the days went on', said by a widow in connection with her belief that her young son's 'bad' behaviour was a direct result of him taking on his father's characteristics – characteristics she didn't like, following his father's death.

Obviously, replacing a relationship with one which is essentially similar to the one which has been lost may be a common pattern amongst people who have been bereaved. The outcome of such a strategy would probably depend upon the appropriateness of the choice of replacement, in the case of those who had lost partners, and the quality of the lost relationship. In adult to adult relationships the recipient of a need for a particular kind of relationship has some degree of choice in the matter. However, in the instance of 'replacement' children, the rights and choices of the child may be severely limited.

THE DEATH OF A PARENT IN ADULTHOOD

This type of loss is one commonly experienced in adult life. Pearlin and Lieberman (1979) found that 5 per cent of the population of the United States of America had experienced the death of a parent in the year of their study. However, despite the relative frequency of parental deaths, little research has been conducted regarding the impact of these deaths upon adult children. There would appear to be a tendency in Western societies to view the loss of parents in adulthood as 'timely' and, therefore, relatively unproblematic. However, several studies have indicated that this may not be the case (Anderson 1949; Bunch 1971; Birtchnell 1975). All of these studies suggest that for some people:

1. a higher tendency towards thoughts of suicide;
2. increased rates of attempted suicide;
3. higher rates of clinical depression

follow the experience of the death of a parent in adult life.

It has also been suggested that the death of a mother may be much harder to adjust to than the death of a father. One reason for this may be that the mother's role as a nurturing caretaker continues with respect to her children into their adult life. Consequently, many adults rely on continuing to receive their mother's unconditional approval which may act as a buffer against the impact of various life events. Also, given current patterns of mortality it is far more likely that a father's death will precede a mother's death. Therefore, reactions to maternal bereavement may involve the adult's realisation that they have lost 'parents'. Furthermore, the death of the mother under these circumstances might reactivate feelings of grief associated with the death of the father as well as death anxiety resulting from feelings concerning being 'the next in line'.

Sanders (1979–80), in comparing different types of loss on the Grief Experience Inventory (GEI), found that the loss of a parent in adulthood tended to be associated with the least levels of disruption when compared to the loss of a partner or the loss of a child. However, comparing Sanders's results on specific scales, it must be said that adults who had lost parents scored higher on both the 'death anxiety' scale and the 'loss of control' scale when compared to adults who had lost partners.

In terms of death anxiety, a possible reason for the difference may be that the deaths of parents are frequently an adult's first experience of loss and thus a reminder of mortality in general. Also, the loss of a sole surviving parent has been associated with the adult child beginning to feel that they are now members of their family's 'oldest' generation.

In terms of loss of control it seems likely that, in some ways, loss of control may be associated with an appeal for comfort. Most adults who had lost parents presumably had someone to whom they could turn to for comfort. While, for those who had lost partners, the loss of the person to whom one habitually turns for support might inhibit or delay the loss of control. Also, those who had lost partners in this study were scoring relatively highly on the 'denial' scale, and denial of the event may have limited the extent to which those who had lost partners felt a need to 'lose control'.

Furthermore, Owen *et al.* (1982–3), in looking at the impact of parental death upon middle-aged people, found the absence of grief to be striking amongst this group. Kalish has suggested that this may be because:

As we enter our adult years we find that our parents are growing older, when we are middle-aged our parents are elderly. As this occurs, most of us become concerned about our parents' health and ability to resist disease. When one parent dies, we become deeply concerned about the other parent. How we respond to these concerns are a function of many factors, including the history of our relationship with our parents, but many middle-aged children begin to anticipate the dying processes and deaths of their parents.

(Kalish 1985: 245)

Moss and Moss (1983–4) have called this process one of anticipatory orphanhood, and Pincus (1976) has pointed out that the death of a parent in adulthood often results in considerable psychological growth among those so bereaved. Specifically:

In looking at the responses of sons and daughters to the loss of a parent however, I could observe none of this need for regression, rather the opposite: there was a need for self-assertion, for taking the dead parent's place both in relation to the surviving parent and the family and in relation to the lost parent's position, his work, his creativity. Therefore, it seems that the loss of a spouse, a sexual partner, raises the need to regress, while the loss of a parent raises the need to progress . . .

(Pincus 1976: 210)

However, the death of a parent can have many meanings for an adult child and not all of them may be unproblematic. In my own study (Littlewood 1983) the majority of the people interviewed had lost parents in adulthood and at least 10 per cent of these people were, in terms of the observations concerning complicated grief referred to in Chapter 3, experiencing relatively severe complications to the grieving process. Furthermore, the majority of these adults experienced the loss of their parent as painful and consequently grieved the loss. Although psychological growth undoubtedly occurred for many people, it was not achieved without a considerable amount of psychological pain.

In terms of the difficulties associated with the loss of a mother or father it would seem, from my study, that both of the previously discussed explanations which have been put forward are partly correct. However, most people spontaneously identified, if they had lost both parents, a preferred parent, and it must be said that this was by no means invariably their mother.

161

However mothers did seem to occupy an important role in the lives of a considerable number of adult daughters. Many of the women in my study associated persistent sadness following a mother's death with their perceptions of their mothers as having experienced 'a hard life'. Many women felt that they had tried to 'make it up to' their mothers and felt anguish over her death. For example.

A woman in her late seventies expressed a pervasive sense of sadness concerning the death of her mother, then in her nineties, two years previously. This woman's mother had spent most of her life caring for her invalid husband and children and had experienced considerable hardship due to her husband's disability (following active service in World War II). This woman felt that following her father's death (ten years before her mother's) her mother had 'had the best, the only good times in her life'. This woman felt very sad that her mother had experienced so little enjoyment and was sorry that she hadn't lived longer.

More commonly, daughters tended to describe poverty and a poor relationship with their husbands as the key factors in their mother's lives, which had to be compensated for. For example:

My dad was always horrible to Mum. I can remember the fights. She never had anything nice when he was alive – he wouldn't let her. When he died I thought she'd get some peace and I could look after her a bit, but she was dead inside six months herself.

It must be said that relatively few sons made similar observations in connection with their mothers' deaths. However, this was possibly because these women tended to compare their own, relatively privileged positions directly with their mothers', and, to a certain degree, felt slightly guilty over what they saw as their mothers' deprivation. It may also be the case that these women's mothers had fostered particularly close relationships with their daughters due to the unsatisfactory nature of their relationships with their partners.

In terms of adult children's difficulties following a parent's death the following situations were the ones which appeared to have the potential for complicating the process of bereavement:

1. relationships in which the adult child feels ambivalent about and/or identifies strongly with the dead parent (associated with subjective feelings of depression);
2. relationships in which the dead parent was seen to represent some kind of protection against a hostile surviving parent (associated with an apparent inability to complete the process of grieving);
3. relationships in which the adult child cared for the dead parent on a day

to day basis (associated with a tendency towards guilt, which may be very marked, depending upon the circumstances).

Ambivalence and identification with the dead parent

Pincus (1976), in discussing her findings in connection with the loss of a parent in adulthood, has described identification with the dead parent during the parent's life as being a potential source of problems for adult sons and daughters following the death of the parent. In her study she cites the example of daughters who identified with their fathers, consequently feeling that their assumption of masculine roles may have caused the father's death.

However, both Raphael (1984) and Rowe (1988) have focused upon identification occurring after loss or death. The tendency to identify and 'take inside oneself' the lost object was believed by Freud (1917) to be the major pathway to the resolution of grief. However, as Bowlby (1980) observed, identification in this sense is probably only one way amongst many ways towards the resolution of a loss. A major problem which has been associated with the process of identification is that of identifying with a dead person with whom one had an ambivalent relationship. Freud was of the opinion that, in such cases, depression would be the likely result as the hostility towards the dead person was turned inwards towards the self.

In my own study (Littlewood 1983) three sons, all in their thirties at the time of the deaths of their fathers, related experiences following the death which seemed indicative of problems associated with ambivalence and/or identification.

The first two sons openly acknowledged their difficulties in terms of their relationship with their fathers. One father had died following a short illness whilst the other had died unexpectedly of a heart attack. Both sons felt that they had not been affected by the death particularly, but both experienced relatively severe episodes of depression some time following the death. One man commented, in connection with his depression that 'I don't know what's the matter with me but I don't like myself any more.' He described in great detail how his father was a petty individual who had various irritating little habits, some of which, to his horror, he found himself taking up after the father died. The final son was a coal miner in his late thirties whose father, also a coal miner, died in his early sixties from lung cancer. Mr C's experiences are particularly interesting.

Mr C was married with three teenage children when his father died, three years before the relevant interview took place. Mr C had no religious beliefs and attended his father's cremation wearing a black tie which he wore for the day of the cremation only. Mr C's father died in his own home from lung cancer after a short illness.

Mr C knew his father was terminally ill. He was not present at his father's death and did not see his father's body after the death had occurred. Mr C's sister and brother-in-law cared for his father during the terminal illness, and both of these people offered condolences to Mr C. Mr C did not tell his neighbours about his father's illness and death, and at the time of the death was awaiting admission to hospital for a routine operation. Consequently he was absent from work. Following his father's death Mr C lost a great deal of weight and maintained some of this weight loss by choice. Mr C's sleep was badly disturbed following his father's death, for just under one year. He reported having difficulty in getting to sleep at nights, and was disinclined to get up in the mornings. He often awoke in the middle of the night perspiring and 'feeling panicky'. He felt his health worsened and he became increasingly withdrawn. 'I couldn't be bothered to talk to anyone.' Also, he suffered severe chest pains which started almost immediately after the death of his father. For some time after his father's death Mr C believed that he too had lung cancer. Despite favourable X-ray results these pains persisted for many months. Mr C's eldest son attended the cremation, but his youngest two sons did not. Mr C said that he had not discussed their grandfather's illness or death with them but that his wife 'might have mentioned it'.

Informal support

Mr C's sister and brother-in-law were cited as being extremely supportive, and helped with terminal care which involved staying overnight with Mr C's father in his home. Mr C's brother-in-law made all of the arrangements associated with the cremation, and the disposal of Mr C's father's possessions and home. Mr C's wife tried to be understanding but apart from these people very few others knew of the death because Mr C felt he could not discuss or mention the subject to anyone, including his wife, with whom 'I could usually talk about *anything* to'. Moreover, he found his wife to be extremely supportive, because she didn't question his social withdrawal and his lack of interest in communication. Four months following the bereavement Mr C returned to work and discussed his feelings with 'one or two really *close* friends – one had lost his father a year or so before'. He found discussing the matter with these friends to be extremely helpful to him.

Professional help

The only professionals Mr C had any contact with were the hospital staff whilst his father was in hospital, and his own and his father's

GP. Mr C's father's lung cancer was discovered on a routine X-ray following a mining accident which resulted in chest injuries. The cancer was inoperable and Mr C's father underwent radiotherapy and died seven months after the diagnosis of his cancer. Mr C was told by a hospital doctor of his father's condition after his father had asked him to make enquiries on his behalf. Mr C's father was being asked to undergo various tests and did not know what they were for. Since he was afraid to ask himself he asked his son to find out.

Mr C found the doctor at the hospital to be unhelpful. 'He said, "You're not seriously telling me you don't know what's the matter with your father".' Mr C said he did not know and was extremely shocked when he was told 'well, it's lung cancer, we're referring him for radiotherapy treatment at —— hospital'. Mr C didn't feel able to ask any more questions, and felt he couldn't tell his father what he'd been told. Consequently, he told his father that his accident may have damaged his lungs and that's what the tests were for.

Mr C found his father's GP 'more concerned and helpful'. This GP explained to Mr C that his father's illness was almost certainly terminal. He also explained, in great detail, about radiotherapy and told Mr C that most people with lung cancer tended not to live for much more than six months following their diagnosis. It was only after this interview that Mr C realised fully that his father was dying. Mr C and his father's GP decided that it would be better if Mr C's father did not know of his terminal prognosis.

Mr C consulted his own GP twice following his father's death. Mr C explained his situation and his fears to his GP who sent him for an X-ray which was 'clear'. However, Mr C returned to his GP as he still suffered from chest pains, and was prescribed 'something to calm me down. He told me not to worry, that it was something which would pass.' Mr C was extremely concerned and felt, at the time, that his GP was 'dodging the question' but on the whole, he found his GP to be helpful and the pains did, in fact, 'pass'.

Mr C was not present at his father's death and was informed over the telephone by his sister. Mr C avoided his father during the last weeks of his terminal illness because he found his father's deterioration too distressing to witness. He said he wished to remember his father 'when he was fit and well – like he always was'. Mr C recalled feeling relieved that he'd successfully avoided his father's last few weeks of life.

Mr C was shocked and numb when he heard the news of his father's death, and a few days afterwards started experiencing chest pains. He recalled being extremely withdrawn for about nine months after the death. During this time Mr C dwelt on happy times he'd spent with his father and recalled no sadness associated with any of his memories.

He felt that he'd always had a lot in common with his father and that they were 'very close'. Although Mr C was of the opinion that his mother's death had brought him closer to his father, he could remember nothing about his own or his father's reaction to her death. During the first year after his father's death Mr C spent a great deal of time alone and expressed a preference for 'sitting in the dark'. Mr C described himself as losing his appetite for everything during this period of time – he became extremely apathetic and 'couldn't be bothered with anything'. Mr C's mother had died eight years before his father. The death was completely unexpected – she died at home of a heart attack. Mr C said he didn't feel 'too bad' about his mother's death, and felt that the death had brought him closer to his father, as they saw much more of each other afterwards. Mr C never discussed the death of his mother with his father and assumed that his father had 'taken it quite well'.

He felt that he could discuss his father's death more openly after the first year of his loss, and identified the earlier discussions he had with his workmates as being particularly helpful in this respect. Overall, he expressed the opinion that he didn't think his father's death had affected him in any long-term way, and three years after the death rarely thought about it any more.

Mr C's experiences were relatively unusual in that he could recall no sadness at all following the death – merely a desire to review 'good memories'. Whilst any interpretation of this person's reaction to bereavement would no doubt depend upon the interpreter's own theoretical orientation, Mr C was of the opinion that he had coped well with the death.

Fear of the surviving parent

Some people described a situation in which they appeared to be stuck in some way in the initial experiences of grief, and unable to move on and adapt to a parent's death. For example:

One man in his mid-twenties upon hearing of the death of his father in a road accident immediately left home and travelled abroad for two years in an attempt to avoid his mother, with whom, four years after the death, he still kept in regular contact by telephone. He felt that his mother had always been extremely hostile towards him since his childhood but he still maintained the contact with her nevertheless. He frequently suffered nightmares about his father's death in which he was at the scene of the crash and was suddenly gripped by an overwhelming fear that 'something terrible was going to happen, that she [his mother] was really going to get me for this.'

166

Another woman in her thirties, Mrs S, reported a good relationship with her father who had died suddenly of a heart attack, but an extremely difficult relationship with her mother, ever since adolescence. Her mother, she felt, had always strongly disapproved of her and had 'never forgiven me for marrying —— [her husband]'. Following her father's death, this woman's mother became extremely demanding and overtly hostile. She responded with considerable anxiety, frantically tried to avoid her mother, and stopped answering the telephone. Eventually, she took the telephone off the hook when her husband was out, because she could not bear to talk to her mother when she was alone. This woman was in the process of being referred for psychiatric help ten months after the death of her father. She had developed an eating disorder shortly after her father's death, and had become obsessed with the idea that she was 'spinning out of control'. Nevertheless, despite her panic-stricken attempts to avoid her mother on some occasions, she remained in regular contact with her, despite the fact of her obvious fear of her.

Another woman in her mid-thirties described a similar situation, although in this instance there was considerably more sadness and guilt expressed over the death of her father. Mrs T was in her mid-thirties when her father died unexpectedly from a heart attack.

Mrs T was married with two stepchildren when her father died, four years before she was interviewed. Mrs T described herself as a Roman Catholic by marriage, and attended her father's Church of England funeral wearing black clothes, which she wore for the day of the funeral only. Mrs T's father died in hospital after a short illness, and Mrs T was not expecting the death. She was not present at the death, and did not see her father's body prior to burial.

Mrs T's husband offered her condolences, but few other people knew of her bereavement. Mrs T socialised much less often following the death, and consequently, saw less of her relatives and friends than she would have done under more normal circumstances. She lost a considerable amount of weight after the death, and persistently and continuously suffered from sleep disturbances. She suffered from recurrent nightmares but did not wish to discuss them in any detail. For about a year after the death Mrs T felt that her physical health had suffered considerably. Although there was nothing specifically wrong with her, she simply felt 'just run down, tired, and depressed'.

Informal support

Mrs T's husband was cited as being extremely supportive and comforting following her father's death. Mrs T said that he'd been extremely fond of his mother, who'd died some years previously, and understood how she felt. Mrs T believed that her husband felt obliged to be particularly helpful because their marriage, five years prior to her father's death, had led to her being virtually ostracised by her family of origin. Only her father continued to visit regularly after the marriage, and he was the only member of her family who would ever speak to her husband and his children.

Mrs T had two aunts whom she saw briefly on the day of the funeral, but subsequently had no contact with them again. Mrs T's mother strongly disapproved of Mrs T's marriage, and would never allow Mrs T's husband or his two children from his previous marriage into her home. Shortly after Mrs T's father died her mother accused her of killing him by putting him under so much strain. Mrs T was 'shattered' by this accusation and still feels sad and guilty about the death of her father. Her father had always hoped for a family reconciliation, and despite being in apparently good health had said on more than one occasion that if 'anything happened' to him he hoped that Mrs T would 'see that mother was all right'. Mrs T has visited her mother regularly since the death of her father and continues to do so. However, she finds these visits to be unhelpful because her mother continues to be very critical of her: 'she is always getting at me – she makes me feel silly.'

Prior to her father's death Mrs T and her only sister had been reasonably close, and Mrs T valued this relationship highly. However, after her father's death Mrs T said her sister also blamed her for the death, and refused to have any more contact with her. Mrs T remembered being more upset by this than she was by her mother's behaviour. Mrs T had asked her mother some time ago if she could have her sister's new address so that she could write to her, or perhaps see her again but was told by her mother that her sister 'never wanted to see her again'.

Mrs T said she 'always got on well' with her father, but was of the belief that her mother had been unduly strict with her and 'didn't like me'. Nevertheless, Mrs T's mother didn't want her to leave home, particularly not with her husband. Mrs T recalled that during adolescence she was rarely allowed to go out alone socially and never permitted to have boyfriends visit her at home. Mrs T has 'never understood this' because her younger sister (by eight years) was allowed to socialise and bring friends home.

Professional help

Mrs T had no contact with the hospital staff, and was not involved in making the funeral arrangements. She recalled little of the funeral service itself but remembered being 'terribly upset' throughout the whole of the day. Mrs T saw her father's GP, on an errand for her mother. She asked him about the circumstances surrounding her father's death and is of the opinion that he too blamed her for the death. She did not, despite feeling 'run down', contact her own GP about her bereavement, and did not mention her father's death to anyone who cared for her during her pregnancy two years after the death of her father.

Mrs T did not expect her father's death at all, although retrospectively she felt that he must have always been at risk because 'heart trouble ran in the family'. She knows few of the details of the death and was informed 'in town' by one of her mother's neighbours that her father was ill and in hospital. She telephoned her mother to confirm this, and visited her father the same day. Mrs T was shocked by the visit because 'it didn't look like him'. He was transferred to another hospital on the day of her visit and died two days later. Mrs T was not told that her father had died until she visited her mother to enquire about his condition. It was at this point that her mother had told her, adding, 'and it's all your fault'. Mrs T would have liked to have seen her father's body before he was buried, but was afraid to ask her mother, who was extremely angry both with her daughter and with the hospital for asking permission to do a post-mortem. Her mother refused to give her permission.

Mrs T was obsessed with reviewing her father's death, and desperately wanted to know why he'd died. She wondered whether or not his redundancy, a year before the death, might have contributed to his illness, because he had suffered from depression following his job loss. Nevertheless, Mrs T continued to feel guilty about what she saw as her own role in his illness. For about a year following her father's death Mrs T remembered 'just sitting and crying all of the time', and feeling, despite her husband's support, desperately lonely. She was also aware of a very strong yearning to 'have him back'. Shortly following his death her recurrent nightmares, which she would not discuss in detail, commenced. She described her nightmares as vivid and 'always about the same thing'. After these dreams she always felt particularly isolated. Mrs T also started to suffer from feelings of panic, and now believes that she has premonitions about events. She recalled trying to explain these things to her mother but remembered her mother being dismissive: 'she always makes makes me feel stupid.' On two occasions Mrs T mistook someone else for her father, the last occasion three weeks prior to the discussion. On both occasions Mrs T was outside her usual environment, and feeling quite happy and relaxed – which she felt was unusual for her. Most of the time she tried not to think about her father but 'sometimes it sneaks up on me'.

Mrs T is of the opinion that she will never fully accept her situation, and, despite feeling slightly better after the birth of her young son, still suffers from nightmares, and feels constantly 'run down.' She felt particularly distressed over the thought that her father would never see her child, and still becomes inconsolable every time she sees daffodils [her father's favourite flower]. She and her husband were hoping to move house, and Mrs T was optimistic that leaving a house which held bad memories for her would help her overcome her sense of loss.

Caring for elderly parents

For many people in my study, the death of one parent effectively left the adult child taking responsibility for the surviving parent. Caring for an elderly parent brought both rewards and problems for people. Some people reported growing much closer to their remaining parent, whilst others felt that the burden of care put a great deal of strain on their other relationships, particularly the one with their partner. Guilt was often associated with the deaths of parents cared for by adult children, either because the child became, or always was, ambivalent towards their parent, or because of a feeling that somehow, the adult child had 'let their parent down'. For example:

A woman in her sixties who had cared for her mother for fifteen years following the death of her father recalled feeling a sense of relief after her father's death, because he had suffered a great deal of pain during his terminal illness. However, she felt extremely guilty over the death of her mother who was in her eighties, very dependent upon her daughter and slightly confused. This woman's husband had suffered a heart attack and, unable to nurse both of them, she had agreed that her mother should be admitted for a short stay to a residential home. Her mother died at the home, without, according to her daughter, being able to fully understand that the arrangement was temporary and that her daughter 'had no choice'.

Whilst many adult children perceived their ageing parents to be extremely dependent upon them, and therefore felt a great sense of responsibility towards them, not all adult children felt that they had the right to make decisions on their parents' behalf. Some people, particularly single people living with their parents, believed that their parents should exercise effective parental authority. For example:

One woman in her forties who had lived with, and cared for, her elderly mother all of her adult life had been extremely concerned over the health of her mother for some months before her death.

170

Her mother was afraid of admission to hospital and had expressly refused to give her daughter permission to consult their GP over her illness. Consequently, her daughter's anxiety grew over the months but she 'daren't go against mother'. When her mother was bedridden she finally telephoned the GP without her mother's permission. He visited and told mother and daughter that a hospital admission 'for tests' would be required. Two days later her mother died, and two years after the death she felt considerable guilt over the possibility that she had contributed to her mother's death by not asking for help soon enough. She also felt that she may have caused the death by confronting her mother with the necessity of a hospital admission. Her situation was further complicated by a lack of informal sources of support (she 'only had mother') and further guilt over her sense of loss about 'never having a life of my own'.

It would seem likely that many adult children in this kind of relationship with their parent might require professional help in order to come to terms with their loss. However, it must be said that caring for an elderly parent following the death of the other parent, whilst always associated with considerable stress, was not invariably associated with guilt following the parent's death.

What follows is an example in which one woman describes the process by which, following the death of her father to whom she was strongly attached, she took responsibility for the care of her mother. Her experiences are representative of the experiences of a great many people in a similar situation who strongly associate parental deaths with psychological growth.

Mrs A was in her late forties when her father, who had always been very active and in good health died unexpectedly. Mrs A took over the care of her ill mother who subsequently died several months later. Both deaths had occurred just over three years before she was interviewed. Mrs A was married with three children.

Mrs A and her father held few beliefs associated with orthodox religion, so she did not undertake any acts of overt mourning apart from attending her father's cremation. Nevertheless, Mrs A saw her father's body and, on the request of her mother, took her mother back to the crematorium on several occasions. Due to caring for her mother Mrs A gave up most of her social and leisure activities after her father's death.

Mrs A's father died in hospital in his seventies. He had been in hospital for three days and died, according to his death certificate, of pneumonia and kidney failure, although Mrs A feels that there was some uncertainty as to the exact cause of death.

Mrs A saw much more of her relatives than she would normally have done in the months following her father's death, and during the

171

first six months of her bereavement put on 'quite a lot' of weight. She also experienced difficulty getting off to sleep for about nine months following the death of her father.

Informal support

Mrs A cited her brothers and sisters as being helpful, with the exception of one sister whom Mrs A had always disliked. This sister attended her father's funeral, but Mrs A refused all contact with her. Apparently, Mrs A never told this sister about the subsequent death of their mother and occasionally feels guilty about this. However, despite the family rallying immediately after the death, Mrs A felt that they 'forgot their offers of help to mother' and effectively left Mrs A to cope. She experienced great difficulty with her relationship with her husband although she described her marriage as good prior to the death, and her husband as helpful in the practical sense, but resentful that they should have to cope alone. Mrs A said that her husband was an only child who had always 'had his own way' and who didn't know how to support her following her father's death. His own family apparently didn't show any emotion, and consequently Mrs A felt that her husband withdrew from her because of fear. Mrs A described the next eighteen months as a nightmare during which time the couple persistently 'got back at each other'. Mrs A felt resentful because she needed comfort and felt her husband was 'cold'. She also reported feeling resentful because her husband's parents who were older than hers were still alive. She felt 'why mine and not his?' Mr and Mrs A argued frequently and all arguments were seen by Mrs A as 'stupid rows about nothing – and they would always go back to the time of the deaths'. Following the first eighteen months of the loss Mrs A felt that her relationship with her husband had steadily improved, and that this had coincided with her decreasing needs for demonstrations of affection and closeness from him.

Professional help

Mrs A was impressed by the hospital staff who had cared for her father. She found a telephone call from the ward sister, warning the family about all of the equipment around her father's bed, to have been particularly thoughtful. She also found one of the hospital doctors, who spent some time sympathising with and talking to the family after the death, to have been helpful. This doctor asked the family for permission to conduct a post-mortem. Permission was given. Mrs A also found her parents' GP to be helpful, particularly over her mother's death, and she found the funeral director to have been very good in both of her parental bereavements.

Mrs A's father had not been ill. He was fit and active and did a lot of walking. He experienced a sudden spasm of pain for no apparent reason and Mrs A's mother telephoned her for help. A doctor was called and Mrs A went to her parents' house to find the doctor arranging to admit her father to hospital. Mr and Mrs A visited in the late afternoon and in the evening, and were told that Mrs A's father had pancreatitis. Mrs A recalls that her husband thought that this was a minor complaint and, consequently, they both felt very light-hearted that evening. However, the following afternoon her father's condition deteriorated and they were told of 'complications' from which he was unlikely to recover. He was breathing with difficulty and had been put on a respirator. Mrs A visited again in the evening and the following morning. She was just about to leave home to visit again in the afternoon when she received a telephone call from the hospital, and was told 'your father has just passed away'. Mrs A wanted to go to the hospital straight away but was asked to wait and collect his things later that afternoon. Despite having some warning of the possibility of death, Mrs A felt that 'They tell you, but it doesn't sink in. I didn't think that he would die. It was a total shock.' Mrs A's mother was staying with her, and was told immediately of her husband's death. Mrs A recalled that 'my mother went to pieces, they had a wonderful marriage and he was everything to her'. Looking back on events Mrs A felt that her father knew of his impending death because he'd told her mother 'I shall never come home any more' at a hospital visit. Mrs A remembered feeling very shocked because of 'all the equipment around the bed' and remembered not being able to look at her father for a long time after his comment.

Immediately after the death Mrs A felt 'total shock. A bit like an excitement'. Many people called and the funeral arrangements had to be made. She felt she was so busy caring for her mother that her own grief 'took months to come out', and three months following her father's death recalled being exceptionally tearful for quite a long time. Following her father's death Mrs A, although growing more distant from her husband, felt she grew closer to her mother, who was very ill and expressed a wish to be reunited with her husband. She finds it difficult to separate her feelings of grief for her parents, but felt great comfort following her mother's death from a belief that her parents had, in fact, been reunited after a relatively short period of separation. Mrs A now makes annual visits to the crematorium to remember both parents. She said the third year's visit was much less painful that her previous visits. She no long felt upset and tearful –

just a quiet sense of remembering. Mrs A thinks of her parents quite often, she can feel sad or happy depending upon what she thinks of. She feels she has some very good and happy memories of her parents and treasures those memories. Overall, Mrs A felt that she'd learned a lot from these bereavements: 'you don't really appreciate what life is about until you've been through it. It brings new depths to life.' She was of the opinion that her relationship with her husband had eventually been strengthened and she had a deeper understanding of him, and she thought he did of her. Mrs A has several friends whose parents have died and she feels it important to talk to them about their experiences because 'There's too much taboo. It's painful but nothing to be frightened of.'

Overall, it would seem that the loss of a parent is associated with the same kinds of contradictory impulses and patterns of outcome as other types of losses which occur in adult life. All of the losses in adulthood, although undoubtedly painful experiences, carry with them the potential for personal growth as well as for perpetual despair. Grief is an inevitable consequence of the death of a loved person and perhaps the fear which often surrounds people who are dying or have been bereaved stems from an attempt by others to avoid the realisation that:

> Anything that you have, you can lose, anything you are attached to, you can be separated from; anything you love can be taken away from you. Yet, if you really have nothing to lose, you have nothing.
>
> (Kalish 1985: p. 181)

BIBLIOGRAPHY

Abse, D. W. (1985) Affects, Mourning and Depression, in Volkan, V. (ed.) *Depressive States and Their Treatment*. New Jersey: Jason Aronson.

Anderson, C. (1949) Aspects of Pathological Grief and Mourning. *International Journal of Psycho-Analysis* 30: 48–55.

Andrews, G., Tennant, C., Hewson, D. M. and Vaillant, G. E. (1978) Life Event Stress, Social Support Coping Style and Risk of Psychological Impairment. *The Journal of Nervous and Mental Disease* 166 (5): 307–15.

Ariès, P. (1974) *Western Attitudes towards Death*. Baltimore. Johns Hopkins University Press.

Ariès, P. (1983) *The Hour of our Death*. Aylesbury. Peregrine Books.

Averill, J. R. (1968) Grief: Its Nature and Significance. *Psychological Bulletin* 70: 721–48.

Bankoff, E. S. (1983) Social Support and Adaption to Widowhood. *Journal of Marriage and the Family* 45: 827–33.

Barbarin, D. A. and Chesler, M. (1986) The Medical Context of Parental Coping with Childhood Cancer. *American Journal of Community Psychology* 14: 221–35.

de Barbot, F. M. (1977) *A Cross-Cultural Study of Attitudes towards Seeking Professional Help*. Dissertation Abstracts International. Series B 38 1875.

Barker, C. and Lemle, R. (1987) Informal Helping in Partner and Stranger Dyads. *Journal of Marriage and the Family* 49: 541–7.

Barraclough, B., with Hughes, J. (1987) *Suicide: Clinical and Epidemiological Studies*. London. Croom Helm.

Barrera, M. (1986) Distinctions Between Social Support Concepts, Measures and Models. *American Journal of Community Psychology* 14: 413–45.

Barrera, M. (1988) Models of Social Support and Life Stress: Beyond the Buffering Hypothesis, in Cohen L. H. (ed.) *Life Events and Psychological Functioning: Theoretical and Methodological Issues*. London. Sage.

Barrett, C. J. (1978) Effectiveness of Widows' Groups in Facilitating Change. *Journal of Consulting and Clinical Psychology* 46: 20–31.

Bell, R. A., LeRoy, J. B. and Stephenson, J. J. (1982) Evaluating the Mediating Effects of Social Support upon Life Events and Depressive Symptoms. *Journal of Community Psychology* 10: 325–40.

Benfield, G., Leib, S. and Volman, J. (1978) Grief Response of Parents to Neonatal Death and Parent Participation in Deciding Care. *Pediatrics* 62: 171–7.

Ben-Sira, Z. (1985) Potency: A Stress Buffering Link in the Coping Stress–Disease Relationship. *Social Science and Medicine* 21 (4): 397–406.

Berg, H., Ekenstein, G., Hofer, B., Sandros, I. and Turrell, R. (1978) Information och stod till foraldra som florat sitt barn vid fodelsoen. *Lakartidningen* 75: 128–32.

Berger, P. L. and Luckmann, T. (1967) *The Social Construction of Reality*. Harmondsworth. Penguin.

Binger, C. M. (1984) Psychosocial Intervention with the Child Cancer Patient and Family. *Psychosomatics* 25: 889–902.

Birtchnell, J. (1975) Psychiatric Breakdown Following Recent Parent Death. *British Journal of Medical Psychology* 48: 379–90.

Bodenham, A., Berridge, J. C. and Park, G. R. (1989) Brain Stem Death and Organ Donation. *British Medical Journal* 299: 1009–10.

Bourne, S. (1968) The Psychological Effects of Stillbirth on Women and their Doctors. *Journal of the Royal College of General Practitioners* 16: 103–12.

van der Bout, J., der Keijser, A. and Schut, H. A. W. (1988) Attributional Cognitions of Widow(er)s and Psychological Functioning. Paper presented to the Second Int. Conference on Grief and Bereavement in Contemporary Society. London.

Bowlby, J. (1969) *Attachment*. New York. Basic Books.

Bowlby, J. (1977) The Making and Breaking of Affectional Bonds: 1 Aetiology and Psychopathology in the Light of Attachment Theory (The Fiftieth Maudsley Lecture). *British Journal of Psychiatry* 130: 201–10.

Bowlby, J. (1980) *Attachment and Loss*, Vol. III. *Loss, Sadness and Depression*. London. Hogarth Press.

Bromley, D. B. (1988) *Human Ageing: An Introduction to Gerontology*, 3rd ed. Harmondsworth. Penguin.

Broverman, I. K., Vogel, S. R., Broverman, D. M. *et al.* (1972). Sex-role Sterotypes: A Current Appraisal. *Journal of Social Issues* 28: 59–88.

Bugen, L. A. (1977) Human Grief: A Model for Prediction and Intervention. *American Journal of Orthopsychiatry* 42: 196–206.

Bunch, J. (1971) The Influence of Parental Death Anniversaries upon Suicide Rates. *British Journal of Psychiatry* 118: 621–5.

Cain, A. C. and Cain, B. S. (1964) On Replacing a Child. *Journal of American Academic Child Psychiatry* 3: 443–56.

Cannandine, D. (1981) War and Death: Grief and Mourning in Modern Britain, in Whaley, J. (ed.) *Mirrors of Mortality: Studies in the Social History of Death*. London. Bedford Square Press.

Caplan, G. (1964) *Principles of Preventive Psychiatry*. New York. Basic Books.

Carr-Gregg, M. and Hampson, R. (1986) A New Approach to the Psychological Care of Adolescents with Cancer. *Medical Journal of Australia* 145: 580–3.

Cartwright, A., Hockey, L. and Anderson, J. L. (1973) *Life before Death*. London. Routledge & Kegan Paul.

Cassel, J. (1976) The Contribution of the Social Environment to Host Resistance: The Fourth Wade Hampton Frost Lecture. *American Journal of Epidemiology* 104: 107–23.

Clarke, M. and Williams, A. J. (1979) Depression of Women after Perinatal Death. *The Lancet* 8122: 916–17.

Clyman, R. I., Green, C., Rowe, J., Mikkelsen, C. and Ataide, L. (1980) Issues Concerning Parents After the Death of their Newborn. *Critical Care Medicine* 8: 215–18.

Cohen, C., Teresi, J. and Holmes, D. (1986) Assessment of Stress – Buffering Effects of Social Networks on Psychological Symptons in an Inner-city Elderly Population. *American Journal of Community Psychology* 14: 75–91.

Cohen, S. and Wills, T. A. (1985) Stress, Social Support and the Buffering Hypothesis. *Psychological Bulletin* 98: 310–57.

Cooper, J. D. (1980) Parental Reactions to Stillbirth. *British Journal of Social Work* 10: 55–69.

Cornwell, J., Nurcombe, B. and Stevens, L. (1977) Family Response to Loss of Child by Sudden Infant Death Syndrome. *Medical Journal of Australia* April 30: 656–8.

Cronkite, R. C. and Moos, R. H. (1984) The Roles of Predisposing and Moderating Factors in the Stress–Illness Relationship. *Journal of Health and Social Behaviour* 25: 372–93.

Dalley, G. (1988) *Ideologies of Caring: Rethinking Community and Collectivism.* London. Macmillan.

Darwin, C. (1872) *The Expression of Emotion in Man and Animals.* London. Murray.

Davidson, G. W. (1979) Hospice Care for the Dying, in Wass, H. (ed.) *Dying: Facing the Facts.* New York. McGraw-Hill.

Dean, A. and Ensel, W. M. (1982) Modelling Social Support, Life Events, Competence and Depression in the Context of Age and Sex. *Journal of Community Psychology* 10: 392–408.

DeFrain, J. D. and Ernst, L. (1978) The Psychological Effects of Sudden Infant Death Syndrome on Surviving Family Members. *The Journal of Family Practice* 6 (5): 985–9.

DeFrain, J., Taylor, J. and Ernst, L. (1982) *Coping with Sudden Infant Death.* Lexington, MA. D. C. Heath.

Deutsch, H. (1937) Absence of Grief. *Psychoanalytic Quarterly* 6: 12–22.

Dimond, M., Lund, D. A. and Caserta, M. S. (1987) The Role of Social Support in the First Year of Bereavement among the Elderly. *Gerontologist.* 25: 599–604.

Dohrenwend, B. P. (1975) Sociocultural and Social Psychological Factors in the Genesis of Mental Disorders. *Journal of Health and Social Behaviour* 16: 365–92.

Donnelly, K. (1982) *Recovering from the Loss of a Child.* New York. Macmillan.

Douglas, M. (1987) *How Institutions Think.* London. Routledge & Kegan Paul.

Durkheim, E. (1915) *The Elementary Forms of Religious Life.* New York. Macmillan.

Dyregrov, A. and Matthiesen, S. B. (1987) Similarities and Differences in Mothers' and Fathers' Grief Following the Death of an Infant. *Scandinavian Journal of Psychology* 28: 1–15.

Eason, G. (1985) Private Communication.

Edelstein, L. (1984) *Maternal Bereavement.* New York. Praeger.

Eisenbruch, M. (1984a) Cross-Cultural Aspects of Bereavement 1: A Conceptual Framework for Comparative Analysis. *Culture, Medicine and Psychiatry* 8: 283–309.

Eisenbruch, M. (1984b) Cross-Cultural Aspects of Bereavement II: Ethnic and Cultural Variations in the Development of Bereavement Practices. *Culture, Medicine and Psychiatry* 8: 315–47.

Elias, N. (1985) *The Loneliness of the Dying.* Oxford. Blackwell.

Emde, R. N. and Brown, C. (1978) Adaptation to the Birth of a Down's Syndrome Infant. *Journal of the American Academy of Child Psychiatry* 17 (2): 299–323.

Engel, G. (1961) Is Grief a Disease? *Psychosomatic Medicine* 23: 18–22.

Engel, G. L. (1962) *Psychological Development in Health and Disease.* Philadelphia. Saunders.

177

Erikson, K. T. (1979) *In the Wake of the Flood*. London. Allen & Unwin.

Feifel, H. (ed.) (1959) *The Meaning of Death*. New York. McGraw-Hill.

Fitchett, G. (1980) It's time to Bury the Stage Theory of Death and Dying. *Oncology Nurse Exchange* 2(3).

Forrest, G. C. (1983) Mourning the Loss of a Newborn Baby Bereavement. *Care* 2: 4–5.

Freud, S. (1917) Mourning and Melancholia, In The *Standard Edition of the Complete Psychological Works of Sigmund Freud*, Vol. 14. London. Hogarth Press.

Fulton, R. and Fulton, J. (1971) A Psychosocial Aspect of Terminal Care: Anticipatory Grief. *Omega* 2: 91–100.

Gauthier, Y. and Marshall, W. (1977) Grief: A Cognitive Behavioural Analysis. *Cognitive Therapy and Research* 1: 39–44.

Gilmore, A. and Gilmore, S. (1988) *Towards a Safer Death: Multidisciplinary Aspects of Terminal Care*. New York. Plenum Press.

Glaser, B. G. and Strauss, A. L. (1965) *Awareness of Dying*. Chicago. Aldine.

Glaser, B. G. and Strauss, A. L. (1968) *Time for Dying*. Chicago. Aldine.

Glick, I. O., Weiss, R. S. and Parkes, C. M. (1974) *The First Year of Bereavement*. New York. Wiley.

Goffman, E. (1972) *Relations in Public: Microstudies of the Public Order*. Harmondsworth. Penguin.

Gogan, J. L., O'Malley, J. E. and Foster, D. J. (1977) Treating the Pediatric Cancer Patient: A Review. *Journal of Pediatric Psychology* 2: 42–8.

Goldberg, D. and Huxley, P. (1980) *Mental Illness in the Community: The Pathway to Psychiatric Care*. London. Tavistock.

Gore, S. (1981) Stress-Buffering Functions of Social Supports: An Appraisal and Clarification of Research Models, in Dohrenwend, B. S. and Dohrenwend, B. P. (eds) *Stressful Life Events and their Context*. New York. Prodist.

Gorer, G. (1955) 'The Pornography of Death' (revised), in Gorer, G. (1965) *Death, Grief and Mourning in Contemporary Britain*. London. Cresset Press.

Gorer, G. (1965) *Death, Grief and Mourning in Contemporary Britain*. London. Cresset Press.

Gottlieb, B. H. (ed.) (1981) *Social Network and Social Support*. Beverly Hills, CA. Sage.

Gottlieb, B. H. (1983) *Social Support Strategies: Guidelines for Mental Health Practice*. Newbury Park, CA. Sage.

Habenstein, R. W. and Lamers, W. M. (1963) *Funeral Customs the World Over*. Milkwaukee. Bulfin Printers.

Hardiker, P. and Tod, V. (1982) Social Work and Chronic Illness. *British Journal of Social Work* 12 (6): pp 639–67.

Hardiker, P., Pedley, J., Olley, D., Littlewood, J. and Walls, J. (1984) *Coping with Chronic Renal Failure*. Leicester. University of Leicester.

Hardiker, P., Pedley, J., Olley, D., and Littlewood, J. L. (1986) Coping with Chronic Renal Failure. *British Journal of Social Work*. 16 (2): 203–22.

Heidegger, M. (1926) *Being and Time* (trans. J. Macquarrie and E. Robinson). Oxford. Blackwell.

Heike, E. (1985) *A Question of Grief*. London. Hodder & Stoughton.

Helmrath, T. A. and Steintz, E. M. (1978) Death of an Infant: Parental Grieving and the Failure of Social Support. *Journal of Family Practice* 6: 785–90.

Hertz, R. (1960) *Death and the Right Hand* (trans. by R. and C. Needham). New York. Free Press.

Hillier, E. R. (1983) Terminal Care in the United Kingdom, in Corr, C. A.

and Corr, D. M. (eds) *Hospice Care: Principles and Practice.* New York. Springer.

Hinton, J. (1967) *Dying.* Harmondsworth Penguin.

Hinton, J. M. (1979) Comparison of Places and Policies for Terminal Care. *The Lancet* 8106: 29–32.

Hodgkinson, P. E. (1989) Technological Disaster – Survival and Bereavement. *Social Science and Medicine* 29(3): 351–6.

Hodgkinson, P. (1982) Abnormal Grief – The Problem of Therapy. *British Journal of Medical Psychology* 55: 29–34.

Hoekstra-Weebers, J. E. W. M., Littlewood, J. L., Humphrey, G. B. and Boon, C. (1989) Parental Reactions to the Death of a Child from Cancer. Paper presented to the 1st International Conference on Children and Death. Athens, Greece.

Horowitz, M. J., Wilner, N., Marmar, C. and Krupnick, J. (1980) Pathological Grief and the Activation of Latent Self-Images. *American Journal of Psychiatry* 137(10): 1157–62.

House, J. S. (1981) *Work Stress and Social Support.* Reading, MA: Addison-Wesley.

Huntington, R. and Metcalf, P. (1979) *Celebrations of Death: The Anthropology of Mortuary Ritual.* Cambridge. Cambridge University Press.

Illich, I. (1977) *Limits to Medicine: Medical Nemesis and the Expropriation of Health.* Harmondsworth. Penguin.

Irwin, M., Daniels, S., Risch, C., Bloom, E. and Weiner, H. (1988) Plasma Cortisol and Natural Killer Cell Activity during Bereavement. *Biological Psychiatry* 24: 173–8.

Jones, M. (1988) *Secret Flowers: Mourning and the Adaptation to Loss.* London. Women's Press.

Jung, C. (1933) *Modern Man in Search of a Soul.* London. Routledge & Kegan Paul.

Jurk, I. H., Ekert, H. and Jones, J. H. (1981) Family Responses and Mechanisms of Adjustment Following Death of Children with Cancer. *Australian Paediatric Journal* 17: 85–8.

Kalish, R. A. (1985) *Death, Grief and Caring Relationships,* 2nd ed. California. Brooks Cole.

Kalnins, I. V., Churchill, M. P. and Terry, G. E. (1980) Concurrent Stresses in Families with a Leukemic Child. *Journal of Pediatric Psychology* 5: 87–92.

Kaplan, B. H. (1975) Toward Further Research on Family Health, in Kaplan, B. H. and Cassell, J. C. (eds) *Family and Health: An Epidemiological Approach.* Chapel Hill: Institute for Research in Social Science, University of North Carolina.

Kaplan, D. M., Grobstein, R. and Smith, A. (1976) Predicting the Impact of Severe Illness in Families. *Health and Social Work* 1: 71–82.

Kastenbaum, R. J. (1975) Is Death a Life Crisis? On the Confrontation with Death in Theory and Practice, in Datan, M. and Ginsberg, L. H. (eds) *Life-Span Developmental Psychology: Normative Life Crises.* New York. Academic Press.

Kastenbaum, R. J. (1988) Safe Death in the Post Modern World, in Gilmore, A. and Gilmore, S. (eds) *A Safer Death: Multidisciplinary Aspects of Terminal Care.* New York. Plenum Press.

Kaufmann, W. (1976) *Existentialism, Religion and Death.* London. New English Library.

Kelly, G. A. (1955) *The Psychology of Personal Constructs,* Vols 1 and 2. New York. Norton.

Kennell, J. H., Slyter, H. and Klaus, M. M. (1970) The Mourning Response of

Parents to the Death of a Newborn Infant. *New England Journal of Medicine* 238: 344–9.

Kerner, J., Harvey, B. and Lewiston, N. (1979) The Impact of Grief: A Retrospective Study of Family Function Following Loss of a Child with Cystic Fibrosis. *Journal of Chronic Disease* 32: 221–5.

Kessler, R. C., Price, R. H. and Wortman, C. B. (1985) Social Factors in Psychopathology: Stress, Social Support and Coping Processes. *Annual Review of Psychology* 36: 531–72.

Kirkley-Best, E. and Kellner, K. (1982) The Forgotten Grief: A Review of the Psychology of Stillbirth. *American Journal of Orthopsychiatry* 52: 420–9.

Klass, D. (1982) Self Help Groups for the Bereaved: Theory, Theology and Practice. *Journal of Religion and Health* 21: 307–24.

Klein, M. (1948) Mourning and its Relation to Manic Depressive States, in *Contributions to Psycho-Analysis*. London. Hogarth Press.

Kübler-Ross, E. (1969) *On Death and Dying*. New York. Macmillan.

Kübler-Ross, E. (1983) *On Children and Death*. New York. Macmillan.

Lansdown, R. and Goldman, A. (1988) The Psychosocial Care of Children with Malignant Disease. *Journal of Child Psychology and Psychiatry*. 29. 555–67.

Lasch, C. (1977) *Haven in a Heartless World: The Family Besieged*. New York. Basic Books.

Lauer, M. E., Mulhern, R. K., Wallskog, J. M. and Camitta, B. M. (1983) A Comparison Study of Parental Adaption – Following a Child's Death at Home or in the Hospital. *Pediatrics* 71(1): 107–11.

Lauer, M. E., Mulhern, R. K., Schell, M. J. and Camitta, B. M. (1989) Long-Term Follow Up of Parental Adjustment Following a Child's Death at Home or Hospital. *Cancer* 63: 988–94.

Lazare, A. (1979) Unresolved Grief, in Lazare, A. (ed.) *Outpatient Psychiatry: Diagnosis and Treatment*. Baltimore. Williams & Wilkins.

Lazarus, R. S. and Launier, R. (1978) Stress-Related Transactions between Person and Environment, in Pervin, L. A. and Lewis, M. (eds) *Perspectives in Interactional Psychology*. New York. Plenum Press.

Lehman, D. R., Ellard, J. H. and Wortman, C. B. (1986) Social Support for the Bereaved: Recipients and Providers' Perspectives on What is Helpful. *Journal of Consulting and Clinical Psychology* 54(4): 438–46.

Leming, M. R. and Dickinson, G. E. (1985) *Understanding Dying, Death and Bereavement*. New York. Holt, Rinehart & Winston.

Leslie, L. A. and Grady, K. (1985) Changes in Mothers' Social Networks and Social Support Following Divorce. *Journal of Marriage and the Family*. 47: 663–73.

Levav, I. (1982) Mortality and Psychopathology Following the Death of an Adult Child: An Epidemiological Review. *Israeli Journal of Psychiatry and Related Sciences* 19(1): 23–8.

Levine, M. and Perkins, D. V. (1987) *Principles of Community Psychology: Perspectives and Applications*. New York. Oxford University Press.

Lewis, C. S. (1961) *A Grief Observed*. London. Faber.

Lewis, E. (1979) Mourning by the Family after a Stillbirth or Neonatal Death. *Archieves of Disease in Childhood* 55: 303–6.

Lieberman, M., Borman, L. *et al.* (1979) *Self Help Groups for Coping with Crisis*. San Francisco. Jossey-Bass.

Lieberman, S. (1978) Nineteen Cases of Morbid Grief. *British Journal of Psychiatry* 132: 159–63.

Lifton, R. J. (1979) *The Broken Connection*. New York. Simon & Schuster.

Lin, N. (1986) Modelling the Effects of Social Support, in Lin, N., Dean, A. and Ensel, W. (eds) *Social Support, Life Events and Depression*. Orlando, FL. Academic Press.

Lin, N. and Dean, A. (1984) Social Support and Depression: A Panel Study. *Social Psychiatry* 19: 91–3.

Lindemann, E. (1944) Symptomatology and Management of Acute Grief. *American Journal of Psychiatry* 101 September: 141–8.

Littlewood, J. L. (1983) *Loss and Change: A Consideration of Death-Related Issues*. Unpublished PhD thesis. University of Leicester.

Littlewood, J., Hardiker, P., Pedley, J. and Olley, D. (1990) Coping with Home Dialysis. *Human Relations* 43(2): 103–11.

Littlewood, J. L., Hoestra-Weebers, J. E. W. M. and Humphrey, G. B. (1990) *Child Death and Parental Bereavement*. Groningen, The Netherlands. University Hospital.

Littlewood, J. L., Cramer, D., Hoeskstra-Weebers, J. E. W. M. and Humphrey, G. B. (1991a) Gender Differences in Parental Coping following their Child's Death. *British Journal of Guidance and Counselling* 19(2): 139–48.

Littlewood, J. L., Cramer, D., Hoesktra-Weebers, J. E. W. M. and Humphrey, G. B. (1991b) Parental Coping with their Child's Death. *Counselling Psychology Quarterly*. 4(2/3): 135–41

Lowman, J. (1979) Grief Intervention and Sudden Infant Death Syndrome. *American Journal of Community Psychology* 7(6): 665–77.

Maddison, D. C. and Walker, W. L. (1967) Factors Affecting the Outcome of Conjugal Bereavement. *British Journal of Psychiatry* 113: 1057–67.

Maddison, D. and Viola, A. (1968) The Health of Widows in the Year following Bereavement. *Journal of Psychosomatic Research* 12: 297–306.

Maddison, D. C., Viola, A. and Walker, W. L. (1969) Further Studies in Bereavement. *Australian and New Zealand Journal of Psychiatry* 3: 63–6.

Magni, G., Silvestro, A., Carli, M. and De Leo, D. (1986) Social Support and Psychological Distress of Parents of Children with Acute Lymphocytic Leukaemia. *British Journal of Medical Psychology* 59: 383–5.

Mandell, F., McAnulty, E. and Reece, R. M. (1980) Observations of Parental Response to Sudden Unanticipated Infant Death. *Pediatrics*. 65: 221–5.

Mann, J. R. (1987) Psychosocial Aspects of Leukemia and Others Cancers during Childhood, in Aaronson, N. K. and Beckman, J. (eds) *The Quality of Life of Cancer Patients*. New York. Raven Press.

Marris, P. (1958) *Widows and their Families*. London. Routledge & Kegan Paul.

Marris, P. (1986) *Loss and Change*. London. Routledge & Kegan Paul.

Martinson, I., Deck, E. and Adams, D. (1986) Statement on the Care of the Dying and Bereaved in Developing Countries: A Working Document. Unpublished Working Document by International Work Group on Death, Dying and Bereavement – Developing Countries Working Group.

Mawson, D., Marks, I. M., Ramm, L. and Stern, R. S. (1981) Guided Mourning for Morbid Grief: A Controlled Study. *British Journal of Psychiatry* 138: 185–93.

Miller, J. (1974) *Aberfan: A Disaster and its Aftermath*. London. Constable.

Moos, R. H. (ed.) (1977) *Coping with Physical Illness*. New York. Plenum Press.

Morrin, H. (1983) As Great a Loss. *Nursing Mirror* February 16: 33.

Morris, D. (1988) Management of Perinatal Bereavement. *Archives of Disease in Childhood* 63: 870–2.

Moss, M. S. and Moss, S. L. (1983–4) The Impact of Parental Death on Middle-Aged Children. *Omega* 14: 1465–75.

Mueller, D. P. (1980) Social Networks: A Promising Direction for Research on the

181

Relationship of the Social Environment to Psychiatric Disorder. *Social Science and Medicine* 14A (1): 147–61.

Mulhern, R. K., Lauer, M. E. and Hoffmann, R. G. (1983) Death of a Child at Home or in the Hospital: Subsequent Psychological Adjustment of the Family. *Paediatrics* 71: 743–7.

Murrell, S. A. and Norris, F. H. (1984) Resources, Life Events, and Changes in Positive Affect and Depression in Older Adults. *American Journal of Community Psychology* 12: 445–64.

Natanson, M. (1970) *The Journeying Self*. Reading, MA. Addison-Wesley.

Nixon, J. and Pearn, J. (1977) Emotional Sequelae of Parents and Siblings following the Drowning or Near-Drowning of a Child. *Australian and New Zealand Journal of Psychiatry* 11: 265–8.

Orbach, S. and Eichenbaum, L. (1980) *Loss in Women's Relationships*. Unpublished paper. BASW Conference on Loss, London.

Osterweis, M., Solomon, F. and Green, M. (eds) (1984) *Bereavement: Reactions, Consequences and Care*. Washington, D.C. National Academy Press.

Owen, G., Fulton, R. and Markusen, E. (1982–3) Death at a Distance: A Study of Family Survivors. *Omega* 13: 191–225.

Palgi, P. (1973) The Socio-Cultural Expressions and Implications of Death Mourning and Bereavement Arising out of the War in Israel. *Israel Annal of Psychiatry and Related Disciplines* 12: 301–29.

Pallis, C. (1984) Brainstem Death: The Evolution of a Concept, in Morris, P. J. (ed.) *Kidney Transplantation*, 2nd Ed. London. Grune & Stratton.

Parkes, C. M. (1970) Seeking and Finding a Lost Object: Evidence from Recent Studies of Reaction to Bereavement. *Social Science and Medicine* 4: 187–201.

Parkes, C. M. (1972) *Bereavement*. New York. International Universities Press.

Parkes, C. M. (1975) What Becomes of Redundant World Models? A Contribution to the Study of Adaptation to Change. *British Journal of Medical Psychology* 48: 131–7.

Parkes, C. M. (1978) Home or Hospital? Terminal Care as Seen by Surviving Spouses. *Journal of the Royal College of General Practitioners* 28: 19–30.

Parkes, C. M. (1980) Bereavement Counselling: Does it Work? *British Medical Journal* 281(4): 3–6.

Parkes, C. M. and Weiss, R. S. (1983) *Recovery from Bereavement*. New York. Basic Books.

Parsons, M. (1982) Imposed Termination of Psychotherapy and its Relation to Death and Mourning. *British Journal of Medical Psychology* 55: 35–40.

Parsons, T. (1951) *The Social System*. Glencoe, I11. The Free Press.

de Paulo, B., Nadler, A. and Fisher, J. D. (eds) (1983) *New Directions in Helping*, vol. 2. *Help Seeking*. New York. Academic Press.

Pearlin, L. and Lieberman, M. (1979) Social Sources of Distress, in Simons, R. (ed.) *Research in Community Health*. Greenwich, CT. Jai Press.

Peterman, F. and Bode. U. (1986) Five Coping Styles in Families of Children with Cancer. *Paediatric Haematology and Oncology* 3: 299–309.

Pincus, L. (1976) *Death and the Family*. London. Faber.

Rando, T. A. (1983) An Investigation of Grief and Adaption in Parents whose Children have Died from Cancer. *Journal of Pediatric Psychology* 8: 3–20.

Raphael, B. (1973) Bereavement: A Paradigm for Preventive Medicine. *Sandoz Therapeutic Quarterly* 2: 1–9.

Raphael, B. (1975) The Management of Pathological Grief. *Australian and New Zealand Journal of Psychiatry* 9: 173–80.

Raphael, B. (1977) Preventive Intervention with the Recently Bereaved. *Archives of General Psychiatry* 34: 1450–4.

Raphael, B. (1984) Personal Disaster. *Australian and New Zealand Journal of Psychiatry* 15: 183–98.

Raphael, B. (1984) *The Anatomy of Bereavement: A Handbook for the Caring Professions*. London. Hutchinson.

Reid, J. (1979) A Time to Live, a Time to Grieve: Patterns and Processes of Mourning among the Yolngu of Australia. *Culture, Medicine and Psychiatry* 3: 319–46.

Richardson, R. (1988a) The Nest Egg and the Funeral – Fear of Death on the Parish Among the Elderly, in Gilmore, A. and Gilmore, S. (eds) *Towards A Safer Death: Multidisciplinary Aspects of Terminal Care*. New York. Plenum Press.

Richardson, R. (1988b) *Death, Destitution and the Destitute*. London. Routledge.

Robson, J. D. (1977) Sick Role and Bereavement Role: Toward a Theoretical Synthesis of Two Ideal Types, in Vernon, G. M. (ed.) *A Time to Die*. Washington, DC. University Press of America.

Rodabough, T. (1981–2) Funeral Roles: Ritualized Expectations. *Omega* 12: 227–40.

Rosenblatt, P. C., Walsh, R. P. and Jackson, D. A. (1977) *Grief and Mourning in Cross-Cultural Perspective*. Washington, DC. H.R.A.F. Press.

Rowe, D. (1987) *Beyond Fear*. London. Fontana.

Rowe, D. (1988) *The Successful Self*. London. Fontana.

Rowland, K. F. (1977) Environmental Events Predicting Death for the Elderly. *Psychological Bulletin* 84: 349–72.

Rubin, S. S. (1984) Mourning as Distinct From Melancholia: The Resolution of Bereavement. *British Journal of Medical Psychology* 57: 339–45.

Sanders, C. M. (1979–80) A Comparison of Adult Bereavement in the Death of a Spouse, Child and Parent. *Omega* 10 (4): 303–23.

Sanders, C. M. (1983) Effects of Sudden vs Chronic Illness Death on Bereavement Outcome. *Omega* 13: 227–41.

Sartre, J. P. (1958) *Being and Nothingness* (trans. H. E. Barnes). London. Methuen.

Schermerhorn, R. A. (1978) *Comparative Ethnic Relations: A Framework for Theory and Research*. Chicago. University of Chicago Press.

Schowalter, J. E., Ferholt, J. B. and Mann, N. M. (1973) The Adolescent Patient's Decision to Die. *Pediatrics* 51 (1): 97–103.

Seligman, M. E. P. (1975) *Helplessness: On Depression, Development, and Death*. San Franciso. W. H. Freeman.

Shanfield, S. B., Benjamin, M. A. and Swain, B. S. (1984) Parents' Reactions to the Death of the Adult Child from Cancer. *American Journal of Psychiatry* 141: 1092–4.

Shanfield, S. B., Swain, B. J. and Benjamin, G. A. H. (1986–7) Parents' Responses to the Death of the Adult Children From Accidents and Cancer: A Comparison. *Omega* 7(4): 289–97.

Shneidman, E. S. (1973) *Deaths of Man*. New York. Quadrangle/New York Times.

Silverman, D. (1972) Some Neglected Questions about Social Reality, in Filmer, P. et al. (eds) *New Directions in Sociological Theory*. London. Collier-Macmillan.

Singh, B. S. and Raphael, B. (1981) Post-Disaster Morbidity of the Bereaved. *Journal of Nervous and Mental Disease* 169(4): 208–12.

Simos, B. G. (1979) *A Time to Grieve*. New York. Family Service Association.

Simpson, M. A. (1979) *The Facts of Death*. Englewood Cliffs, NJ. Prentice-Hall.

Sireling, L., Cohen, D. and Marks, I. (1988) Guided Mourning for Morbid Grief: A Controlled Replication. *Behaviour Therapy* 19: 121–32.

Smith, C. R. (1976) Bereavement: The Contribution of Phenomenological and

Existential Analyses to a Greater Understanding of the Problem. *British Journal of Social Work* 5(1): 75–92.

Smith, C. R. (1982) *Social Work with the Dying and the Bereaved*. London. Macmillan.

Spinetta, J. J. (1982) Behavioural and Psychological Research in Childhood Cancer. *Cancer* 50 (Supplement 1): 1939–43.

Spinetta, J. J., Swarner, J. A. and Sheposh, J. P. (1981) Effective Parental Coping Following the Death of a Child from Cancer. *Journal of Pediatric Psychology* 6(3): 251–62.

Standish, L. (1982) The Loss of a Baby. *The Lancet* March 13.

Stedeford, A. (1984) *Facing Death: Patients, Families and Professionals*. London. Heinemann.

Stein, H. F. and Hill, R. F. (1977) *The Ethnic Imperative*. Pennsylvania University Park. Pennsylvania State University Press.

Stringham, J., Riley, J. H. and Ross, A. (1982) Silent Birth: Mourning a Stillborn Baby. *Social Work* 27: 322–7.

Sudnow, D. (1967) *Passing On: The Social Organisation of Dying*. Englewood Cliffs, NJ. Prentice-Hall.

Tatchell, P. (1986) *AIDS. A Guide to Survival*. London. Gay Men's Press.

Taylor, L. (1983) *Mourning Dress: A Costume and Social History*. London. Allen & Unwin.

Taylor, R. B. (1980) *Cultural Ways*, 3rd ed. Boston, MA: Allyn & Bacon

Tebbi, C. K., Zevon, M. A., Richards, M. E. and Cummings, K. M. (1989) Attributions of Responsibility in Adolescent Cancer Patients and their Parents. *Journal of Cancer Education* 4(2): 135–42.

Thoits, P. A. (1982) Conceptual, Methodological and Theoretical Problems in Studying Social Support as a Buffer against Life Stress. *Journal of Health and Social Behaviour* 23 (June): 1145–59.

Thomas, C. D. (1928) *Life Beyond Death, With Evidence*. London. Collins.

Tillich, P. (1952) *The Courage to Be*. New Haven, CT. Yale University Press.

Tod, J. L. and Shapira, A. (1974) U. S. and British Self-Disclosure, Anxiety, Empathy and Attitudes to Psychotherapy. *Journal of Cross-Cultural Psychology* 5: 364–9.

Towse, M. S. (1986) 'To Be or Not to be' – Anxiety following Bereavement. *British Journal of Medical Psychology* 59: 149–56.

Turner, B. S. (1987) *Medical Power and Social Knowledge*. London. Sage.

Turner, V. (1969) *The Ritual Process*. Chicago. Aldine.

Vachon, M., Lyall, W., Rogers, J., Freedman-Letofsky, K. and Freeman, S. (1980) A Controlled Study of Self-Help Intervention for Widows. *American Journal of Psychiatry* 137: 1380–4.

Vachon, M. L. S., Sheldon, A. R., Lancee, S. L., Lyall, W. A. L., Roger, J. and Freeman, S. J. (1982) Correlates of Enduring Distress Patterns Following Bereavement: Social Network Life Situation and Personality. *Psychological Medicine* 12: 783–8.

Vachon, M. L. S. (1983) Bereavement Programmes and Interventions in Palliative Care. *Proceedings 13th International Cancer Congress*. New York. Alan R Liss.

Vachon, M. L. S. (1987) Unresolved Grief in Persons with Cancer Referred for Psychotherapy. *Psychiatric Clinics of North America* 10(3): 467–86.

Van Gennep, A. (1960) *The Rites of Passage* (trans. M. B. Vizedom and G. L. Caffee). Chicago. University of Chicago Press.

Verbrugge, L. (1985) Gender and Health: An Update on Hypotheses and Evidence. *Journal of Health and Social Behaviour* 26: 156–82.

Veroff, J., Kulka, R. A. and Douvan, E. (1981) *Mental Health in America: Patterns of Help-seeking from 1957–1976*. New York. Basic Books.

Videka-Sherman, L. (1982) Coping with the Death of a Child: A Study over Time. *Americal Journal of Orthopsychiatry* 51(4): 699–703.

Viorst, J. (1986) *Necessary Losses*. New York. Ballantine Books.

Vizedom, M. B. (1976) *Rites and Relationships: Rites of Passage and Contemporary Anthropology*. Beverly Hills, CA. Sage.

Volkan, V. D. (1970) Typical Findings in Pathological Grief. *Psychiatric Quarterly* 44: 231–50.

Volkan, V. (1975) Re-grief Therapy, in Schoenberg, B. *et al.* (eds) *Bereavement: Its Psychosocial Aspects*. New York. Columbia University Press.

Volkan, V. D. (1981) *Linking Objects and Linking Phenomena*. New York. International Universities Press.

Volkan, V. D. (1985) Psychotherapy of Complicated Mourning, in Volkan, V.D. (ed.) *Depressive States and their Treatment*. New Jersey. Jason Aronson.

Volkan, V. D., Cillufo, A. F. and Sarvay, T. L. (1975) Re-grief Therapy and the Function of Linking Objects as a Key to Stimulate Emotionality, in Olsen, P. T. (ed.) *Emotional Flooding*. New York. Human Sciences Press.

Walker, K. N., MacBride, A. and Vachon, M. L. S. (1977) Social Support Networks and the Crisis of Bereavement. *Social Science and Medicine* 11(1): 35–41.

Waller, D. A., Todres, I. D., Cassem, N. H. and Anderton, A. (1979) Coping with Poor Prognosis in the Pediatric Intensive Care Unit. *American Journal of Diseases of Childhood* 133: 1121–5.

Weiss, R. S. (ed.) (1974) *Loneliness: The Experience of Emotional and Social Isolation*. Cambridge, MA. MIT Press.

Weiss, R. S. (1975) *Marital Separation*. New York. Basic Books.

Wellman, B. (1981) Applying Network Analysis to the Study of Support, in Gottlieb, B. H. (ed.) *Social Networks and Social Support*. Beverly Hills, CA. Sage.

Wilcox, B. L. and Vernberg, E. M. (1985) Conceptual and Theoretical Dilemmas Facing Social Support, in Sarason, I. S. and Sarason, B. R. (eds) *Social Support: Theory, Research and Applications*. The Netherlands. Martines Nijhoff.

Wilson, A. L., Fenton, L. J., Stevens, D. C. and Soule, P. J. (1982) The Death of a Newborn Twin: An Analysis of Parental Bereavement. *Pediatrics* 70: 587–91.

Witte, R. A. (1985) The Psychosocial Impact of a Progressive Physical Handicap and Terminal Illness (Duchenne Muscular Dystrophy) on Adolescents and their Families. *British Journal of Medical Psychology* 58: 179–87.

Wolff, J. R., Nielson, P. E. and Schiller, P. (1970) The Emotional Reaction to a Stillbirth. *American Journal of Obstetrics and Gynecology* 108: 73–7.

Woodfield, R. L. and Viney, L. L. (1982) Bereavement: A Personal Construct Approach. *Omega* 12: 1–13.

Worden, J. W. (1976) *Personal Death Awareness*. Englewood Cliffs, NJ. Prentice-Hall.

Worden, J. W. (1982) *Grief Counselling and Grief Therapy*. New York. Springer.

Wortman, C. B. (1984) Social Support and the Cancer Patient: Conceptual and Methodologic Issues. *Cancer* 53 (May 15 Supplement): 2339–60.

Wright, M. (1987) *A Death in the Family*. London. Macdonald.

Young, G. (1981) Hospice and Health Care, in Saunders, C., Summers, D. H. and Teller, N. (eds) *Hospice: The Living Idea*. London. Edward Arnold.

Young, M., Benjamin, B. and Wallis, C. (1963) The Mortality of Widowers. *The Lancet* 2: 454–6.

NAME INDEX

Abse, D.W. 23
Anderson, C. 159
Andrews, G. 79
Ariès, P. 1–3, 4, 5, 15, 18–19, 29
Averill, J.R. 53, 62

Bankoff, E.S. 85
Barbarin, D.A. 70
Barbot, F.M. de 98
Barker, C. 98
Barraclough, B. 83, 135
Barrera, M. 79, 82, 83
Barrett, C.J. 88
Bell, R.A. 82
Benfield, G. 125, 144
Ben-Sira, Z. 81
Berg, H. 144
Berger, P.L. 72
Binger, C.M. 133
Birtchnell, J. 159
Bodenham, A. 142
Bourne, S. 124
Bout, J. van der 69
Bowlby, J. 40, 43, 50, 51, 56, 62,
    65–6, 82, 108, 115, 148, 163
Bromley, D.B. 69
Broverman, I.K. 155
Bugen, L.A. 11
Bunch, J. 159

Cain, A.C. 26
Cannandine, D. 30, 31, 32–3, 35
Caplan, G. 69
Carr-Gregg, M. 136
Cartwright, A. 4
Cassel, A. 79
Clarke, M. 136
Clyman, R. 70, 146

Cohen, C. 82
Cohen, S. 79, 80, 82
Cooper, J.D. 136
Cornwell, J. 131–2
Cronkite, R.C. 70

Dalley, G. 106–7, 121
Darwin, C. 62
Davidson, G.W. 16
Dean, A. 83
Defrain, J.D. 70–1, 144
Deutsch, H. 56
Dimond, M. 86
Dohrenwend, B.P. 79
Donnelly, K. 131
Douglas M. 11
Durkheim, E. 36–7
Dyregrov, A. 70, 144–5

Eason, G. 43
Edelstein, L. 89, 92–3, 98
Eisenbruch, M. 62, 76–7
Elias, N. 4
Emde, R.N. 130
Engel, G. 41, 60–1
Erikson, K.T. 26–7

Feifel, H. 4
Fitchett, G. 14, 15
Forrest, G.C. 144
Freud, S. 63, 64, 163
Fulton, R. 11

Gauthier, Y. 86–7
Gilmore, A. 16
Glaser, B.G. 4–6, 8–9, 10–11
Glick, I.O. 24, 54, 152, 154–5
Goffman, E. 20, 36–7

Gogan, J.L. 133
Goldberg, D. 97
Gore, S. 82
Gorer, G. 2, 3–4, 22, 29, 30, 31, 32, 35, 54, 57, 83, 108, 118
Gottlieb, B.H. 82

Habenstein, R.W. 20
Hardiker, P. 72, 102
Heidegger, M. 74
Heike, E. 4
Helmrath, T.A. 144
Hertz, R. 27–30
Hillier, E.R. 15
Hinton, J. 5, 16
Hodgkinson, P. 91
Hodgkinson, P.E. 143–4
Hoekstra-Weebers, J.E.W.M. 145
Horowitz, M.J. 57, 68, 80–1, 158
House, J.S. 79–80
Huntington, R. 23, 36

Illich, I. 3, 6, 32
Irwin, M. 61

Jones, M. 44
Jung, C. 28
Jurk, I.H. 136, 146

Kalish, R.A. 4, 11, 17, 18, 35–6, 41, 53, 57, 58, 68, 83, 89, 92, 160–1, 174
Kalnins, I.V. 133
Kaplan, B.H. 99
Kaplan, D.M. 133
Kastenbaum, R.J. 17–18, 83
Kaufmann, W. 4
Kelly, G.A. 67–8
Kennell, J.H. 125, 144
Kerner, J. 138–9
Kessler, R.C. 79
Kirkley-Best, E. 123
Klass, D. 89
Klein, M. 63–4, 159
Kübler-Ross, E. 5, 10, 13–15, 17, 23–4, 53

Lansdown, R. 133
Lasch, C. 99
Lauer, M.E. 134–5
Lazare, A. 57, 58
Lazarus, R.S. 80
Lehman, D.R. 83–4
Leming, M.R. 22, 37, 100, 102–3, 104

Leslie, L.A. 83
Levav, I. 142
Levine, M. 97
Lewis, C.S. 4, 43, 49
Lewis, E. 124–5
Lieberman, M. 88–9
Lieberman, S. 90–1
Lifton, R.J. 99
Lin, N. 79, 83
Lindemann, E. 11, 41, 56, 58, 60
Littlewood, J.L. 7, 11, 24–5, 37–9, 42–3, 44, 47, 58, 71, 83, 87, 92, 93–4, 102, 108, 109, 115, 128, 132, 136, 138, 143, 145–6, 152, 155, 158, 161, 163
Lowman, J. 131, 144

Maddison, D.C. 41, 69, 86, 107, 108
Magni, G. 85
Mandell, F. 70, 146
Mann, J.R. 133
Marris, P. 18, 30, 31, 49, 54, 55, 56, 57, 99–100, 100–1, 103, 109, 151–2
Martinson, I. 22
Mawson, D. 91–2
Miller, J. 26
Moos, R.H. 72
Morrin, H. 129
Morris, D. 124
Moss, M.S. 161
Mueller, D.P. 80
Mulhern, R.K. 133
Murrell, S.A. 80

Natanson, M. 73
Nixon, J. 144

Orbach, S. 141–2
Osterweis, M. 61, 71–2, 146
Owen, G. 160

Palgi, P. 142–3
Pallis, C. 142
Parkes, C.M. 6, 7, 11, 16, 18, 22, 30, 41, 47, 48, 50, 51, 53, 58, 66–7, 82, 87, 107
Parsons, M. 65
Parsons, T. 101
Paulo, B. de 97
Pearlin, L. 159
Peterman, F. 70
Pincus, L. 43, 64–5, 103, 117, 158, 161, 163

Rando, T.A. 140, 145
Raphael, B. 55, 56, 57, 58, 69, 82,
  87–8, 99, 108, 123, 130, 131, 132,
  135–6, 142, 144, 147, 149, 152,
  157, 163
Reid, J. 99
Richardson, R. 29–30, 31
Robson, J.D. 101–2
Rodabough, T. 102
Rosenblatt, P.C. 99
Rowe, D. 75, 81, 163
Rowland, K.F. 41
Rubin, S.S. 65, 68

Sanders, C.M. 12, 132, 160
Sartre, J.-P. 9, 74–5
Schermerhorn, R.A. 76
Schowalter, J.E. 137
Seligman, M.E.P. 9, 81
Shanfield, S.B. 140–1
Shneidman, E.S. 14
Silverman, D. 94
Simos, B.G. 58
Simpson, M.A. 58
Singh, B.S. 57
Sireling, L. 92
Smith, C.R. 4, 27, 54, 66, 69, 72, 84,
  88, 107
Spinetta, J.J. 133–4
Standish, L. 144
Stedeford, A. 53
Stein, H.F. 76
Stringham, J. 124
Sudnow, D. 5, 10

Tatchell, P. 4

Taylor, L. 30, 31
Taylor, R.B. 21
Tebbi, C.K. 136–7
Thoits, P. 79
Thomas, C.D. 34
Tillich, P. 75
Tod, J.L. 98
Towse, M.S. 74, 75
Turner, B.S. 4, 27, 37
Turner, V. 26–7

Vachon, M. 11, 12, 58, 65, 86, 88, 99
Van Gennep, A. 22–7, 30
Verbrugge, L. 70
Veroff, J. 97
Videka-Sherman, L. 25, 89, 138
Viorst, J. 65
Vizedom, M.B. 22
Volkan, V.D. 11, 46, 48, 56, 90

Walker, K.N. 85
Waller, D.A. 127
Weiss, R.S. 45
Wellman, B. 83
Wilcox, B.L. 80
Wilson, A.L. 125, 144
Witte, R. A. 139–40
Wolff, J.R. 124
Woodfield, R.L. 67
Worden, J.W. 41, 42, 45, 46, 48, 50,
  57, 72, 88
Wortman, C.B. 83
Wright, M. 88

Young, G. 15
Young, M. 41

SUBJECT INDEX

A, Mrs (death of parents) 171–4
abortions 123
absent grief 56–7
acceptance: stage of dying 14
accidents, fatal: of children 132; of
   adolescents 135; of adults 140
acknowledgement of relationship: lack
   of, 108, 118–20
adolescent deaths 135–40; accidents
   135; cystic fibrosis 138–9; Duchenne
   muscular dystrophy 139–40;
   malignancies 136–8; suicide 135–6
adoption 129–30
adult child deaths 140–7; accidents 140,
   142; disasters 143–4; malignancies
   140–1; organ donation requests 142;
   war deaths 142–3
AIDS 4, 120
ambivalence 48, 158–9; ambivalent
   relationships 57, 162, 163
Anatomy Act 29–30
anger 45–6; stage of dying 13–14; 53
anticipation: grief 11–13; orphanhood
   161
anxiety 42–3; death anxiety 160;
   existential anxiety 75; separation
   anxiety 66, 75
apathy 52
appetite disturbances 48
Armistice day 34
attachment theory 65–6
attitudes towards death 1–4; primitive
   attitudes 3
avoidance: bereaved 38–9, 83; coping
   style 70
awareness contexts: dying 8–9, 10, 13

B, Mrs (death of partner) 112–14

bargaining: stage of dying 14, 53
bereavement role 101–2
biological explanations: grief 61–2;
   fight-flight 61, 62; conservation
   withdrawal 61, 62
brain death 142
buffering effects: social support 79–81
bureaucratisation: death 35
burial 28–9

C, Mr (death of father) 163–6
calendrical rites 21
Cenotaph 34
chief mourner 103–4; social support
   105–6; family disputes over 114–15;
   brothers/sisters 115–17; adult
   children/parent's partners 117;
   partners/parents 117–18
child deaths see also adolescent deaths
   and adult child deaths 123–35;
   abortions 123; accidents 132;
   adoption 129; cystic fibrosis 138–9;
   fostering 129–30; handicap 130–1;
   malignancy 132–5; miscarriage
   123; perinatal 125–7; SIDS 131–2;
   stillbirth 123–5; 'replacement' after
   child death 26
chronic grief 57
cognitive models: grief 66–9
complicated grief 55–9; absent
   56–7; chronic grief 57; latent
   self-images 68, 158–9; delayed
   grief 56; determinants 57–8;
   distorted 56–7; mummification 57,
   74
confusion 45
conservation–withdrawal 61–2
conservative impulse 18

189

coping: crisis 69–72; gender styles 70–2; potency 81
cremation 28–9
crisis intervention 69–72
crying 43, 52
cystic fibrosis, 138–9

death: adolescents 135–40; adult child 140–7; anxiety 42–3, 160; attitudes 1–4; bureaucratisation 35; child 123–35; denial 3, 4, 18, 35, 123, 127, 155–6; glorification 33; 'good' 17–19; hospital 4–11; 'modern' 3; obsessive review 46, 69; old age 6–8; parents in adulthood 159–74; partners 148–59; pornography 3, 35; 'romantic' 3; 'safe' 17–19; sexuality 44; 'tame' 2, 8, 17, 18; timely 6–7; unanticipated 58; Victorian celebration 29, 31–3, 34; voyeurism 35, 38, 39; war 33, 142–3
death awareness movement 35–6
death education 4
delayed grief 56
denial: death 4; dying 13, 53; parental 123, 127
depression: 61, 64; feelings 162, 167; stage of dying 14, 53
depressive position 64
deterioration: social support 83–4
direct effects model: social support 82
disasters 26–7, 143–4
disbelief 42
disease model: grief 41, 60–1
distorted grief 56–7
dreams: dead person 48–9
Duchenne muscular dystrophy 139–40
dying process: awareness 8–9, 10, 13; control 2, 9–10; routinisation 5; stages 13–15, 17, 53; trajectories 5–6

ethnicity 76–7
euphoria 43–4
existential anxiety 75
existential models: grief 74–5

F, Mrs (death of partner) 152–4
family model: caring 106–7
fear: surviving parent 162, 166–7
fight–flight 61, 62
forced mourning 90–1
forgetfulness 48

fostering 129, 130
funerals 21, 27–30; perceptions 37–9; political 22; roles 102

G, Mrs (death of fostered child) 129–30
gender: coping styles 70–2; parental grief 144–7; widowhood 149, 154–6
glorification of death 33
'good' death 17–19
grief: absent 56–7; chronic 57; cognitive models 66–9; complicated 55–9; delayed 56; determinants 57–8; disease models 41, 60–1; distorted 56–7; gender differences 144–7, 149, 154–6; mummification 57, 74; phenomenological and existential models 72–5; physical sensations 41; psychodynamic models of 63–5; re-grief therapy 90; resolution 54; stages 53–4; therapeutic interventions 58–9; uncomplicated 54–5
guided mourning 91–2
guilt 46

hallucinations 47, 48; pseudo-hallucinatory thought echoes 74
handicapped children: death 130–1
helper: 104–5; social position 120–1; social support 106
home care: terminal illness in children 134–5
honorary experts 105, 106
hospice movement 15–17
hospital deaths 4–11

identification: lost object 63; dead person 162, 166
illness and disease models: grief 41, 60–1
incorporation: rites 24–6
informal support: distress alleviation 97–100; lack of 108–9 interviews Mrs A 171–4; Mrs B 112–14; Mr C 163–6; Mrs F 152–4; Mrs G 129–30; Mr L 109–12; Mr N 156–7; Mrs O 149–52; Mrs R 137–8; Mrs S 138; Mrs T 167–70; Ms W 125–7; daughter who cared for elderly mother 170–1; daughter of sole surviving parent 116–17; elderly couple 10; bereaved

husband 155; parents of dead
  child 128–9

L, Mr (death of partner) 109–12
latent self images 68, 158–9
learned helplessness 9–10, 81
loneliness 45

malignancies: adolescents 136–8;
  adults 140–1; children 132–5
master status 102–3, 104
meaninglessness 45
miscarriages 123
morbidity: bereavement 41
mortality: bereavement 41
mourning; forced mourning 90–1;
  guided mourning 91–2; time-
  limitation 30
mourning dress 30, 31–2, 38
mummification 57, 74
murder 58

N, Mr (death of partner) 156–7
numbness 42

O, Mrs (death of partner) 149–52
obsessive review of death 46, 69
old age: deaths 6–8; bereavement
  108–14
organ donation 142

parent; death 159–61; death anxiety
  160; dependent elderly 162, 170–1;
  fear of surviving 162, 166–7;
  identification 162, 163; mothers
  161–2
partner; death 148–9
perceptions of professional support;
  92–6; practical help 94–5; emotional
  support 95; need for support
  95–6
perinatal deaths 125
personal construct theory and cognitive
  models: grief 66–9
phenomenological and existential
  models: grief 72–5
physical sensations: grief 41
Poor Law (Amendment) Act 29
pornography and death 3, 35
post-mortem psychology 69
pregnancy following bereavement
  25–6

preoccupation; with events prior
  to death 46; with thoughts of
  deceased 46
presence of dead; experiences 47;
  sensing presence 47
preventive programmes 87–8
professional interventions 87–8;
  complicated grief 89–92; forced
  mourning 90–1; guided mourning
  91–2; re-grief therapy 90
psychodynamic explanations: grief
  63–5

R, Mrs (death of adolescent child)
  137–8
re-grief therapy 90
relationships; ambivalent 57, 162,
  163; lack of acknowledgement
  108, 118–19; highly dependent 57;
  narcissistic 57
relief; after death 43; euphoric 43–4
religious beliefs 37–8; systems of rites
  and beliefs 27–30
reminders of dead 49–50
replacement child 26
restlessness 51
rites of passage 21, 22–7; separation
  23–4; transition 23, 24, 26–7;
  reincorporation 23, 24–6
rituals 21–2; everyday life 20; calendrical
  rites 21; rituals and social support
  36–7
rites and beliefs: systems 27–30
'romantic' death 3

S, Mrs (death of adolescent child) 138
sadness 43
searching 50–1
secularisation 27, 37
self-help groups 88–9
separation anxiety 75
sexuality and death 44; bereavement
  157–8
shadow grief 147
sibling rivalry 115
sickness role 101–2
SIDS 131–2
sleep disturbances 47–8
social relationship, lack of acknowledgement 108, 118–20
social role 100–2
social status: dying 5; bereavement
  102–5

social support deterioration model 83–4
social support direct effects model 82
social withdrawal 52–3
social worth 5
spiritualism 33–4, 38
stages: dying 13–15; grief 53–4
stillbirth 123–5
stress-buffering 79–81
stress prevention 82
substance abuse 53
suicide 5, 58, 83, 135–6
surviving parent, fear of 162, 166–7

T, Mrs (death of father) 167–70
'tame' death 2, 8, 17, 18
terminal illness 6, 9–11
therapeutic interventions: complicated
    grief 58–9; forced mourning 90–1;
    guided mourning 91–2; preventive
    87–8; re-grief therapy 90
time-limitation: mourning 30

timeliness: death 6
Tomb of the Unknown Soldier 34

unanticipated deaths 58
uncertainty: death 57
uncomplicated grief 54–5

Victorian celebration of death 29,
    31–3, 34
voyeurism 4, 35, 38, 39

W, Ms (perinatal death) 125–7
War deaths 33–4, 142–3
widowhood; gender differences
    149, 154–6
withdrawal; conservation–withdrawal
    61–2; social 52–3
World War I 33–4
World War II 34

yearning 46–7